Workers and Revolution
in Iran

Workers and Revolution in Iran

A Third World Experience of Workers' Control

Assef Bayat

Zed Books Ltd.
London and New Jersey

Workers and Revolution in Iran was first published by
Zed Books Ltd., 57 Caledonian Road, London N1 9BU and
171 First Avenue, Atlantic Highlands, New Jersey 07716,
USA in 1987.

Cover design by Andrew Corbett
Printed and bound in the UK by The Bath Press, Avon.

British Library Cataloguing in Publication Data

Bayat, Assef.
  Workers and revolution in Iran : a
  Third world experience of workers'
  control.
  1. Iran—Politics and government
  —1941-1979 2. Works councils
  —Iran
  I. Title
  955'053   DS318

  ISBN 0-86232-389-4
  ISBN 0-86232-390-8 Pbk

Contents

Tables

Figures

Preface

This book originated from my PhD thesis which I submitted to the University of Kent at Canterbury (England) in July 1984. I have substantially revised the text, adding two new chapters and condensing a few others.

I have benefited from the help and opinions of many people, both in Britain and in Iran, while writing this work. My thanks are due to Frank Furedi, my supervisor, and David Reason, the Director of the Interdisciplinary Studies Programme, University of Kent, for their intellectual assistance and stimulation. I owe a special debt to Henry Bernstein, a very good friend, who at every stage advised and encouraged me, and whose scrupulous readings and criticisms did much to improve the content of the book. Professor Robin Cohen, Professor Ervand Abrahamian and A. Hatef read large parts of the manuscript and made valuable criticisms and suggestions. S.A. Smith kindly allowed me to see his very interesting unpublished (at the time) thesis, and A. Ghotbi helped in preparing the first draft of the questionnaires – to all these my especial thanks.

Finally, I would like to express my appreciation to the many friends and associates, both in England and in particular in Iran, who despite the difficult political conditions did not hesitate to assist me in various ways. Notwithstanding the hostile attitude of the state bureaucracy in Iran, I have been able to obtain valuable information with the help of a number of worker militants and state employees. Although I cannot name them individually here, I do wish to record my gratitude to them all. It only remains to say that I alone am responsible for any errors of fact and judgement this book may contain.

Assef Bayat
Berkeley, California

1. Introduction

The Problem and its Significance

Post-war capitalist expansion has been marked by an extensive integration of the remotest areas of the Third World into the world capitalist system. The development of capitalist relations in the peripheral countries has dramatically altered the class structure and, more specifically, has produced within those countries working classes of a considerable size.

Whether these newly emergent urban wage-labourers and immigrant poor constitute *the* working class or proletariat *per se* has been a matter of controversy among scholars. Some dispute it; see, for example, *Third World Proletariat?* (Lloyd, 1982). Others (without actually defining their terms) assimilate the working classes under the blanket term of the urban poor, whose grievances and actions are supposed to be without any of the characteristic features of class struggle.

Whatever the conceptions of scholars, the working classes of the Third World do continue to wage their own struggles. These are in response to their actual position as wage-earners who are exploited by capital and who are oppressed both by the political form of the peripheral capitalist states and by the pre-capitalist remnants of domination embodied in the ruling ideologies and institutions. Third World working-class struggles have been spreading in recent years from the mines of South Africa to those of Bolivia, which have been the stronghold of resistance against successive military coups; from the Egyptian strike movement in January 1977, which escalated into an uprising of the rural and urban poor, to the insurrection one year later by the Tunisian national Trade Union Centre (Cohen, 1982, p. 285); from the Iranian oil workers' strike, which played a crucial part in bringing down the *ancien régime* to the current struggle against the military regime in Chile which is virtually led by the militant workers of the copper mines.

An alternative radical approach is being developed which, on the evidence of extensive field research, attempts to go beyond the phenomenal forms of Third World working-class practices to examine their real dynamics. R. Cohen (1972, 1979, 1980), R. Sandbrook (1975), P.

1

Waterman (1979, 1983), C. van Onselen (1976), among others, have made valuable contributions to this area in recent years.

The present study is concerned with the workers of Iran and their experience of workers' control during the revolutionary period following the insurrection of February 1979. It attempts to examine the objective existence of the working class in terms of its economic identification and significance (Chapter 3) and the process of its proletarianization (Chapter 4). It gives a sociological analysis of the divisions in the labour market and looks at conditions of work and the workers' struggle to organize themselves in the workplaces (Chapter 5). It then goes on to investigate the actual role of the workers in the anti-Pahlavi revolution (Chapter 6). But the major substance of the book concerns the emergence of particular forms of work and workers' organizations, *shuras* or factory committees, in the industrial workplaces; these called for the extension of the revolutionary process and for a permanent class struggle. The *shuras* were institutions of workers' control; they wanted to modify the division of labour in the workplace and to give workers control over the processes of production, distribution and exchange (Chapters 7 and 8).

I attempt to evaluate the experience and demise of the *shuras* (Chapter 9). I attribute their defeat both to their internal contradictions and to external pressures, in particular those imposed by the new state.

It seems, rather regrettably, that this work is the only systematic research which has been carried out (at either the theoretical or the empirical level) on the position of the Iranian working class both in normal circumstances and in a revolutionary crisis.[1] Its relevance is therefore twofold. On the one hand, there is a serious lack of analysis of the working-class experience of the Iranian labour movement and the inability of workers to carry out a substantial reappraisal of the predicament of the working class in all its economic, sociological, politico-ideological dimensions. I hope that the present work will act as a spur to further investigation on the position of the Iranian working class. Yet, I must stress that this book is not a history of the Iranian working class in the three years after the Revolution. It is simply concerned with one important and novel aspect of struggle: workers' control.

On the other hand, and no less significantly, I wish to consider the international dimension of the working-class movement. The expansion of world capital has generated as its counterpart a world working class. The struggle of the Iranian workers is a part of the global and, in particular, Third World, labour movement. An analytical approach to particular labour issues will serve as a contribution towards a better understanding of all Third World workers' movements. Thus this book is not merely the story of the Iranian workers' struggle for workers' control. It attempts to go further and relate this experience to the idea of workers' control *per se*.

2

Workers' Control and the Third World Experience

The question of workers' control in the Third World is particularly interesting. At first glance it might appear that the idea of workers' control is specific to the proletariat of the advanced capitalist countries. That is because much less attention has been paid to the general conditions of workers' struggles in the periphery, let alone their particular experience of workers' control. Any consideration of Third World workers in academic circles is quite recent; and this neglect is compounded by academic doubts as to whether Third World workers really form a working class.

On the other hand, in the West, various forms of workers' organizations and practices such as 'consultation', 'co-determination', 'job-enlargement', 'productivity bargaining' and 'works councils' to settle grievances at plant level have been erroneously identified with the concept of workers' control. The terms industrial democracy, workers' participation and so on, have been confused with workers' control proper. Here, we must note that these industrial institutions and practices in the West were distinct from the radical rank and file organizations of *workers' councils* which emerged in European countries in the revolutionary situations of the 1910s, 1940s and the late 1960s.[2] (In the following Chapter I attempt to clarify the concept of workers' control.) In this book, workers' control is used in the 'strong' sense of demands by workers to exert control over the processes of production and administration of production, and the implications generated by such demands.[3]

In this sense, the possibility of struggles for workers' control in the Third World countries tend to be denied (when it is acknowledged at all) on the following grounds:

a) The repressive and authoritarian nature of management regimes in the industries of countries dominated by foreign capital (Mapolu, 1976, p. 200).

b) The fact that political democracy generally is less deeply rooted in Western countries, or is absent altogether.

c) Workers' control is too 'advanced' a demand for the 'young' or 'backward' workforce of the Third World to mobilize around.

The above arguments appear to be based upon a problematic assumption that workers' participation is a policy initiated from above, supported by the state legislations, and not a struggle from below. Also, in this sense of the term, which takes an ILO-type corporatist approach, the extent of workers' participation does not go beyond that represented by trade union participation; unlike workers' control, in trade unions it is the union officials who conduct limited, joint consultation with the management. In fact, the historical examples I shall provide below challenge these views. The relevant question is thus, not whether Third World working classes do experience workers' control, but rather how and in what conditions they are materialized, and in what ways they are distorted and fail.

As an alternative to the above line of argument (and the assumptions it is based upon) I would argue that there are some specific structural features of capitalist development (and socio-economic development in general) in the periphery that provide conditions favourable to demands and movements for workers' participation and workers' control:

a) One feature is the chronic inability of capitalist states in the periphery to establish ideological hegemony (i.e. ruling through consensus), thus providing special opportunities for oppositional movements, including those of the working people.

b) Similarly, economic 'backwardness' (low level of capital accumulation) inhibits any significant cooption of workers through economic 'incentives'. Together with almost perennial crises of ideological hegemony, this means that reformist measures have little chance of success. Independent trade unionism, for example, tends to assume a highly critical and political character.

c) Together with their general 'backwardness' within the world economic system, Third World countries experience the unevenness of capitalist development especially sharply, above all with new industrial technologies — and their attendant labour processes and management regimes — introduced by multinational companies. The strains and conflicts associated with such unevenness are much less easily contained within 'business unionism', and are more likely to generate demands for workers' control.

d) The capitalist state, capitalist class and bourgeois values are generally weak and less deeply rooted in the Third World countries. The weakness of these structural factors and their related social forces, which tend to preserve the *status quo*, means that resistance against change and alternative socio-economic structure is concomitantly weaker.

e) Although, generally, the working classes of the Third World have less experience of organization and political education, the relatively simpler organization of work and the labour processes can make possible a higher degree of control by the working classes over the organization of work and production, as the following examples illustrate.

Following the French withdrawal from Algeria in 1962 workers and peasants took over control of production, at a time when the absence of colonial managerial elements created a vacuum which had to be filled by the native producers (Clegg, 1971). Later, however, through the institutionalization of self-management, the state granted real (as opposed to formal) power of control to the new managers.

In 1972 in Tanzania, following President Nyerere's declaration for 'workers' participation' (*Mwongozo*), a series of workers' occupations of the factories took place. The workers demanded full and legal control of the workplaces. The action surprised many observers who had not anticipated that the workers would even strike. Nyerere's *Mwongozo* was in fact *trade union* participation. It was a manifestation of a radical populist policy which aimed to raise productivity and to create a corporatist ideology (i.e. cooperation of workers, management and the state for the good of the nation) in the industry by securing the cooperation of the unions (Nyerere, 1970 in Mapolu, 1976), whereas the workers' demands in 1972 reflected a desire for real control (Mahyo, 1975; Mapolu, 1976).

A few years later in the aftermath of the downfall of the dictatorial Portuguese regime (1974), a movement for mass participation escalated and organs of workers' control were set up. Pressure from below and desire for a self-managed economy was so strong that it forced the constitution to recognize the principle of workers' control. But this was restricted to the sphere of production and was successful mainly in small-scale enterprises. This workers' control was in conflict with un-altered bourgeois modes of distribution and exchange, which remained outside workers' control (Goodey *et al*, 1980; Wise, 1975). The capitalist states, the multinationals and the domestic industrialists undermined the movement by resorting to economic sabotage. The state at first acted merely as an axis of balance of class forces. But as the moment of revolutionary enthusiasm passed, an essentially capitalist strategy was adopted which entailed a *de facto* dismantling of the workers' committees.

In Chile, the victory of the Popular Unity in the 1970 general election created a political situation in which the working class initiated expropriation of private enterprises and multinationals, taking them into workers' control. Allende's socialist party had already envisaged a pro-gramme of workers' participation, based on the formation of *cordones industriales* at the enterprise level. The three years of *Unidad Popular* government were marked by an intense class struggle, as the power and initiative of the working class was released and the bourgeoisie and its international allies resisted by organizing the subversive strike of the bourgeoisie in 1972. The workers extended the social property sector (state-owned nationalized and expropriated enterprises) and took control of planning. *Cordones industriales* were set up to co-ordinate the opera-tions of enterprises and provincial *co-ordinadora* planned their activities. *Commondas* or communal councils were created to integrate the workers, peasants, students, housewives, unions and the committees for the control of food supplies and prices as a single body (Raptis, 1973, p. 54; also Zimbalist & Petras, undated; Zimbalist and Espinosa, 1978; and Smirnov, 1979). A further instance is provided by the experience of the Iranian workers to the examination of which this book is devoted.

These examples show the desire of workers to exert control over their work environment. This challenges the view that workers, especial-ly in the developing countries, are merely interested in bread-and-butter issues. In some cases allied political parties played an important part in spreading the idea of workers' control and in others the movements were entirely spontaneous. In all cases the achievements were short-lived and were eventually either crushed or transformed. A crisis of hegemony and a low level of capital accumulation may be conducive to the emergence of workers' control, but the very same factors may act as obstacles to both its emergence and development, especially in the context of capitalist economy. In a capitalist, developing country, a competitive and weak position of capital leaves little room to accommodate the initially disruptive and restrictive effects of workers' control *on capital*. Nor does such a method of production seem politically viable; the undemocratic character of developing states cannot accommodate institutions of workers' control. (The conditions in which workers' control may develop in a developing country are discussed in the final chapter.)

Yet the short life and eventual disintegration of these movements should not be wholly attributed to their location. They were undermined by physical liquidation (Chile), the politics of integration and transformation (Portugal, Algeria), and lack of clear political perspective. These factors can also operate in advanced capitalist countries.

A crucial factor needing investigation is the inner contradiction and shortcomings of the movements themselves. Some scholars limit themselves to merely praising the workers' control struggles, assuming that their failure cannot lie with the workers themselves. They attribute the failure exclusively to external factors: suppression or betrayal. In this study, I shall deal with the internal problems of workers' *shuras* in Iran. My emphasis is not the incompatibility of workers' control with efficiency, but the problem of the persistence of a predominantly capitalist division of labour which conflicts with the logic of workers' control. How is it possible to modify and eventually eliminate the division of labour? It is this problem, I would suggest, that should be the focal point of both theoretical discussion and empirical investigation.

Field Research

I originally planned to do research on the historical development of the Iranian working class. From its inception this was a hard task, especially in view of the severe limitations of sources. I had already begun to do the relevant general reading when I made a return visit to Iran some three months after the Revolution. The few months I spent there changed my plan of research on the working class. The *shuras*, the grass-roots popular institutions which had developed in offices, schools, districts, farms, factories and in the armed forces, were generating a widespread interest. I was more or less familiar with a rather romanticized view of factory *shuras* through the left-wing papers and my activist friends who were directly involved. When I came back to England I pursued the idea of researching these developments. My second long visit to Iran from October 1980 to June 1981 led me to engage with the more immediate question of what the factory *shuras* were (in this period), and it was then that I managed to conduct my field research, despite enormous difficulties.

To obtain first-hand information I conducted field research mainly in four institutions:

a) The Institute of Industrial Hygiene and Protection of Labour Force, Ministry of Labour, where I managed to obtain data on conditions of work. I examine this issue in Chapter 5 in the section on physical oppression.

b) The Ministry of Health, which provided documents concerning the frauds and overcharges levied against industrial workers under the medical insurance scheme.

c) Three hospitals for industrial workers in Teheran, where I formally interviewed 120 industrial workers, obtaining detailed information about the process of their proletarianization in economic, cultural and ideological terms. The analysis in Chapter 4 rests heavily on this data.

d) Fourteen modern plants in Teheran (and one in Tabriz) which specialized in four main sectors of industrial production: domestic appliances, electronics, metal and cars. These factories provided the major source material of my study.

Visiting factories was my prime objective and obtaining official permission to do so my major concern. Frankly speaking, I had at the outset little hope of obtaining a permit card. But I tried and succeeded — but only after fifty days. During this period my request was rejected outright several times by the Deputy Minister of Labour with such excuses as 'you might be a communist', 'who knows, you might be a CIA agent', 'honestly, believe me, factories are explosive'. I persisted and answered every question. Eventually, after nearly two months, during which I learnt a great deal about the Ministry, an official assumed the 'responsibility' of issuing the Letter of Permit. According to our arrangement, I produced two kinds of questionnaires. The first was the formal questionnaire, copies of which were to be sent, via the Ministry of Labour, to 30 modern factories in three industrial zones throughout the country; the completed forms were to be received by the Ministry. I therefore produced 2,000 copies of these questionnaires. The second questionnaire was to be completed by myself inside selected factories. Questions in this were grouped in two sections addressed to workers and management.

The agreement of the Labour Ministry was conditional on the limitation of my questionnaires to the past, to the Shah's regime; no questions about strikes were allowed, or about the profit-sharing scheme.

The response to the formal questionnaires was almost nil. In some plants the workers had torn the questionnaires in half — a show of distrust of the Ministry of Labour. I had to complete a limited number of them afterwards by direct interviews with workers in the hospitals in Teheran.

The results of the informal interviews and open questions were, on the other hand, quite satisfactory. While conducting interviews I asked about the issues which really interested me: the formation and composition of the *shuras*, the political situation in the past and present, management strategies against the *shuras*, and so on. This method was effective despite the fact that, in some cases, the management and the zealots of the Islamic Associations were scrutinizing me very closely. I would direct the discussion, but I would allow the workers to say what they wished to. In some cases the interview would develop into a discussion involving all the workers in a shop, with their differing politico-ideological orientations; I would tape-record the whole conversation. The most useful interview sessions were concerned with the *shura* leaders of the factories; at times these lasted for many hours.

My success in conducting investigations in the plants was conditional mainly on the political atmosphere. If a democratic *shura* was in power, as at Metal Works, Fanoos, it would provide further facilities helpful to my research without the requirement of the management's consent. In contrast, where there was no factory *shura* (perhaps as a result of forceful dissolution) and the management was the absolute power, genuine investigation was either entirely impossible (as at Eadem Motor Diesel and Tractor Sazi, both in Tabriz) or was very restricted. In either case management would refuse to allow me to visit the workshop and talk to the workers, on the grounds that 'if you go inside, the workers will stop work; you don't know; the workers have changed.' And indeed, stoppages did happen in a few cases after my interviews. To avoid a potential threat of problems in these situations, I had to adopt a guerrilla-type tactic of research — ask and run.

The pattern of informal interviewing and the number of workers interviewed therefore varied plant by plant. On the whole I managed to interview some 150 workers, including 22 *shura* leaders. I managed to make closer contacts after the official interview with the militant workers whom I had met inside the factories. I would contact these workers outside the workplace in their free time and we would have long conversations. These workers in particular provided valuable information concerning the functions of *shura* and management.

I had planned to visit 30 large industrial units. But the dramatic political change during the June Days of 1981 which led to the dismissal of President Bani'Sadra and widespread violence against militant workers and the forces of opposition halted my study. In those days, I could only watch the militant workers with whom I had talked being arrested. It should be noted that all names of people, and of some factories, are fictitious.

Notes

1. Although there are useful contributions by, for example Ghotbi (1979, 1980), Ghasim (1979), *Rah-i Kargar* (1981) in Farsi; and Goodey (1980) and Azad (1980) in English.
2. For the study of a few cases, see Lomax, 1976; Comfort, 1966; Hoyles in Coates, 1969; Tampke, 1979.

3. In this book the term workers' participation is used to denote the *general problematic* of participation of workers in the decision-making of enterprises. In this sense, workers' participation may refer to participation in various degrees, from above or below, embodied in mere consultation or genuine workers' control.

Table 1
Details of Plants Investigated

Plant*	Date of establishment	Capital	No. of employees	Product
Amazon	1937	Domestic	2,268	Domestic appliances
Arasteh	1959	Domestic	950	Domestic appliances
Bloom Helm	1960	Multinational	168	Television sets
Fanoos	1962	Multinational	645	Television and radios
P.R. Plant	1966	Domestic/ multinational	880	Domestic appliances
I.T.N.	1966	Domestic/ multinational	735	Electricity transformer
Behshahr	1961	Multinational	958	Cars
Turkman	1966	State/ multinational	2,670	Industrial tools
Metal Works	1963	Domestic	895	Metallic and cement pipes
R.C. Chemicals	1965	Multinational	602	Dry batteries
Teheran Auto	1967	Multinational	2,600	Cars
Teheran Steel	1960s	Domestic	850	Metallic pipes
Alvand	1960s	Domestic	400	Commercial refrigerators
Iran Cars	1960s	Multinational	?	Cars

*The names here are all fictitious to preserve anonymity of informants.

2. Control Relations in a Capitalist Enterprise

The notion of workers' control has been surrounded by confusion. Its meaning is never really defined and the extent, degree and spheres of workers' discretion are obscure. The idea is at times identified with the limited trade unionist gains made under capitalism, and at times is associated with a major revolutionary social transformation in which workers play a prominent part. Workers' control is taken to indicate such a variety of practices that we may wonder whether it is an objective fought for by workers or introduced by capital itself. This chapter attempts to deal with these issues. In the first instance I shall examine the abstract notion of control in a capitalist enterprise and then the historicity of control. Certain concepts will be introduced to establish an historical, as opposed to formalistic, approach to the issue of control in capitalism.

The reader interested only in specifically the Iranian experience of workers' control may skip this chapter without a loss of continuity.

What is Control?

The notion of control in a capitalist enterprise implies the adoption, by both capital and labour, of certain decisions and practices in the workplace. Capital's control is maintained by various managerial strategies which are examined in Chapter 10. Here I am concerned with the notion of *workers'* control.

By workers' control in industry, I mean the effective control by workers over the processes of production, and administration of production, and the implications generated by such practice. I shall for the moment concentrate my analysis on the sphere of production. In itself, control over the production process is an abstract notion. Workers' control is assumed to mean that workers take certain decisions about the production process, divorced from their historical time and place. This study is concerned with specifying the historical determinants of worker control. But before so doing, we still have to characterize it at a general level, which involves looking at the salient features of the capitalist production process.

The capitalist production process is really two unified processes: the labour process and the valorization process. The labour process is the way in which use-value is produced; it is related to concrete labour. Concrete labour differentiates the various tasks to be performed. It is characterized by the quality of work and the technical aspect of production by skill and expertise. The valorization or surplus-value-extracting process is concerned with the production of exchange-value or the process of abstract labour as a quantitative expenditure of energy or effort. The two processes are separable only in the abstract and for the sake of analysis (see column 1 in Figure 1.1).

If we examine the class relations within the production process at a high level of generality, it may be suggested that those involved in the surplus-value-extracting process are agents of capital. Their function is to maintain and create the conditions for maximum surplus-value production (which may involve various strategies from repression to industrial democracy). They may be identified as owners, exploiters, and non-producers. In contrast, those involved in the labour process carry out the function of labour; they are the non-owners, the exploited and the producers (see column 4 and Carchedi, 1975a and 1975b).

It is easy to identify, theoretically, the functions of capital and labour in a capitalist enterprise characterized by the formal subordination of labour to capital. Following Edwards, 1979, we may refer to an uncomplicated organization of production in which the relationship between exploiter and exploited is direct and unmediated control (see also Chapter 5).

But with the development of capitalism and a growing complexity of organization of production, the identification of the two functions also becomes complex. Conditions of real subordination (the development of modern technology), prevalence of bureaucratic and structural control in place of simple control and the development of monopoly capitalism from competitive and individual capitalism are accompanied by a substantial transformation in both the labour and valorization processes. On the capital side, the category of ownership of the means of production gives way to that of possession (Poulantzas, 1975; Bettelheim, 1979). This refers to control by non-owners (of the means of production) i.e. managers, who determine how capital functions through the managerial structure. On the labour side, under monopoly capitalism collective labour emerges to replace workers scattered round individual and competitive capitalist enterprises. It also refers to the combined social labour which in its totality performs the total function of labour (i.e. producing total surplus value) in the whole capitalist economy in industry, in services or in the office.

The functions of both capital and collective labour are each characterized by technical and social aspects. Any position in the production process has, on the one hand, a technical aspect and, on the other, a social aspect of power and authority. This differentiation has a more immediate relevance to the function of capital. The functionaries of capital (managers)

Figure 2.1 Relations of Control

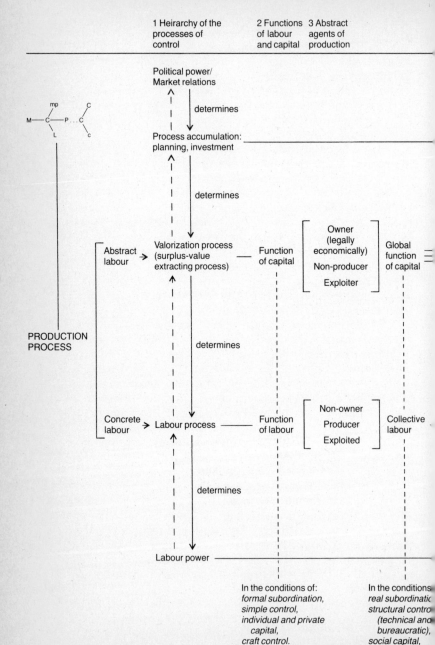

tents	5 The Heirarchy of concrete (class) agents in production	6 Concrete and potential areas of class struggle for control

ons

Share-holders —— determine —— Real and
legal ownership

Board of Directors
Chairmen of Board
Chief Executive —— determine ——
Divisional Management
Factory Management
etc.

Finance
Choice of technique
Choice of products
Sales (marketing)
Purchases
etc.

Work of
nt of — control
on (authority)

Department Managers
Planners
Designers —— determine ——
Supervisors
etc.

Planning
Function of
designing
Supervision at
the shop floor

ical
t of — Work of
n coordination

Productive and
unproductive
workers

Skilled workers

Control over
organisation
of work

(restrictive
practices)

Semi-skilled
workers

Unskilled
workers

For example:
Job demarcation
Self-supervision
Regulation of
manning and pay
Rejection of
measured daywork
Control over
conditions of work
etc.

Control over the supply of labour

Hiring
Firing
Wages
Hours of work
etc.

perform two kinds of work in the production process simultaneously: on the one hand, they perform a work of control which is designed to ensure the maximum production of surplus-value; and on the other, they carry out the work of co-ordination which is a technical necessity in any complex labour process (Marx, 1977, pp. 382–5). In fact, a hierarchy of functionaries perform these tasks, from top directors and managers to the planners, designers and supervisors listed in column 5. As the figure makes clear, since certain functionaries perform the functions of both capital and collective labour (planners, supervisors, foremen), they are in a contradictory class position which is a peculiarity of the 'new middle class' (Carchedi, 1975a).

If we assumed full control by capital, it would follow that workers would only do what the functionaries of capital ordered them to, without any struggle. Reality, however, diverges from this assumption. Workers do resist the full control of capital in various areas and through different strategies. To consider this matter, let us this time start with the right-hand side of the figure and move to the left, from the concrete to the general levels. This will help us evaluate the extent of workers' struggles for control and the effectiveness of these struggles; are they, for instance, in the sphere of labour supply, of the labour process, of the production process or of the state?

Column 6 of the figure illustrates a variety of areas which are sites of struggle between capital and labour in both normal and critical and revolutionary conditions. The areas of struggle (or the frontiers of control) have been arranged so that the upper areas indicate areas of wider control than the lower ones and so that each practice in the column relates to respective levels of the hierarchy of control (in column 1). For instance, struggles over wages or a closed shop concern the conditions under which the labour is supplied; job-demarcation and gang-systems are in the sphere of the labour process; workers' management, control over planning, and such like, is in the sphere of resource allocation and planning.

Can the workers of an enterprise gain full control of the production process through cumulative struggle at the workplace? Not *full* control. With the concentration and centralization of capital, individual capitalists themselves can exert only partial control over their enterprises. If workers' control were set up in a single enterprise, it would be severely limited by the capitalist environment and its laws. The second point suggested by column 1 of the figure is that there is a process of determination between the levels of control. The arrow → indicates that the top levels determine all of the lower levels of the hierarchy of control directly or indirectly. Control over the supply of labour is constrained by the mechanisms of the labour process; these, in turn, are constrained by the logic of the surplus-value-extracting process, and the latter is constrained by the accumulation process (planning and resource allocation); all of them in turn are constrained by the dictates of market relations upheld by state power (see Baumgartner in Burns, 1979, pp. 185–7).

These determinations, however, are by no means one-directional. Class struggle from below restricts the scope of capital. (The arrows —→ point to the limited restrictive effects of the lower levels on the higher ones.)

Struggles in the sphere of the labour process can impose serious limitations on accumulation; if, for example, workers in all capitalist enterprises were to carry out a concerted battle, it would be likely to disrupt the whole of market relations. Though such a concerted action can hardly materialize in a practical political struggle, the point nevertheless illustrates the impact workplace struggles can have as part of the wider labour struggle to restrict accumulation.

The Historicity of Control: Some Relevant Concepts

So far we have discussed the abstract concept of control. We must now look at some workers' control in concrete historical settings. If we consider a model at a level of abstraction in which capitalists exercise *full* and unchallenged control over the production process, then any action which workers take to challenge authority, at whatever level (from struggle over wages to demands for control over the work process and finance) has to be seen as a battle for control. This is how Goodrich has proceeded in his classic work *The Frontier of Control* (1975). Such vagueness and ahistorical abstraction is misleading in several respects. It does not distinguish struggles in qualitatively distinct spheres. It tends to confuse, for instance, wage battles with struggles for control or the organization of the labour process. It also fails to distinguish between defensive (reactive) control — which aims to preserve certain already achieved advantages — and offensive control — struggles waged to advance the authority of workers against that of management; and it ignores the distinction between control as an end and control as a means. Control as an end refers to the attempt to win a certain limited control over a particular work area; control as a means sees workers' control as a stage on the journey to undermine capitalism. Finally, and most importantly, such an approach ignores the contradictory strategies of control from below originating from rank-and-file initiatives and pressures, and control from above which is introduced by capital in various forms (e.g. British Whitleyism, German co-determination, the Iranian corporatist *shuras*, Tanzanian *Mwongozo*).

Defensive Control vs Offensive Control
Defensive control is an attempt by the workforce to defend an existing position threatened by the encroachment of capital. A typical historical instance was the position of the powerful British craft unions of the 1910s which struggled against the novel strategies of capital during wartime. The new strategies aimed to qualitatively transform the organization of

15

the production process by introducing new technology, by a more extensive division of labour, a simplification of executive jobs, the recruitment of a mass of less skilled and cheaper labour, and, most important, by undermining the position of those workers whose skill and knowledge of production underlay their strong bargaining power. Wartime imperatives provided an appropriate opportunity for such an offensive by capital when the rapid expansion of the armaments industry generated growing demands for labour. These developments fostered the grievances of skilled workers (Hinton, 1973, p. 14).

At the same time, several factors led to the emergence of the shop-steward movement. These included the 'especial helplessness of the trade union leaders' who had 'responded to the declaration of war with promises of industrial truce' (Goodrich, 1975, p. 7); the introduction of conscription; the rapidly rising cost of living in the war period; the Munitions Act of 1915–16 and wartime discipline, especially the militarization of the workplace (Hinton, 1973, p. 34). 'In general redress could be obtained only through action at workplace level' (Hyman, 1975b).

Although skilled craft workers supported shop-steward committees in their efforts to reorganize the work process, their involvement was in defence of their position as skilled craftsmen. This position was being threatened by the wartime measures, in particular, dilution (Monds, 1976). 'In the end craft conquered class goals among the rank and file of the movement, and the anticipated strike against the war in January 1918 collapsed into a sectional struggle in defence of the (novel) craft privilege of exemption from military conscription' (Hinton, 1973, p. 16).

Apart from this well-known historical case, numerous sporadic incidents have happened since then that, despite their apparent militancy, have been merely defensive; various episodes of factory occupations and work-ins have occurred in response to lock-outs and to save jobs in periods of economic recession (for example, occupation of the Talbot car plant in France, in 1985).

The struggle for offensive control is struggle by workers in the production process waged in order to further the aim of workers' control. This offensive acts as both a means (confronting the power of capital at the point of production) and an end (it satisfies certain rights).

The Russian factory committees of February–October 1917 were set up and developed to express the opposition of the factory workers to bourgeois management (Smith, 1980, pp. 145–51); so it was in Italy (Milan and Turin) in 1919–20 when *commissioni interni* led to the factory occupations (Spiriano, 1975; Williams, 1979). In Allende's Chile 'the workers, through their political organization, successfully translated their technical skills in production into social control over management' (Zimbalist and Petras, 1972, p. 2). In Britain in the 1920s the miners' statement that 'the organization of industry is right enough as it is, what we want is to eliminate private ownership', or the demands of the National

Union of Railwaymen and Miners Federation for 'nationalization and joint control' point to an offensive tendency (Hyman, 1975b).

A struggle for defensive control can rapidly be transformed into an offensive one as a result of the direct involvement of the militant rank-and-file workforce in an unprecedented terrain of struggle. Part of the experience of the Iranian factory *shuras* may be such a rapid metamorphosis.

Control as an End vs Control as a Means
Control as an end refers to restricted attempts by the workforce to get certain areas of managerial control into their own hands; the struggle is designed to end as soon as the objective, however limited, is achieved. This is what Goodrich terms 'control for control's sake' (1975). The impulse behind these sorts of demands arises from the authoritarian, alienating and dehumanizing features of the workplace. The union policies of industrial democracy exemplify these limited perspectives which seem to characterize the strategies of the social democratic trade unions and which may well be accommodated within the boundaries of capitalist domination.

Control as a means seeks to advance towards further definite objectives and to inflict pressure on capital by means of restrictive practices. The concept of control as a means is a fundamental principle of the Alternative Economic Strategy in British politics, which envisages it as the cutting edge of an offensive against capital. An offensive control strategy both undermines the authority of capital and establishes alternatives. The rationale of such practices is to limit capital's economic power of manoeuvre, and hence, by gradual but persistent measures, place capital in an impasse.[1] This view of the possibility of an incremental weakening of capital is economistic and even in this respect is rather inadequate when we consider the hierarchy of control (illustrated in Figure 1.1). It is economistic because it ignores political and ideological dimensions of struggle against capital; and inadequate, because market forces and political power impose a severe limitation on such practices.

Control from Below vs Control from Above
By control from below I mean the independent struggle of the workers to gain more control in the capitalist workplace, contrary to, or irrespective of, the desire and interests of managers.

Any struggle of this sort may or may not achieve its objective. If it does, and capital agrees to concede, this means either that capital is able to concede or that it has no alternative but to give in. As long as the initiatives of the control struggle are in the hands of the workers, control is from below. In the case of pre-war craft-control in Britain, control was demanded and practised from below, with the agreement of capital, because a) British capitalism was globally dominant; b) the industrial employers lacked competence and self-confidence; c) a relatively high demand for skilled and competent labour strengthened the workers' position and d) the self-disciplining character of craft-control at that period was compatible with the profitability of capital (Hyman, 1975b). But after the war, with intensifying competition on the world market and Taylorism beginning to dominate the work process, the material basis of craft-control tended to diminish. In contrast, control from below in the post-February Russia of 1917, in Chile (1973) or in Iran (1979) materialized simply because capital was in retreat and workers were on the offensive.

Capital never wants to lose control over work relations, nor does it want to recognize even a limited control by labour. Some historical evidence points to the ceding of control to the workers. Yet capital designedly sustains its control by freely introducing or conceding under the pressure of the class struggle workers control.

Control from above thus explains the distortion by capital of the genuine movement (from below) for control by forcefully introducing a limited version with the intention to 'regain control by sharing it' (Cressey and MacInnes, 1980). Such strategies are adopted as a response to the growth of a genuine movement and the contradictions arising from the strategy of direct control by capital reflected in alienation of workers, absenteeism, sabotage, etc.

One expression of capital's response to the revolutionary shop-steward movement was the introduction of Whitleyism in 1916 as an aspect of its more general strategy for post-war reconstruction. It was the strategy of J.H. Whitley, chairman of the committee that recommended creation of permanent joint bodies of employers' representatives and union officials (Hyman, 1975a, p. xix; Coates, 1968, p. 228). One of its main targets was to 'head off and contain any independent and aggressive movement for workers' control' (Hyman, ibid). In Germany, in 1905, some 220,000 out of 270,000 miners went on strike for the reduction of working hours and to question capitalist control. The state responded by introducing labour committees in the mines with limited power (Bologna, 1976, p. 27). In Iran, following the emergence of independent workers' committees (*shuras*) after the overthrow of the Shah's regime, the state itself introduced its own (distorted) version of the Islamic *shuras*.

Control from below can also be fostered by the contradictions inherent in capital: on the one hand it must subsume labour to the means of production in order to maximize surplus-value and on the other, it 'seeks a purely cooperative relationship in order to abolish the antagonism between the worker and the means of production that its capitalist form throws up' (Cressey and MacInnes, 1980, p. 15). Thus the strategies of 'responsible autonomy' (Friedman, 1977), co-determination, the Japanese solution, and so forth, are introduced on the one hand to avert the contradictions of scientific management and direct control, i.e. generating alienation at a high level, which would result in absenteeism, high turnover, strike action (see Walker, 1981, p. 53; Palloix, 1976), and on the other to generate an ideology of mutual interest, interdependence and responsibility through the participation of the workforce in decision-making, autonomous practices and so on.

Some Factors Influencing Control

Four main factors influence the possibility of workers' control over the capitalist production process. These may be classified into two broad categories of capital accumulation and workers' struggles.

Uneven Development of Capitalist Organization of Production

The classic historical development of capitalist work organization may be characterized by the following stages:

i) craft production, with a high level of control by skilled craftsmen over the simple process of production;

ii) the manufacturing system, which brought those skilled craftsmen under one roof where they were still able to exercise a high degree of control from below;

iii) large-scale industry characterized by a more extensive compartmentalization which set the ground for the development of Taylorism. Taylor's system was based upon and extensively fostered the detailed division of labour, culminating in the complete separation of conception from execution;

iv) the post-war systems of organization of production, notably 'neo-Fordism' or 'responsible autonomy' which *appear* to confer a certain degree of autonomy on the workforce;

v) current computerized systems which extend the alienation of shop-floor workers to even professional designers and planners (Murray, undated, p. 13; Cooley, 1981).

The segmental presentation of thse systems does not, of course, imply that they do not co-exist, rather that, at each stage, one system is dominant.

This historical transformation of the labour process has incrementally restricted the control of labour and extended that of capital over the labour process. Workers have responded differently to this process. For instance in Britain, at the turn of the century, workers formed craft unions to protect their relatively strong discretion over the matter of hiring and firing, manning and organization of work.

The development of the contemporary industrializing countries in the Third World is markedly different. There, the most advanced forms of work organization tend to co-exist with an historically backward economy. Fordism is abruptly introduced into economies dominated by peasant production. In such situations almost all of the workforce of the new industries are recruited from the countryside and lack any familiarity with industry, let alone industrial skills and claims for control. A production organization is established without the historical precedent of a control-oriented resistance.[2]

The Technical Content of the Labour Process
As we have noted, the labour process refers to the ways in which use-values are produced with concrete labour. It differentiates various functions and tasks, has varying levels of division of labour, skill and expertise and kinds of organization of work. The feasibility of workers' control is greater in an industrial enterprise with a simpler labour process, simpler division of labour and with a highly-skilled labour force. These would not only enable the workforce to sustain their control following a revolutionary upheaval against the capitalist class, but would act as a factor of control and a bargaining point in normal conditions since capital would need and could not easily replace certain workers' expertise.[3]

The Position of a Given Industry in Competitive Markets
Column 1 of the figure suggests how control over each of the spheres of production activities is constrained by higher levels of determination, and ultimately by market forces.

   While a strong market position could be a reason for not resisting the control demands of the workforce, a weak position would impose serious limiations on such accommodation.[4]

Effective Workers' Organization before the Introduction of New Technology, and the Unity of Workers
The necessity of organized opposition to the employers' strategies to introduce ever more subordinating work organization is self-evident. Resistance by craft workers in Britain led to the shop-steward movement during the First World War. At the same time in the USA employment of an unorganized immigrant workforce facilitated the new strategy of capitalist control.[5]

   That section of the working class which, owing to the particular objective power their skills give them, is able to advance and even lead a movement for control, does not necessarily work for the liberation of the rest of the workforce. The sectarian mentality of the British craftsmen led eventually to 'the collapse of the shop-steward movement' (Hinton, 1973, Chapter 10). Because of occupational differences within the working class, a conscious unity is a prerequisite of workers' control.

Notes

   1. This argument seems to be similar to that put forward by Banaji in his *Communist Platform*, No. 1.
   2. The radical transformation of work organization in American industries, such as the introduction of Taylorism, was facilitated by the massive numbers of immigrant labourers. Some six million of them entered the USA from Europe between 1900 and 1906 (Bologna, 1976, pp. 76–7). See also Montgomery, 1979, pp. 32–47.

3. The highly specialized German tool-makers in the 1910s possessed quite a high degree of power. They were the ones who forced the employers in the Busch Company to introduce the 8-hour day for the first time in 1906 and the free Saturday in 1910. They were also in the forefront of the workers' council movement (Bologna, 1976, p. 68).

4. For the historical facts see Hyman and Elger, 1981, pp. 115–49.

5. Unions like the NGA in Britain fight to retain traditional control over work organization, while the AFL-CIO (American Federation of Labour) has implicitly accepted such encroachment by capital (Davis, 1982).

3. Industrial Development and the Working Class in Iran

Industrial Development

Pre-War Period

The economy in the inter-war period was one in which state capitalism and the oil industry predominated. During the 1930s Reza Shah sought to rebuild Iran in the image of the West by means of secularism, anti-tribalism, nationalism, educational development and state capitalism (Abrahamian, 1982, p. 140). The state played a multiple role in the development of wage-labour relations. It laid the infrastructure for economic, especially industrial, development by the construction of transnational railways and roads and by modernizing the state bureaucracy. The state itself initiated direct industrial investment. By the end of the 1930s it had established 64 factories and was allocating about 20% of its budget to industrial development (Bharier, 1971, pp. 176, 178). The third role of the state was to be a 'class-creating force', the agents of this process being top-ranking state personnel and big landowners and merchants who formed an economically close-knit group. The Shah remained in control though he sometimes came into bitter conflict with the ruling class (Abrahamian, 1982, pp. 149–52).

This phase of industrial development began in the early 1930s as the Great Depression drastically reduced the price of capital goods. The state encouraged industrialization by imposing high tariffs and fiscal policies. It also established state-owned industries. The number of modern industrial plants (excluding oil installations) increased from 20 in 1925 to 346 in 1941 (Abrahamian, 1982, p. 146). The wage-labour sector expanded with the oil industry; many of the small workshops (shoemaking, carpentry and tailoring) merged, each employing over thirty workers. Workers in the oil industry, modern factories, fisheries, railways, coalfields, docks and construction formed a small working class of over 170,000. Concentrated nearby in a few urban centres, this working class was less than 4% of the total labour force. It was surrounded by an ocean of rural workers (11.35 million) whose life and labour were regulated by pre-capitalist relations.

The Post-War Period
The post-war period until the 1953 coup, which was organized by the CIA and toppled the nationalist government of Dr Mosadegh, was characterized by confusion and uncertainty. Reza Shah had been forced to abdicate, being replaced by his son Muhammed Reza Shah. The war had weakened the state and various forms of political, ethnic and working-class struggles flourished. The state was not only inactive in the industrial arena, but government plants were bankrupted by mismanagement and competition from the foreign products which had flooded into the country at the end of the war (Bharier, 1971, p. 183). But later in this period there was a considerable expansion of private industry. A shortage of foreign exchange raised the domestic price of imported goods. Private investment was further encouraged by tariff concessions for importers of machinery. Between 1948 and 1952 nearly 10,000 factories of all sizes were established; in the following four years nearly double this number were set up (Bharier, 1971, p. 184).

After the overthrow of Mosadegh, owing to his independent political stance, the state played a major role in integrating Iran into the world economy. It was from this period on that industrial growth gathered momentum. Three strategies of industrial development were followed: the encouragement of foreign capital investment, import substitution and state capitalism.

Before the 1950s foreign investment outside the oil sector was minute. In the period following the coup it developed rapidly, mostly in the form of investment in subsidiaries of multinationals, in partnership with the state or with indigenous private capital. By the end of the 1960s there were 90 foreign firms in Iran, and by 1974 the number had reached 183 (Halliday, 1978a, p. 153). Nevertheless, overall foreign direct capital investment remained a small proportion of capital investment (3.8% in the 1973–8 Development Plan).

The strategy of industrial expansion was carried out in a series of 5-year development plans. Putting over $9.5 billion into the economy, the third (1962–8) and fourth (1968–73) plans helped GNP to grow at the annual rate of 8% in 1962–70, 14% in 1972–3 and 30% in 1973–4 (Abrahamian, 1982, pp. 427–8). Between 1963–78, the share of manufacturing in GNP increased from 11 to 17%, and the annual industrial growth rose from 5 to 20%. In the same period the value of total industrial output rose almost twelvefold, with an average rate of growth of 72% per annum (Table 3.1). The table shows that the highest rate of growth was in the water and power and construction sectors, with an average annual rate of growth of 104.2% and 78.2% respectively. This growth was due to the rapid construction of hydroelectric dams, power stations, ports and later nuclear power stations, as well as roads, railways, schools, hospitals, public and private housing, offices and factories.

Table 3.1
Industrial Output Between 1963 and 1978 (1,000 million rials)

Industrial sectors	1962–3	1967–8	1972–3	1977–8	Annual rate of growth
Manufacturing & mining	41.5	72.5	224.8	468.2	68.5
Construction	14.1	24.9	91.4	179.5	78.2
Water & power	2.2	8.9	17.2	36.6	104.2
Total	*57.8*	*106.3*	*333.4*	*684.3*	*72.2*

Source: Based on Bank Markazi Iran, and Katouzian (1981, p. 276).

The role of the state in promoting commodity relations was determining both economically and politically. In economic terms the state built up the infrastructure of capital development — which the weak bourgeoisie would have been unable to do. Between 1963 and 1977, dams were built in a number of provinces and helped to increase electrical output from 0.5 billion to 15.5 billion Kw hours. New port facilities were developed, roads and railways were constructed, and the mass media mushroomed. The state was involved in direct as well as infrastructural investment. Thanks to its oil revenue it was responsible in 1975 for some 60% of all industrial investment; through its fiscal policies it encouraged private domestic investment and provided funds for industry through various institutions and specialized banks.

The political role of the state was no less significant. It swept away the old production relations that had hampered the expansion of commodity relations. Encouraged by the US, the state in 1962 introduced a series of reform programmes, the most important of which was the Land Reform. The implementation of the Land Reform ended pre-capitalist land tenure and transformed 'feudal' relations. Unequal distribution of land in the rural areas entailed the formation of a rural bourgeoisie, middle and poor peasant land holders, and a rural proletariat. Commodity relations were expanded in the countryside, as well as between peasants and the urban population.

The Shah's régime was undoubtedly dictatorial. But the repressive nature of the state and the tensions between it and the bourgeoisie in both economic and political spheres by no means hindered the process of capitalist expansion. An observer commented that 'private industry was encouraged and capitalist forms developed in their hundreds during the 1950s and 1960s, precisely due to the growing role of the state in the overall management of the economy' (Nima, 1983, p. 14).

The Growth and Size of the Working Class

The number of industrial workers naturally grew as industry expanded. In 1962–3 the share of industrial labour in the total workforce was 20.6%. By 1977–8 the proportion had reached 33.2%, with an annual rate of growth of 9.3%. The service sector also experienced a substantial rate of expansion — 11.3% per year during 1962–77. In 1977, the share of the service sector in the total GNP amounted to 34.6% (see Table 3.2).

Table 3.2
Sectoral Distribution of Total Labour Force 1963–78 (thousands)

Sector	1962–3 No.	Total (%)	1967–8 No.	Total (%)	1972–3 No.	Total (%)	1977–8 No.	Total (%)
Agriculture	3,672	55.1	3,861	49.0	3,600	40.9	3,200	32.2
Industry	1,372	20.6	1,947	24.7	2,550	29.0	3,300	33.2
Services	1,584	23.8	2,020	25.7	2,600	29.5	3,379	34.0
Oil	36	0.5	46	0.6	50	0.6	60	0.6
Total	*6,664*	*100.0*	*7,874*	*100.0*	*8,800*	*100.0*	*9,939*	*100.0*

Source: Katouzian, 1981, p. 259.

In 1977 about 54% of the total economically active population (EAP) of 8.8 millions were subsisting through wage-labouring. The rest of the population were divided between four working groups: landed peasants using family labour (2.3 million, 26% of the EAP), non-agricultural self-employees (1.1 million, 12.5%), non-agricultural family workers (0.43 million, 4.9%), and employers.

Most wage-earners were directly involved in industrial activities (2.38 million), such as manufacturing, mining, construction, utilities, transport and communications. Over 66,000 workers were engaged in agricultural production; this included those employed in the mechanized agribusiness enterprises, and the collective agri-industries such as the farm factories. The third component of the working class was the service workers, which in the official categorization covered those in modern commercial, insurance and banking enterprises and the public service state bureaucracy (including the police and the army). The total number of employees in this sector in 1978 was 1.65 million, a considerable number of whom were 'white-collar' workers. Subtracting some 400,000 military personnel from the category of service employment, since they were not involved in economic activities, it follows then that some 1.25 million employees were engaged in service, of whom 68% were in the state sector as teachers, clerical workers, health workers or civil servants; and the rest of the 213,000 were employed in the private sector.

If we take a broad economic definition of the working class as including all productive and unproductive wage-labourers who in the processes of production, distribution and exchange collectively contribute to the creation and the realization of surplus-value, then we can roughly estimate that the total number of working-class people in Iran would probably exceed four million; well over 50% of the EAP. The figure points to a relatively large Iranian working class in comparison with other Third World countries (see appendix).

Table 3.3
The Sectoral Distribution of Labour Force 1977

1. Wage-Labourers	Number (000)	%
Agriculture	662	7.5
Industry:	2,388	27.1
Manufacturing*	900	(10.2)
Mining	88	(1.0)
Construction	1,065	(12.1)
Utilities	61	(0.6)
Transport & Communication	272	(3.0)
Services:	1,660	18.7
Commerce, Finance, Insurance	260	(2.9)
Public & Private Services†	1,400	(15.9)
Other	34	0.39)
Total fully or seasonal wage-labourers	4,744	53.9
2. Self-employed (non-agricultural)	1,100	12.5
3. Family workers (non-agricultural)	430	4.9
4. Employers	220	2.6
5. Peasants (with family labour)	2,300	26.0
6. Other	34	0.3
Total Economically Active Population	8,799	100.0

*Excluding self-employed rural and urban manufacturing units.
† Including defence (400,000), state bureaucracy, social services and domestic servants (some 165,000).

Source: Statistical Year Book, 1979–80. Teheran: Plan and Budget Organization.

The Industrial Labour Market

One characteristic of the capitalist industrial labour market is its segmentation into primary and secondary markets. The primary sector is the modern, capital-intensive and monopoly sector with skilled, relatively privileged and stable workers with high wages and job security. The primary sector may evolve within itself an internal labour market from which employees are reproduced and recruited. On the other hand, the secondary labour market is composed of the small-scale, traditional and competitive industrial units, services with low wages and insecure and unstable employment.[1]

The primary sector in Iranian industry consists of oil, state-owned enterprises, multinational firms, joint ventures and other large-scale units of which there were 923, including 162 multinationals, in 1973 (Daftary and Borghaii, 1976, pp. 28–9). The integration of the Iranian economy into the world market brought it into contact with modern technological development, whose operations in a backward economy gave the primary sector a distinct character of its own.

The Primary Labour Market

The strategy of import substitution involved the production of a mass of non-durable and durable consumer goods with a protectionist state policy; it also involved production through periphery Fordism, that is, labour-intensive assembly lines. On the other hand, large-scale heavy industry was producing capital goods such as basic metals which by nature required an expanded and scattered work process (as distinguished from an assembly line) and thus a certain degree of craft-work.

Two trends emerged: on the one hand, import substitution and state protection, together with the existence of a relatively small market for these products, placed some industries in a monopoly position. This potentially enabled them to pay higher wages and provide better conditions. On the other hand, the rapid pace of industrialization produced a high demand for skilled labour. The ILO planners estimated that some 250,000 skilled workers were needed in the manufacturing sector between 1973–7 to be engaged almost entirely in the modern plants (ILO, 1973, p. 74).[2]

The shortage of skilled labour in industry coincided with a political repression which hindered the organization of the workforce into independent unions. Strike action was assumed to be an act of violence against the state. The actual ban on any union organization seems to be quite reasonable from the state's viewpoint, in a country like Iran, since trade union action is very likely to assume a political character (see Chapter 5). Lacking an organizational medium for bargaining, skilled labourers resorted to individual resistance which led to a high labour turnover. My own sampling of the workers of modern factories in Teheran showed that (on average) workers changed their jobs 2.6 times during their industrial work, and 15% of them 4–5 times. In selected multinational companies, the rates of turnover of skilled workers were registered as 25%, 18% and 15% respectively for textiles, chemicals and transport equipment (Daftary and Borghaii, 1976, p. 62).

The Internal Labour Market and Wage Differentials

The need for skilled and stable labour on the one hand, and the monopoly position of industries in the primary sector on the other, laid the foundation for the development of an internal labour market in this sector. The average wage in this sector was undoubtedly higher than that in the small-scale units in the secondary sector. Yet the internal labour market generated a wider wage-differential within itself than that between the primary and secondary sectors.

In the internal labour market, capital makes the wage-differentiations according to skill and education (which are scarce) and length of service (owing to a need for a stable workforce). Wage-differentiation on these grounds was introduced in 1970, under the policy of job classification, *Tabaghebandi-e Mashaghel*. This policy laid down regulations concerning job qualifications and skills, job evaluation, wage-levels, promotion and on-the-job training (Institute of Labour and Social Security, 1976, pp. 102–10). Skilled labour was to be supplied from within a firm or industry by fixed promotion and seniority rules. As a necessary component of the scheme new fringe benefits and bonuses had to be introduced. Such allowances for housing, marriage, childbirth and child benefit are non-existent in the secondary sector.

Table 3.4
Wage Differentials Among Manual Workers of Two Factories in Teheran (March 1981)

Monthly earning (Rls)*	Metal Works % of workforce	Fanoos % of workforce
Under 12,000	2.0	22.5
12,000–20,000	43.2	
20,000–30,000	41.0	62.5
30,000–45,000	8.0	10.0
45,000–65,000	2.5	5.0
65,000–95,000	1.6	
Total	no. = 557	no. = 422

*Rate of exchange in 1981 was $1 = Rls 79.5.

Source: provided by the respective companies.

From the 1973 oil boom until the eve of the Revolution (1973–8), the formal wages of industrial workers rose by an average 30% each year. But wages among the working class were highly unequal and differentiated according to sector. There were significant divisions between a) old and new workers, b) skilled and unskilled, c) permanently employed and contract workers and d) male and female workers. Table 3.4 shows the wage-differentials among the manual workers in two firms.

The disparity between manual workers and white-collar and the highly skilled technicians still tends to be much higher than between manual workers. For instance, in Arj factory in 1981, the white-collar workers were earning on average twice as much as the manual workforce (see Table 7.4).

Inter-Industry Wage Differentiations in the Primary Sector

According to the Job Classification Scheme, length of industrial work (experience) and skill were the main factors in determining wage policy in the primary sector. Yet the strategic position of an industry and its particular labour process are additional factors determining wages. At least four distinct types of industries may be identified; despite their positions as large-scale employers of stable workforces, they adopt different patterns of pay.

a) Industries with a strategic and monopoly position such as the oil industry, employ workers who, for some observers, are a labour aristocracy. Paying the highest average wages in the industrial sector, the oil industry has developed a fully-fledged internal market with an enormous wage disparity within itself (Table 3.5).

b) Industries such as the tobacco industry, with long services involving heavy and unpleasant labouring pay high wages with much lower differentials.

c) In industries characterized by a Fordist labour process the extensive division of labour provides various simplified jobs which can be performed by a cheap semi-skilled workforce who usually get on-the-job training. The automobile industry in Iran is an example. While the average wages in this sector are higher than in the secondary sector, the differentials within it are also high. In 1973, skilled workers earned 3.5 times as much as the unskilled, foremen 2.4 times as much as skilled workers and highly-skilled technicians 5.6 times as much as foremen. This pattern, in general, continued after the 1979 Revolution. This wage pattern is a contradiction of the labour aristocracy thesis which views modern sector workers as a homogeneous privileged workforce without internal divisions.

d) Some large-scale firms in the textile industry are characterized by Taylorism. The work process requires a fairly homogenous skilled workforce to perform quite simple, repetitive tasks.[3] The wages here are the lowest in the primary sector, but their differentiation is relatively small; women, children and migrant peasant workers are the main employees.

The Secondary Sector

This sector falls into three sub-sectors. One is made up of small-scale units (with fewer than ten workers) of either traditional or modern origin.

Table 3.5
Wage Differentials Among Four Categories of Industries,* 1972–3 (Rls per hour/per worker)**

Industry	Total average wage		Unskilled		Skilled		Foremen		High technicians		Total annual average in large units 1979–80 1,000 rials
	Wage	% LF†	Wage	% LF	Wage	% LF	Wage	% LF	Wage	% LF	
Oil & Coal											
Exploration	82.7	100.0	20.4	26.5	86.3	57.8	178.3	13.5	243.0	1.3	1,006
Refining	67.6	100.0	19.8	13.2	59.2	72.1	—	—	209.3	9.5	790
Tobacco	37.5	100.0	24.7	21.0	34.3	69.6	100.8	9.3	—	—	
Transport equipment	16.7	100.0	5.7	19.1	17.9	77.4	42.9	3.0	241.4	0.4	597
Textile	12.9	100.0	11.9	6.7	12.1	84.0‡	19.5	8.8	106.2	0.1	236

*The table has been compiled on the basis of wage differentials in *all* industries (large- and small-scale) in the urban areas. Almost all industries (except textile) are in the large-scale category. Yet, the *Central Bank Bulletin*, Vol. 12, No. 69. supports this intra-industry wage disparity. The disparity within the textile industry remains an estimate.

**Rate of exchange, 1972–3, $1 = Rls 76.66.

†LF = Labour Force.

‡This high proportion of skilled workers in the textile industry seems to be misleading. The figure is probably the result of an inaccurate definition of skill by the official surveyors.

Source: Ministry of Labour, *Natayeg-i Amargiri-e Niroy-e Ensani 35* (Statistics of Labour Force), pp. 208–9.

Using simpler technology, the units produce consumer goods (such as sweets, printing, baking or footwear), do small-scale processing (cement, wood-sawing), or provide transport (buses, taxis, trucks), services, commerce or construction. The second sub-sector is the petty-entrepreneurial, in which the owner may or may not employ his family and one or more apprentices. This sector employs over 1.5 million, some 17% of the total EAP (see Table 3.6). The most common trades here are tailoring, carpentry, goldsmithing and repair. The final sub-sector of wage-employees is domestic servants.

The secondary sector originates historically from existing petty-commodity production and has been reproduced as a consequence of the capitalist accumulation in a broader scale.

Table 3.6
The Position of Workforce of Secondary Sector in Total Employment, 1976–7

	No.	%
1. Small-scale industry	602,000	6.8
(Urban)	(333,000)	(3.7)
(Rural)	(269,000)	(3.0)
2. Petty-entrepreneurial sector	1,104,455	12.0
Petty-self-employed*	433,783	4.9
3. Domestic servants	165,000	1.8
Total wage-labourers	*4,745,000*	*53.9*
Total EAP	*8,799,420*	*100.0*

*In *all* sectors except agriculture and hunting.

Source: Based on *Statistical Year Book, 1979–80*, Teheran, Plan and Budget Organization.

The figures indicate that the secondary sector grew at a higher rate than the primary sector (12.1% and 9.3% respectively in 1963–77). This was for various reasons. The monopoly sector was not developed enough to suppress all branches of traditional production and indeed small-scale units produced some of the raw materials or intermediate goods required by the large-scale ones. Some units, like repair shops, were a direct outcome of the requirements of the modern sector. For certain commodities such as carpets and works of art, the exchange-value of which depends almost entirely on the concrete living labour-time expended. Moreover, some small-scale units employed machines and modern Taylorite (not craft) methods of work. This tendency, combined with low wages, enabled them to compete against the modern industry.

Enterprises in this sector are highly competitive and, in comparison with the enterprises in the primary sector, have a low level of productivity. They pay low wages, offer few benefits, and have poor conditions of work and little job security, the consequences of an effort to reduce costs. The secondary sector is usually regarded by the (mostly migrant) workers as the first place to find a job. In the case of the Teheran marginals, however, research suggests a very limited occupational mobility, especially into the primary sector (Kazemi, 1980, pp. 56–8). But the majority of this class, notably the non-squatting migrants, were fully employed wage-earners and about 48% were working in the private sector (ibid., p. 56).

The dispersed conditions of work made it increasingly difficult for the workers in this sector to organize. Above all, the small size of the workshops and the simple control patterns within them fostered a paternalistic relationship between the workers and the employers, which was a serious obstacle to the development of a labour organization.

The Rural Origin of the Working Class

The working class in Iran has strong rural ties. This is especially true of the workforce in the newly-established industries; labour in older industries such as oil, textile, sugar and tobacco is, on the other hand, mainly second generation from an urban background. Two patterns of labour migration from countryside to town may be identified, roughly corresponding to the periods before and after land reform.

The first may be described as a migratory pattern of formal subordination. This refers to migrations which are not directly caused by capitalist development, but by such push factors in the rural areas as natural disasters, famine and drought. Yet, for the migration to occur at all, there have to be some developing urban centres to absorb the migrants. Such conditions usually begin to develop in the early stages of the transition to capitalist relations, during the period of formal subordination. In Iran, the period from the 1930s up to the late 1950s may be characterized in this way. From the second half of the 1930s migration from the countryside to the cities was around 25,000 a year. The figure jumped to 130,000 for the subsequent period of 1941–56. By 1964, 48.8% of the population of Teheran (1,115,286) were immigrants, of whom 60% were searching for a job or a better job; the rest were dependants (Ministry of Labour, 1965, pp. 1601, 1608).

The second post-land-reform population movement may be characterized as a migratory pattern of real subordination. It refers to a major urban migration movement which was substantially caused by the development of capitalist relations (in both places of origin and destination) which drew the mass of rural labour into its network. By the 1970s, the land reform programme had accomplished its task of altering the socioeconomic structure of the countryside, integrating it into the capitalist

Table 3.7
Annual (Compound) Rates of Population Growth

Period	Urban	Rural	Total	Annual no. of urban migrants
1900–26	0.08	0.08	0.08	0.0
1927–34	1.5	1.5	1.5	0.0
1935–40	2.3	1.3	1.5	25,000
1941–56	4.4	1.4	2.2	130,000
1957–66	5.3	1.7	2.9	250,000
1967–76	4.8	1.2	2.7	330,000

Source: Bharier, 1972.

market. It transformed the class structure of rural ares. A rural bourgeoisie and proletariat were created; land became a commodity, production tended to be carried out not for subsistence but for sale, exchange relations between town and country and in the rural areas expanded. The pre-capitalist organizations of production were transformed into individual petty production and a few agribusinesses. As a result of the land reform, some 73% of the peasants received land of less than 6 hectares and about 35% received virtually nothing or less than one hectare (Hooglund, 1982, p. 91). This unequal allocation of land, together with the privatization of farming water, the rising need of the peasant family for cash (because of its integration into the market) and the forceful expropriations of peasant land for agribusinesses started a massive urban migration, and proletarianization of migrant peasants.

As a result, urban migration continued to rise during the 1960s and 1970s as industrialization proceeded. During the period 1966–76, over 300,000 rural people were pouring into the cities every year (Table 3.7) together with another 10,000 foreign migrants. The major urban centres were transformed. The rural areas lost many more of their people in this period than in the previous one. In 1972, immigrants were 13.8% of the urban population, some four million. Industrial centres like Teheran attracted the highest proportion of immigrants. With an annual rate of growth of 5.3% between 1976 and 1980, it had 13.4% of the total population in 1976–7.

Notes

1. I am aware that the terms 'primary' and 'secondary' labour markets, which are used as equivalent to 'formal' and 'informal' sectors, are merely descriptive terms.

2. The debates on shortage of skilled labour were reflected in a great deal of literature: see ILO (1973), Bartsch (1971) and Elkan (1977). The shortage was such that the government imported some 15,000 skilled workers from, among other places, South Korea, the Philippines and Pakistan.

3. Generally the workers in textile manufacturing (not craft) are quite rightly characterized by *unskilled* labour. The 'paradox' in Iranian textile industry is due to the official, formal definition of 'skill' as a capacity to perform one particular task, no matter how much knowledge the task requires.

4. Proletarianization

The term 'proletarianization' generally refers to the process of the emergence and development of a class whose subsistence depends on the sale of its labour power (manual and intellectual). An examination of proletarianization is also an analysis of the economic aspect of working-class formation.

An analysis of the emergence of the working class should also include a study of its cultural/ideological and political domensions. In this chapter I shall discuss the problems inherent in the socio-cultural position of the Teheran factory workers. The political struggle of the working class will be outlined when we deal with the struggle for the formation of the *shuras* in Chapters 7–9.

The Determinants of Proletarianization

In examining the proletarianization of the labouring classes in capitalist production, writers have expressed rather different views. Studying the proletarianization of the factory workers of Petrograd from the beginning of the First World War until 1917, S.A. Smith (1980) has used three criteria to distinguish two strata of Russian workers: worker-peasants and cadre-workers (proletarianized wage-labourers). The criteria are a) the scale of the worker's landownership in the countryside and whether or not s/he is engaged in both agricultural and industrial production, as a seasonal labourer; b) the length of residence in the city, the degree of urbanism and detachment from rural culture; and c) the extent to which s/he comes from prior generations of working-class families (pp. 22–6).

A general application of these criteria to identify a proletarianized working class is problematic. At least two meanings can be attributed to the concept of proletarianized worker. On the one hand the term refers to a change in consciousness by urbanized, class-conscious workers with a long period of industrial work and a high degree of organization. On the other hand, it also refers to a change in the objective conditions of labourers who, a) have lost control over the means and conditions of production which they had previously exercised, b) have nothing but their labour power to sell in the capitalist free market, and c) are freed from their pre-capitalist ties (change in objective conditions). Smith's criteria confuse these two conceptually distinct changes.

The criteria, however, are useful in examining the initial stages of a class in the making and class formation in present-day Third World countries where the dominant feature of working-class development is worker consciousness. This changed consciousness means that 'workers' identities and societal imagery based on their places in systems of work relations . . . override the identities of kinship, ethnicity, or other non-work roles and affiliations . . . Workers may express it by acting collectively or as individuals' (Simpson and Simpson, 1981, p. ix).

As for working-class formation, Hobsbawm, examining the development of the English working class in the late 19th Century, held that the working class could be said to have been formed only when its members began to feel the identity of their interests in all economic, political and cultural spheres, and to act accordingly in their daily lives. He demonstrated historically that the English workers assumed their class character only in the second half of the 19th Century.[2] Such an approach, however, would lead to denying the existence of a working class in many backward capitalist countries, as well as in the most advanced capitalist society, the USA. American labour lacks political organization; only a minor part of it (16% of workers in private industry) is organized in trade unions (Davis, 1982, p. 45).[3] As Cohen et al rightly argue (1974, p. 14), the essential issue is not so much *whether* there is a proletariat in countries like Iran or Nigeria; the incorporation of those countries in global capitalism has inevitably created one. The essential issue is rather *how* a proletariat is formed in a complex of religious, linguistic, ethnic differentiations; how divided it is, and how, despite the divisions, it reveals a class identity and political consciousness.

Rural Origins

With regard to Smith's criterion of land ownership in the countryside, we may argue that the Teheran factory workers, especially in comparison with other Third World workers, are entirely proletarianized. Rural origin and migration are marked peculiarities of the Iranian working class. In Teheran our sample revealed that 94% of the workers had been born in places other than Teheran; 7% of these were from the suburbs of the capital. This trend is supported, to a large extent, by the data from single factories. Of the 900 workers in Metal Works factory for instance, only 13% were from Teheran and 3.6% from its suburban areas. As Table 4.1 indicates, over 80% of the workers in this factory were peasants or sons of peasants who had migrated to Teheran because of landlessness, shortage of land or insufficient income. They had mostly migrated after land reform, when commodity relations were spreading rapidly in the countryside. In comparison with the Petrograd workers of 1917, and workers in the rest of today's Third World (except probably in some Latin

American nations), Teheran factory workers have to a large extent broken their economic ties with the village.

Table 4.1
The Causes of Migration According to Workers

The causes expressed	%
Loss of land	
(*Khusnashins*, agricultural and other rural labourers)	39.1
Shortage of land (less than 5 hectares per family)	29.1
Scarcity of water, drought leading to low income, oppression	15.0
Migration with family	5.8
Low income despite sufficient land	2.5
Workers born in towns and unspecified	8.3
Total	*100.0* (N = 150)

Iranian pre-capitalist relations in the countryside, unlike European feudalism, lacked legal barriers preventing the free movement of the peasants. This facilitated rural-rural and rural-urban migration even before land reform. But the post-land-reform migratory process was quantitatively and qualitatively different. The new wave of capitalist development and industrialization from the 1960s onward had a profound influence on the proletarianization process in that it 'liberated' free labour (see Chapter 3).

Our survey revealed that some 90% of the workers lacked any form of ownership in the villages. The rest owned a small plot (less than two hectares) or a tiny orchard which had been let to other villagers. Only 7 out of 88 entirely propertyless workers said that their relatives, parents or brothers possessed a small plot (up to three hectares). This lack of workers' economic interest in the village militated against the development of seasonal factory labour. In this respect, the African countries provide a rather different picture. In West Africa, for example, some three-quarters of a sample of industrial workers in the late 1960s and early 1970s claimed some sort of land ownership in the countryside (Simpson and Simpson, 1981, p. 3). But the Teheran factory workers are not representative of the whole working class. The construction workers, for instance, provide a good example of seasonal labour. Nonetheless, wage-relations are now the predominant characteristic of the entire Iranian social economy.[4]

Length of Industrial Service and Urbanization
A long residence in the town would tend to undermine any inclination to return to the village. Some workers even stressed that they had forgotten

how to do farm work. If the length of service in wage-work is regarded as a positive indication of proletarianization, Teheran factory workers score highly. Over 35% of them had been wage-labouring for over 15 years; and fewer than 10% for less than 5 years. Yet the factories under investigation were mainly the product of the industrialization process of the 1960s.

The importance of length of service in wage-work as a factor of proletarianization is disputed. As Smith reports, Soviet historians have argued that it takes at least five years for a new wage-labourer to develop into a fully-fledged proletarian (Smith, 1980, p. 32). While Lenin, on the one hand, described workers as 'those who, as a result of the conditions of their lives, have gained a proletarian mentality', he also argued that such a mentality required at least ten years of work in large industry to develop (1973b, pp. 254–6). Although the length of industrial service may be significant, proletarian mentality does not depend on it. There may be workers who carry out both industrial work and agricultural production, and who reside virtually in the countryside. This is a quite frequent tendency (in our sample 4%). Other factors must be considered in order to find out the extent to which workers have lost negative rural mentalities (those which tend to restrain the migrants from acquiring new values) and gained an industrial consciousness.

Table 4.2
Length of Industrial Service Among Teheran Factory Workers

Length of service	1. My sample %	2. Factory (A) %	3. Factory (B) %
15 years and over	45.3	} 7.3	16
Between 10 & 15 years	22.6		30.5
Between 5 & 10 years	22.6	51.0	} 53.5
5 years or less	9.3	42.0	
Total	*100.0*	*100.0*	*100.0*
Total workers	*N = 150*	*N = 800*	*N = 750*

Factory (A) established in 1966; Factory (B) established 1960.

Sources: Column 1, my own sample; Columns 2 and 3 provided by the factory managements.

As we have said, some 80% of Teheran workers are of rural origin. Yet nearly half of them have been urban residents for 5–20 years; and on the whole, fewer than 10% of them had experienced urban life for less than five years. Not surprisingly, only 4% of the workers lived in the villages around Teheran. But a relatively long stay in the city does not necessarily imply urbanism — the acquisition and practice of urban-industrial values. It is therefore necessary to examine the cultural/ideological relationship between the workers and rural life.

Rural Links

We shall concentrate here on the degree of severance of the cultural/ideological ties between the worker and his village, without making any value judgement about the cultures and the ideologies. (This issue will be examined later when we deal with the factors preventing proletarianization.)

Quite a large majority, 75% of the respondents, had relatives and friends in a village, though these links were mainly remote. A quarter of the sample denied any link with a village, whether moral — the obligation to friends or relatives — or economic — the remittance of, or receiving, money, goods or presents in any form. This group of workers included those of urban origin, and those who lacked any reason for continuing links with the village. While, as we learnt earlier, around 85% of the sample lacked any form of property in the villages, a limited proportion, of 25%, said they did not have any form of link. The difference between these two figures points to the part played by familial and moral/cultural elements in linking workers to the village world.

Yet the rural link of the Teheran workers seems much less significant than that of African workers or Istanbul shanty-town dwellers.[5]

Table 4.3
The Rural Link of Teheran Factory Workers (1981)

Forms of linkage	%
Totally rural resident	3.3
Regular visit (once a month)	8.0
Irregular visit (3–4 times a year)	14.0
Rare visit (1–2 a year for holidays or cultural visits)*	39.3
Without any links	24.0
Other	10.0
Total	*100.0*
	Number of workers = 150

*Cultural visits are those made on such occasions as deaths, marriages, etc.

Table 4.3 shows that an insignificant proportion (10%) retained strong ties with a village. Leaving aside the workers who lived in villages, those with ties were those who were economically unable to have their families living in the town or single persons who supported their parents, brothers or sisters. This group had to remit a considerable amount of their income to the village. Irregular communications characterized those workers who visited friends or relatives or paid visits on occasions like marriages and deaths and those whose connection was for practical reasons, such as to inspect belongings which they had left behind.

Yet the financial remittances of the workers were meagre: only 12% sent a part of their income to the village, and 16% sometimes, some presents. In addition, predictably, financial assistance from the countryside to the workers was even more insignificant. The fewer the workers' links to the village, the more tenuous the kinship identity.

The migration pattern is useful in examining workers' connections with the village before 1980. Some workers, when leaving the village, brought their families; others emigrated by themselves. Individual migration is followed by an inevitable persistence of rural links; whereas the migration of the entire family leads to a gradual breaking off of the relationship. Some 45% of the migrant workers brought their entire family with them, even though in most cases they had to endure the risk of possible unemployment or insecure jobs. The rest had initially migrated on their own and after a while (1–10 years) had their families join them or were single. The interesting thing about this group was their tendency to marry urban girls in the city (though the pattern of marriage in the village has not withered away). This points to the gradual reproduction of urban social relations among the immigrant workers. The domination of male household heads of these families meant that children were brought in line with the father's wishes in cases where the wife was brought from the native village.

Family Background
One of the most important determinants of proletarianization is the family background of the worker. A working-class family tends to transfer its proletarian experience and mentality to the next generation. This mediation becomes more significant in conditions where non-family cultural and neighbourhood organizations are almost non-existent.

The survey revealed that the socio/cultural background of a large majority of the Teheran factory workers was non-proletarian. Only 7% of workers' fathers had engaged in industrial labour, though over a quarter were involved in wage-labouring in one way or another: in construction, railways and inferior jobs in the government ministries. The rest were independent workers (14%) and peasants (both landed and landless, over 55%) (Table 4.4). From this perspective, we may conclude that the working class in modern manufacturing industry, unlike that in oil and textiles, is still historically young.

The children of the workers (the second generation) in our sample were not numerous enough to enable us to examine class mobility accurately. Nonetheless, the occupations of this small number were evidence of working-class reproduction: of 23 workers' children, 20 were factory workers, one a taxi-driver, one an army sergeant and one a college student. Comparing this occupational composition with that of

Table 4.4
Occupations of the Fathers of the Teheran Workers (1981)

Occupations	1961 %	1981 %
Peasants (landed or landless)	65.1	55.8
Independent workers*	21.5	14.1
Wage-labourers	1.7	26.6
(Industrial workers)	?	(7.5)
Unspecified	2.0	3.4
Total	100.0	100.0
Total no. of workers	N = 239	N = 120

*Including: *Mulla*, barber, carpenter, shepherd, petty-trader.

Source: Vielle, 1980, p. 75, for 1961 figures; my own sample for 1981.

1981 presented in Table 4.4 attests to the accelerating growth of the class. A sample survey of 1,189 households in Teheran in 1981 indicated that the rate of reproduction of the two generations in the working-class (skilled and semi-skilled) families, was much higher than that in the upper or middle classes, i.e. over 240% (Table 4.5).

Table 4.5
Class Mobility in Two Generations, Teheran, 1981

Class position	Father's generation %	Childrens' generation %
Upper classes	7.1	11.9
Middle classes:	46.7	37.5
New middle class	(9.7)	(19.1)
Traditional middle class	(37.0)	(17.9)
Traders and craftsmen	(24.1)	(17.0)
Landed peasantry	(12.9)	(0.9)
Working class:	46.3	50.5
Skilled and semi-skilled	(19.8)	(33.4)
Unskilled and the like	(10.3)	(16.6)
Agricultural and husbandry	(26.2)	(0.5)
Total	100.0	100.0

Source: Tabrizi, 1981, p. 48.

Resistance and Metamorphosis

So far we have examined the indices of the process of proletarianization among Teheran factory workers. This is only one aspect of the question. The other is resistance to the process. If we do not assess the contradictions and tensions within this process of transformation and if we do not acknowledge its complexities, a study of proletarianization will be incomplete.

We have so far pointed out the predominantly peasant origin of the Teheran industrial workers. On the other hand, we mentioned that one aspect of the metamorphosis of a rural migrant to a fully-fledged proletarian was not only physical migration, but the acquisition of an urban industrial mentality. We shall deal with two issues: first, the characteristics of the cultural/ideological load which a migrant carries with him and secondly, the process of its metamorphosis in the town. The metamorphosis proceeds by a dialectical interaction between the inherited cultural/ideological load and the cultural/ideological forms which emanate from the mode of life in the new environment, and from the new position of the migrant in industry.

The Legacy of Rural Culture

Our study showed that workers of Turkish origin (from Azerbaijan, and other areas) and Shomali workers (that is, those from the northern provinces of Gilan and Mazandaran) were the main ethnic components of the workforce in Teheran factories. Data on the whole workforce of a few factories demonstrate the same pattern (Table 4.6).

Although only a small number of factory managers could provide accurate sociological data on the workers' origins, almost all of them expressed their surprise at the high concentration of Turkish-speaking[6] and Shomali workers.[7]

The managers could not conceal their dissatisfaction at such a composition. To what extent class identity has been able to transcend these ethnic/cultural groupings is a matter of debate.[8] But the reason behind managements' displeasure is the persistence of a rural cultural form of kinship or ethnic solidarity, which together with proletarian militancy — the product of the wage-labourer's position in the production process — acts against management authority. This form of traditional solidarity, however, may also have narrow sectarian and disunifying characteristics. Workers from the same village may unite against their boss; but this does not imply unity with other workers against the same boss.

Stratification inside the factories can be attributed to the particular mode of labour recruitment. Several factors caused the labour force to be recruited directly at the factory gates, and/or introduced by fellow-villagers. Among these were the rapidity of industrialization and the need for cheap labour; the 'irrationality' of most of the traditional factory-

Table 4.6
Ethnic Composition of Teheran Factory Workers (1981–2) %

The areas of origin	Sample survey	Metal Works	Teheran Auto	P.R. Plant	Sample survey 1961
Turkish speaking:	36.6	27.6		?	37.2
(from Azerbaijan)	(?)	(25.6)		?	?
(Hamadan, Ghazvin, Saveh)	(?)	(2.0)	70.0	?	?
Shomali					
(Gilan & Mazandaran)	14.6	16.3		30.0	4.7
Teherani Persian	13.3	16.5	?	30.0	11.6
Central areas of country	14.6	?	?	?	?
Other areas	20.6	39.3	30.0	40.0	40.4
Total	*100.0*	*100.0*	*100.0*	*100.0*	*100.0*
Total no. of workforce	*150*	*720*	*2,600*	*900*	*293*

Sources: The first column are figures from my own sample; data on the factories was provided by factory managers, and the last column is from Vielle, 1980, p. 75.

-owners for whom cheap labour and a rapid rate of return were preferable to the careful selection of competent labour with a higher productivity potential. In any factory, ethnic/cultural groups from the same village were formed. In our survey, it was revealed that some one-third of all workers had been recruited by friends and relatives; and less than 15% of workers, mostly skilled, through newspaper advertisements. Over half the workers were simply hired at the factory gates. For this group information on the availability of jobs would probably have been provided by friends or acquaintances.

We now should consider the cultures of our migrant workers (Azeri, Shomali and Yazdi) and how and to what extent these cultures have resisted or been undermined by the dominant urban culture. None of these questions can be answered accurately in the abstract without a specific empirical investigation. It is important that we should not make canonical statements such as that workers with a rural culture are conservative and full of petty-bourgeois values, though of course this may well be the case.

Two things may be relevant here. First, the above approach assumes 'peasantry' as a homogeneous socio-economic category which possesses fixed and inscribed ideological characteristics, e.g. adherence to property ownership, individualism, narrow-mindedness, a belief in the immutable nature of things. The category of peasantry is not homogeneous or neatly stratified. Ideological/cultural differentiation can be amplified by regional variations. A lack of clear understanding of workers' culture could lead to a misconception of their socio-political behaviour. All traditions and cultural symbols possess historical character. As Stuart Hall rightly argues, it is false to 'value tradition for its own sake, and treating it in an ahistorical manner, analyse popular cultural forms as if they contained within themselves, from their moment of origin, some fixed and unchanging meaning or value' (Hall, in Samuel, 1981, p. 237). What is significant is, first, the very act of metamorphosis, and secondly, the mode and form of this process. Is a given traditional form reactionary? In itself, this is an irrelevant question. The answer can only be historically conditioned: where? when? under what conditions? and what is its implication? An interesting study on the Petrograd working class of 1917 revealed that nearly 20% of the workers in the gigantic steel mill, Putilov, with a 30,000 workforce, and the headquarters of the Petrograd Soviet, were in fact peasant-workers; that is, wage-labourers who, while working in the factory, were also involved in agricultural work in their villages. Towards the end of the war, as the demand for labour in the armament industry rose, this tendency became even more marked (Smith, 1980, pp. 35–9). This is in addition to the fact that a large majority of the workforce were from rural backgrounds. In another instance, in the inter-war period in Britain when the car was becoming a general consumer commodity, a large part of the Coventry automobile industry was absorbed from the most backward agricultural and mining areas of South Wales. These immigrant workers retained their original culture and formed one of the most militant sections of the working class in the industry (Zeitlin, 1980, p. 10).

These examples do not imply that rural culture plays a positive role in the development of workers' militancy. Their objective is simply to dispute the false generalization that peasant culture is always conservative. The organized militancy of the workers of Petrograd was facilitated because they brought with them the village tradition of *astorcy* (the election of the headman of the village or a council or elders) into the factories. This tradition inside the factory was turned initially into the tradition of election of workers' delegates, and later in the revolutionary period of 1917, into the formation of the *fabzavkomy*, factory committees. Secondly, they were militant because their resentment against the system derived not only from their position in the industry as wage-labourers but also from their position as peasants or peasants' sons within oppressive relations in the village (Siriani, 1982, p. 32). In Britain the South Welsh immigrant workers to Coventry brought with them a strong tradition of trade unionism from mining areas into the factories of Coventry.

Cultural form and symbols can be class-pervasive. Classes speak the same language, hold the same religion, and share other aspects of a common culture. Each class attempts to transform not only the content, but even the appearance of the symbols or traditions according to their own interests. In this sense, culture becomes an arena of class struggle. In this process the ruling classes advocate their dominant culture, while the subordinate classes strive (consciously or spontaneously) to transmute them in accordance with their own aspirations. In the case of the Russian *astorcy* we could observe how it was carried from one class (peasants) to another (factory workers); from one historical situation to another; and how in this process it was itself transformed.

The Cultural Loads of the Teheran Factory Workers

General Features The social organization of Iranian villages has historically been based upon a kinship system and kinship relations. Two of the most significant attributes of kinship relations, as far as our discussion is concerned, are patriarchy and conflict. One of the principles and social implications of patriarchy is the idea that the status of an individual male is judged by his age. This idea paves the way for a culture of subordination, respect for elders and legitimation of their authority. The translation of this particular ideological/cultural form into the factory and society at large would, from the workers' viewpoint, raise questions about the legitimacy of labour and political leadership. The elderly workers would cast doubt on the legitimacy of a young radical leader; an old conservative union leader might be acceptable (the case of Amazon factory, spring 1981).

The dialectic of co-operation and conflict is a characteristic feature of rural social relations in Iran: co-operation, closeness and solidarity *within* the kinship structures, and conflict, confrontation and competition for power *between* them.[9] According to Paul Vieille's survey (Teheran, 1980) 67 of 199 workers of rural origin in Teheran factories in 1962 remembered bloody confrontations in their villages. The same survey reports that the conflicts were on such issues as the allocation of irrigation water, land, harvesting, the landowner's policy of divide-and-rule, and cultural differences (pp. 14–17). The transfer of this particular cultural characteristic to the factory floor may lead to the creation of traditional solidarity among particular groups of workers against the management (the case of ITN) but to cultural divisions between the workforce as a whole (eg. P.R. Plant).

Particular Characteristics We shall be concerned here with two workers' groupings — Shomalis and Yazdis, and with the degree of militancy among them.

Almost all our observations in various factories suggest a high degree of militancy among Shomali workers who were mostly rebellious, enlightened, usually the vanguard in protest actions, and sensitive to the issue of democracy. They were militant not only in their own region (Gilan and Mazandaran) but also in some other industrial centres where they were concentrated. My study of the whole labour movement in the year immediately following the revolution confirms that, in terms of the nature of demands and the forms of struggle, Shomali factory workers were the most radical. The long strike of the Chuka wood industry in Asalem in spring and summer 1979 for workers' control and other demands is an example (see also Table 4.7). A clear distinction should be made between these, and, for instance, Yazdiese with their conservative views and susceptibility to paternalism.

We would suggest that the radicalism of Shomali workers arises from the socio-economic and historical peculiarities of the Caspian Sea coastal region. Because of its fertile land and sufficient rain, the Caspian Sea coastal area was one of the first regions where large-scale agriculture and production for the market developed. This implied, on the one hand, loss of land and smallholding, and a gradual process of proletarianization; and on the other, more rapid development of commodity production and wage-labour relations.

Table 4.7
Regional Variations in the Participation of Units in Radical Protests in the Five Months Following the Revolution

Region	No. of units which protest	No. of units making radical protests	Percentage of units making radical protests
Shomal	63	35	55.5
Teheran	90	31	34.4
Azerbaijan (Tabriz)	35	14	40.0
Ghazvin	9	5	55.5
Khuzistan (oil fields)	26	12	46.1
Other areas*	64	13	20.3
Total	*287*	*110*	*38.3*

*Including: Isfahan, Shiraz, Arak, Kurdistan and Gonbad.

Note: Radical demands are specified in Chapter 7, Table 7.1.

Source: Compiled on the basis of Labour Reports in papers *Kar* and *Paykar*.

The hasty expansion of tourism from the 1960s onwards had a dramatic cultural effect on the region. It expanded small-scale trade and involved villages in the economy of the town. This in turn meant the establishment of strong links between the rural areas and the towns, de-isolation and a consequent urbanization, in a socio-cultural sense, of rural life. This pattern is not found in other regions of the country. This background may explain why the people of this region are more flexible and open to new cultural forms and ideas. In Gilan there is a long tradition of anti-clericalism evidenced in alcohol drinking in market-towns (Kazemi and Abrahamian, 1977).

The region has a tradition of militancy, shown by the anti-imperialist and anti-dictatorial struggles of the late 1910s embodied in the Jangali Movement which, together with Communists established the embryonic Soviet Republic of Gilan in 1919; the Seyahkal Movement, a left-wing guerrilla group which started a new wave of armed struggle against the Shah's regime in the 1960s. These events are an important part of the people's written and oral history. This cultural/ideological load was carried by the migrants into the factories of Teheran (as well as into the industrial units of the region itself).

In contrast, the Yazdi workers came from areas on the margin of the central desert where in dusty and isolated villages the traditional values and superstitions still persisted. In the P.R. Plant the conservative and traditional sectarianism of this group of workers became an obstacle in the way of workers' struggle.

Acquisition of New Cultural Traits?

In a cultural metamorphosis, the dialectic of abandonment and acquisition occurs in a unified process. We shall now look at the process of the acquisition of urbanist norms and values. The term urbanism implies that the social division of labour in urban life undermines self-sufficient and individualistic mentalities; that the spectrum of people, occupations and ideas with which s/he comes into contact opens up the closed world of the peasant migrant; an unequivocal demonstration of social contradictions and inequalities; an awareness of the concentration of power in the hands of a few vs the powerlessness of many; and lastly that the direct or indirect involvement of the migrant in these conditions, will shatter his conception of the eternity and naturalness of the world. The argument that the urban migrant may in certain conditions develop new forms of rural culture in urban centres, and that the urban life may produce new kinds of individualism, may well be valid in some circumstances. But Teheran factory workers do not exhibit this tendency. According to our survey, beside the fact that all of the workers had radios, some 80% possessed television sets; and two-thirds of them had obtained them *before* the Revolution when the main addressee of the programmes was the new middle class.

Yet aspirations, ethnic identities and traditional values may be preserved and practised alongside new beliefs. This, however, is not simply because of psychological/cultural reasons, i.e. survival of traditions and values for the sake of traditions and values. It is rather 'a direct response to the exigencies of survival in the competitive urban economy where economic opportunities are scarce' (Robert, 1978, p. 141). In a

47

society which lacks any form of social security familial and kinship ties tend to become stronger; and family/kinship institutions play the roles of the agencies of economic, social and moral security. Cohen's study of African societies has discovered that among the African workers, tribal cultural forms reappear as a reaction to industrial discipline (1981, p. 198).

Religious Workers?

This leads us to examine the conception of the religious character of the Iranian working class. In our view, the application of this vague concept, without clear definition, to Teheran industrial workers, would reflect a misconception of workers' social behaviour and their particular mode of conceptualization. By being religious we mean having a belief in a metaphysical force which is assumed to determine the relations between men on the earth. Given this conception, we would not regard Teheran industrial workers as religious *per se*; rather, we would suggest that for them religion is a cultural form whose content changes with historical situations. This should not be taken to imply that they are aetheist or faithless, but their religion is determined by the relations between men, not the other way round. The reaction of the workers in the Azmayesh factory to Khomeini's famous statement that 'we have not made revolution for cheap melons, we have made it for Islam' was

> they say we have not made revolution for economic betterment! What have we made it for, then? They say, for Islam! What does Islam mean then? We made it for the betterment of the conditions of our lives.

In an historical situation when a secular modern political language has not yet become popular, the language, the terms and the symbols of the predominant popular culture, religion, have become political. Political behaviour is clothed in religious language and slogans and even in sermons. Religion (as popular culture) is no longer simply an instrument of class domination, but rather a subject of class struggle.

In the early stages of capitalist expansion in England, where a new proletariat was emerging, religion, as a cultural form, was transformed to serve as a socio-political expression of the working class. Thus Primitive Methodism and the Labour Church with radical political connotations emerged in the working-class districts, especially of mining areas, in opposition to the conservative Church of Wesley. In France, where the dominant (Catholic) Church was a strongly conservative force, the labour movement remained independent of religion. Here, instead, the great image of the Jacobin Republic, or personified republic was invoked (Hobsbawm, 1964, pp. 375–6). The relevance of the point is much more obvious in today's world. Religion as the arena of class struggle is seen most unequivocally with the emergence of 'liberation theology' in Latin America, in particular in revolutionary Nicaragua: we see the Church of the Poor vs the Church of the Rich.

The Teheran workers have not yet developed a labour religion or a coherent radical religion. At the same time, they lack secular traditions to express their immediate aspirations (mass trade unions, workers' parties or socio-cultural associations). As a consequence, the working class has tended to change the content of established religion, and has had to borrow certain elements of the dominant cultural forms which do not historically belong to it.

This dialectic of change by means of 'traditions' is quite similar to the one by which E.P. Thompson described plebeian culture of 18th-Century England: 'the plebeian culture is rebellious, but rebellious in defence of culture' (1970: p. 154).

This incapacity of the workers to develop their *own* cultural expression points to their weakness. It is here — in this limbo of being religious and not being religious, in the struggle against dominating religion by religious language — that obscurities, ambiguities, mistakes and deceits can easily take root. These are the characteristics of a class in the formative transition.

Limitations on the Development of a Class Culture

One of the most important variables influencing the development of a class culture is the expansion of communication through the organization of political, welfare, cultural or artistic activities, pamphleteering papers, local meetings, associations and self-help activities. The working class in Iran, including the Teheran factory workers, lack such facilities. According to my survey and a few others (Ershad, 1978; Javadi Najjar, 1974), over one-third of the workers (37%) are totally illiterate, some one-quarter have little ability to read and write, and only one-third (another 37%) are literate. Of 120 workers, only 15 had read as far as high-school courses, of whom 6 had graduated. In such circumstances, the possibilities of acquiring modern and detailed knowledge become very limited. This limitation is aggravated by political repression (an attribute of both the pre- and post-revolutionary regimes). The presence of television sets in the houses of 80% of the workers only served to reinforce established culture. Out of forty literate workers, 40% stated that they read newspapers 'at times', and only 17% 'regularly'. The latter group tended to be of urban origin, skilled and with relatively higher education.

Class struggle — i.e. the struggles that the workers wage as a result of their positions as *workers* in the social organization of production — precedes class formation in the sense of the maturity of the working class to achieve identity and hegemony. In Europe independent out-of-work organizations, societies and gatherings among the working class have been manifestations of the process of class formation. They grew rapidly when the capitalist state was in the initial stage of its formation. In England, for instance, independent working-class associations and activities developed extensively after 1780: the workers constructed schools, literary societies, sports clubs, cultural clubs and political associations; published papers and books, and formed self-help organizations which all together constituted the expression of class formation and class struggle (Thompson, 1979, pp. 781–820). But the advanced form of the capitalist state which was the product of an accelerating rate of capital accumulation following two world wars was characterized by more intervention of the state in the economy, and the development of the welfare state in the form of social security policies, free education and health care. This expansion in the functions of the capitalist state erodes the material basis of traditional independent working-class activities (Jones and Novak in Corrigan, 1980). The new state could present itself as supra-class and exert ideological domination over the working class, particularly in periods of economic boom. In the Third World, on the other hand, material circumstances requiring self-help activities still prevail.[10]

In Iran there is some evidence of working-class self-help activities in particular districts.[11] But the scale is limited and the potential meagre, despite the evident need. For Teheran industrial workers, free time is hardly ever spent in gatherings for discussion and chat about work and daily life. My survey, along with other studies (Ershad, 1978; Javadi Najjar, 1974), points to the fact that most industrial workers (according to my survey, 80%) spent their leisure time almost exclusively at home in isolation. Another survey dealing with Arak industrial workers in 1978 indicated that over 90% were interested in home-oriented leisure (Ershad, 1978, p. 217).

This implies that the workplace is almost the only place of collectivity. In Teheran, there is almost no equivalent of the labour clubs, Sunday Schools or traditional pubs of the early English working class. The *ghahveh khanes* (coffee shops) in Teheran are *not*, contrary to popular view, gathering places of *industrial* workers. Only 2 out of 120 industrial workers stated that their free time was spent at the *ghahveh khane*. These are used on the one hand as residences for migrant construction workers in the initial stages of their arrival at the city and on the other, in the bazaar areas, as the place where the workers in traditional workshops and trade enterprises spend their lunch-time break.

Since the workers lack any secular independent institutions of their own through which to express their culture and class feeling, they have had to borrow institutional devices from the dominant cultural form, religion. The mosque and *hey-ats*[11] have become institutions of leisure. In my sample survey, those (20%) who stated that they had leisure time were oriented more than anywhere else toward mosques and *hey-ats*. Another survey in 1974 reached the same conclusion. It found out that of leisure-time pursuits such as going to bars, cabarets, theatre, sports centres, parks, *ghahveh khane*, *hey-at* and *emamzadeh* (shrines of pilgrims), mosque attendance with 21.4% of positive responses was the most popular form of leisure (Javadi Najjar, 1974, p. 69). Research in the town of Arak showed that 40% of workers spent their free time in the mosques (Ershad, 1978, p. 305). It is worth mentioning that in the above list of leisure pursuits, mosque and *hey-at* were the only places which were free. Just as the mosque could be converted to be a public place for leisure, the holy cities (like Qum and Mashad) could be places for holidays. Of those workers who could afford to take holidays, 83% had been to Mashad at least once, and 49% had been exclusively to the cities of Qum and Mashad.

This reflects the contradictory position of the workers toward Islam. They both are and are not religious. They may be religious in the sense that the point of reference of their socio-cultural activities is religious-oriented. On the other hand, they are not religious because they are prepared to change the implications and distort the meaning of their religion to fit with their own socio-economic and political ends.

Notes

1. The present study is based on a sample survey of 120 male workers in large factories in Teheran, conducted through the formal questionnaires and informal interviews during July–August 1980. Each interview lasted 30–40 minutes. We were able to interview the same workers and a further 30 on specific issues, such as migration, length of industrial service, etc.

2. Professor Hobsbawm's lecture at Birkbeck College (History Society), London University, Summer 1982.

3. In another lecture, he implicitly rejected this view. See Hobsbawm, 1973, p. 15.

4. A survey of 210 peasant families in Isfahan showed that over 50% of the income of families came from wage-working in industry.

5. This figure for the Istanbul shanty-town dwellers is 22% (male) and 38% (female) (Karpat, 1979, p. 170); and in West Africa such links are widespread (Sandbrook and Cohen, 1975, p. 3).

6. As the table points out, Azeri Turkish workers were the largest single ethnic group before land reform.

7. It is interesting to note that there was almost no sign of other main ethnic minorities: Arabs, Baluchis, Turkmans and Kurds. In a sample of 150, there was only one Kurd and one Turkman.

8. Our observations suggest a strong tendency to overcome such divisions. It may be worth pointing out the prevalence of ethnic jokes against the Shomalis and Azeri Turks, two main groups of Teheran industrial workers during the Shah's time.

9. As a villager, I myself have observed the conflicts and bitter and bloody confrontations between kinship groups in villages. For a comprehensive list of divisions in rural (and urban) Iran, see Abrahamian, 1974, pp. 3–31.

10. For an account of such activities in Latin America, see de Chungara, 1978.

11. A casual semi-regular religious sermon. The *hey-ats* are often organized on the basis of common ethnic or geographical origin of the members. They promote religious observance and celebrate major Shi'i festivals; see also Kazemi 1980, p. 63.

5. Pre-Revolutionary Factories

The objective of this chapter is to analyse the peculiarities of labour relations in the pre-revolutionary factories. The pre-revolutionary forms of labour relations were the product of the particular form of capitalist development in Iran and the particularities of the Iranian society. Without going into detail, suffice it to suggest here that Iranian society on the eve of the Revolution could be characterized as a backward capitalist society integrated into world capitalism. Pre-capitalist institutions, ideology and rationale were, in varying degrees, still functioning. Another major characteristic was political dictatorship which interacted with the whole structure of society.

We can identify three forms of oppressive labour relations in Iranian factories, which are characteristic of all such societies. They manifest themselves in administrative, political and physical forms. We shall examine these in turn.

Administrative Domination: Management System

Marx argued that in the capitalist production process, management is necessary, firstly, because any production process in any mode of production requires co-ordination to harmonize the combined labour of individual labourers; and secondly, because capitalist production relations are intrinsically antagonistic since the ultimate objective of capital is a successful rate of accumulation. This second function of management, necessary in all modes of production characterized by antagonism between labourers and controllers of the means and conditions of production is also termed control.[1] This is the function which rests, at the point of production, upon the social division of labour among various agents. In capitalism, the function of control, a form of discipline, designed to further the extraction of surplus-value, dominates the function of co-ordination. The form of the labour process is thus subordinate to the requirements of the accumulation process which itself is determined by the overall movement of market relations as well as politics. Thus discipline characterizes any capitalist workplace in any society. It assumes, however, different forms in different capitalist social formations, depending on a variety of historical and socio-political factors. This section aims to explore the bases of the oppressive forms in the pre-revolutionary Iranian factories.

Uneven development of social forces and relations of production in different economic sectors in societies where industrialization is quite recent is a common phenomenon. Iran is no exception. The uneven development of industry in Iran has led to uneven forms of organization of production and work processes, as well as uneven forms of control and co-ordination. In the Iranian factories, on the eve of the Revolution, three forms of management could be identified: semi-craft management, traditional management and modern or scientific management.

Semi-Craft Management
In the term semi-craft management, I am not referring to the organization of production in a *craft* system *per se*, in which artisans and skilled craftsmen exert a high degree of control over the organization of the labour process, even though they may be wage-labourers. Semi-craft management refers to the decentralized mode of organization of production in small-scale, technically backward and organizationally simple units of production in which the worker-capitalist relations assume the appearance of the patron-client relation of the classic craft system. Such units are found in a large number of small-scale industrial enterprises (with less than ten employees) accounting numerically for more than 98% of the industrial units and employing about 36% of the total manufacturing employees. These enterprises are involved in the production of consumer goods (sweets, printing, baking, footwear), in processing (cement, wood) and petty-entrepreneurial workshops.

The control system is semi-craft because not all of the units in this category are characterized by the craft system proper, in the sense of the formal subordination of labour to capital in the production process (as in the traditional cottage industries of carpet and textiles and in almost all self-employed industrial establishments which employ family labour). Uneven development produces a tendency in these small establishments to employ relatively modern machines — such as turning-machines, sewing-, melting- and printing-machines — which perform a considerable number of the tasks previously performed by labour. These transform the craft-based organization of production into a Taylorite system (see Chapter 3). However, in the case of Iran, the main and common characteristics of these semi-craft enterprises have remained rather unaltered: a simple division of labour, a decentralized organization of production, and a relatively high degree of labouring skill. A still commoner feature is the personalization of the capital-labour relation. The owner is at the same time the manager, designer, seller of the product and buyer of raw material; he is master. He keeps a skilled, experienced, trustworthy and usually bullying hand as a foreman who exerts a great deal of control in discipline, in hiring and firing, in determining overtime rates, bonuses and pay-rises.

The continual presence of the patron in the workshop, combined with the simple organization of production and of labour relations, and the fragmentation of the workforce, laid the base for direct control over the workforce. There was no mediatory element in the form of a managerial hierarchy, nor any organ of structural control between the owner and the labourers. The direct relationship would generate on the one hand, a feeling of close, paternalistic and even family relationship between the labourers so that they identified their interests more with their master than with their fellow workers in the next workshop. On the other hand, the bare exploitation and physical oppression generated antagonism.

The owners/managers of these units originated either as bazaar merchants or as labourers who had, by taking a partner or by saving, got enough capital together to start a business. They were entirely aware of how to run business by paternalist discipline. There were hardly any signs of workers' rights such as normal working-hours, accident insurances, holidays or minimum wages here.[2]

In these enterprises, the employers' unions in the form of guilds (*asnāf*) were more active than the workers' unions. The workers did not constitute an economic force because of the insignificant position of the sector (secondary sector) in the whole national economy. In 1976 the contribution of these enterprises to the total manufacturing value added was only 22.8% of the total, even though the units numerically accounted for about 98% of the total number of manufacturing units.

In Britain in the 1910s, the introduction of new technology and deskilling threatened the basis of the heavily organized and economically vital craftsmen in the armaments industry. They could and did resist the new processes for some years. Craftsmen in Iran could not and did not oppose any innovation in the manufacturing labour process. The new forms of work processes were rather abruptly and rapidly imported and introduced from without; the workforce was not organized and economically strong enough to resist; and it was affected *indirectly*, that is, it had concentrated mainly in the small-scale sectors whose total existence was jeopardized by the establishment of modern large-scale sectors; among other areas, the most obvious example may be the shoe industry. Instead of resistance, the skilled workers of these sectors would be absorbed in the modern sector for higher wages.

Traditional Management
The pre-capitalist socio-economic background of the domestic industrial bourgeoisie resulted in the transfer of irrational pre-capitalist methods of extraction of surplus-labour into the industry. As an observer suggested, 'the owner-managers of these factories were former bazaar merchants who regard factory operation as merely uninteresting preliminaries to the

sale of the product in pursuing their traditional interest of quick turnover at high margins' (Bartsch, 1971b, p. 28).

In the process of class formation, transformation of economic positions occurs much faster than political and ideological change. Just as we still await an ideological transformation of the working class in Iran, so we have yet to see the bourgeoisification of the industrial bourgeoisie. The private industrialists (who mainly perform a traditional management role) have in recent years emerged from three distinct socio-economic backgrounds.

The first stratum is of ex-landowners, who, during land reform, were offered a certain number of shares in state-owned industries as part of their compensation. They swelled the group of already existing industrialists from the same background. The second group were the bazaar traders. And finally there were the top civil servants who, under the Shah, and through corruption made sufficient money to put up the initial capital to engage in industrial production (see also Halliday, 1978a, pp. 151–2). The industrial bourgeoisie tends to proceed by the logic of rapid turnover and short-term investment, preferring to employ less-skilled and mostly unskilled peasant labour to lower the cost of production with little attention to long-term profitability. Few elements of modern and rational capitalist management such as programmes of work-study, skill training, long-term planning (structural strategies of control) are to be found.

Most of the industries run by traditional management were labour-intensive, like textiles, leather, clothing, wood, non-metallic products, and, to a lesser extent, food. In 1976, there were about 4,500 units with 10–50 employees each, accounting for 7.8% of the manufacturing work-force. In such units, direct control was dominant; there was no structural-hierarchical mediating element between labour and capital. The industrial relations prevailing in these industries could well be characterized as 'feudal'. For an ex-landowner who had become an owner-director, the factory was most likely to be viewed as a village and workers as the subordinate peasants who were to be coerced to work harder. There were certainly examples of beating, physical punishment, and imprisonment even in the modern factories.[3] In Sepenta, a metal plant, there were workers who would call the boss *arbāb* (master). This was the term used by peasants to landowners in the villages.

The supervisors, the boss's hands, exerted an effective and extended control over the disciplinary process of the workshop, in terms of hiring, firing, wage-increases, promotion, overtime, punishments and penalties. There was little security for the labourers in their relations with their supervisors. 'Even a delay in saying a hello to the supervisor or laughing in the workshop could be an excuse to dismiss the workers' (Sanavandi, 1974, p. 63). A report about the conditions of women workers in such factories in 1974 pointed out that owing to the [authority of] foremen, the female workers are rapidly trapped by *fahshāā* [sexual abuse]. They have to be subordinate to the foreman, otherwise they would be fired or transferred. The *fahshāā* is so widespread that the girls deny their working in the factories, since they would be called "factory girls". (Sanavandi, 1974, p. 63.)

Even though the conservatism of such industrialists was based on pre-capitalist methods of exploitation, there was also a resistance on the part of workers to any 'change in the methods to which they have become accustomed during long years of employment' (Bartsch, 1971b, p. 26).

Modern Rational Management
There was a third type of factory which had been established recently by private, joint-venture, multinational or state capital, located in the primary sector. This employed a rational form of management, by which I mean methods of organization and production which, while raising the productivity of labour, at the same time sought the co-operation of the workforce, attempting to avoid as far as possible naked antagonism between labour and capital. The strategy thus aimed at, in the words of Burawoy, 'obscuring and securing surplus-value' (1978, pp. 247–312).

This objective can be achieved only when a structural strategy is adopted — a strategy which rests on both technical change, disciplining the workforce by automation and real subordination, and 'relational change', managerial tactics to regulate the relations between the workers and the employer. These policies tend to be accompanied by restrictive practices, workers' participation and experiences of control from above (see Chapter 10). The strategy of 'obscuring and securing surplus-value' does not depend simply on the subjective decision of an employer. It requires ideological commitment on the part of workers, a recognition of free unionism on the part of capital and capital's capacity for technical control.

During the old regime in Iran, only some patterns of rational management were in place: modern techniques of production and machinery and centralized and hierarchical structures of the management functions. The hierarchical/technical division of labour corresponds to a hierarchical/social division of labour according to authority and power. As well as being controlled through technical change in the work process, the workers were controlled socially through the hierarchical relations — through structural control.[4]

In such modern large-scale enterprises, supervisors assumed contradictory positions. Their role as agents of capital was to assure an appropriate extraction of surplus-value from the workers, while being themselves subjected to a higher control by a higher agent within the hierarchy. Their actual relations to shop-floor workers appeared to be contradictory too. An old worker in the Metal Works Plant was describing his feelings about the supervisor:

I used to distribute bottles of milk; a worker was to get his bottle of milk. But we were short of a bottle. Now at that time we had a supervisor called Abbas Kasaii. I told him we had "a bottle too few and that lad wants his milk". He [the supervisor] said to him: "What the hell do you want?" I said to him [supervisor]: "It's his right!" But again the supervisor told him: "You get out of here", and grabbed his hand and pushed him to the factory gate! Believe me, I swear to God, by my conscience.

Another line worker in Arasteh, however, expressed his support:

The supervisors wouldn't make any trouble for us, they're OK. It was the *engineers* who did bother us much. We are pleased with our supervisors both under *Taughout* [the Shah] and now.

The position and the role of the engineers and higher technical staff were radically different from those of workers. In a relatively simple managerial hierarchy their positions both technically and socially were at much higher levels of the managerial bureaucracy. The relationship between the engineers and the shop-floor workers was tense and anta-gonistic. After the revolution their social, technical and ideological positions in the production process played a significant part in the defeat of the *shuras* (see Chapter 9). In the Leyland Motor firm a worker expressed his resentment towards them after the revolution in the follow-ing way:

Q. Do you think the SAVAK agents were active here during the Shah?
A. They're active even now. The engineers: all of the engineers in this factory were SAVAK agents . . .
Q. Do you think the workers themselves can perform the tasks of the engineers?
A. Of course they can, we've got a lad here who can do the job much better than the engineers . . .

The behaviour of supervisors and engineers was endorsed by law. Two years before the revolution, when sabotage in the factories assumed a new momentum, new disciplinary measures were introduced. Cash fines and dismissals became the penalties for such misdemeanours as

absenteeism for more than three days; disruption of workplace affairs; smoking in specified areas; sleeping while on duty; causing noises; disrup-tion in the factory; not respecting the supervisor; refusal of the orders of *entezāmāt* guards when entering or exiting from the workplace. (*Kayhan*, 26 March 1977.)

The pattern of modern rational management existed only in the large-scale and technically modern factories (probably with more than a hundred employees). In 1973 there were 340 such units or 5% of the total number of manufacturing establishments, accounting for some 16% of manufacturing, and employing 11% of the total industrial workforce in

1976.[5] A significant number of such factories (the chemical sector almost totally) were owned by the multinationals (in 1973, some 118 units). In such firms the crucial technical and financial decisions were made by the foreign managers. A case study in 1973 revealed that, out of 114 managerial positions in 22 multinational firms, only 43 insignificant positions were filled by Iranians (Daftar, 1980, p. 19) and that almost all of the technical administration had been taken over by foreign experts.

So, even though the firms were mainly owned, managed and operated by multinationals, that is, despite the existence of rational experienced managers and experts, and of technical possibilities, industrial relations did not change, but remained sharply antagonistic and backward. This proposition should not be taken as indicating any illusions about capital's humanitarian tendency to produce better industrial relations. Nor, on the other hand, does the argument that capital is exported to underdeveloped countries to achieve higher profitability through harsher exploitation. The productivity of labour in the home countries was much higher than that in Iran.[6] The point, however, is that technical change does bring about a (reformist) medium for real subordination. But its scope is too limited to provide industrial peace for capital in the developing countries. Industrial peace is dependent on the political form of the state, and the organization of the working class itself.

Table 5.1
The Skill Composition of Workforce in Selected Modern Factories in Teheran, 1980

	Workers %			Experts and engineers %	Admin. personnel %	Total no.	Number of women
Factories	Un-skilled	Semi-skilled	Tech'ly skilled				
Large workshop system							
Turkman	31.3	15.0	37.4	3.0	13.1	2,680	135
Metal Works	9.9	76.9		1.3	11.7	895	8
Teheran Steel	75.7	16.2		0.4	7.5	924	0
Assembly line system							
Amazon	26.1	20.0	36.0	0.6	17.2	2,301	90
Alvand	12.4	49.7	33.3	0.0	4.4	402	0
Fanoos	44.0	40.3		3.1	12.7	645	157

Source: Based on data directly obtained.

What were the possibilities of and limitations on workers' organization and resistance in the face of technical change? As we have mentioned earlier, the British shop-steward movement of the 1910s emerged as the consequence of workers' resistance to the introduction of new techniques in the production process which would result in the deskilling of highly-skilled craftsmen so that women and the less skilled could be recruited (Hinton, 1973). The emergence of factory committees in Germany was led by the most skilled section of the tool-makers in 1918 (Bologna, 1976). Such forms of organization could hardly take shape in Third World countries such as Iran where a high proportion of the workforce came directly from the countryside and were devoid of any experience of industrial work and organization. Since more than 80% of Teheran modern factory-workers were of rural origin, only an insignificant proportion had any kind of industrial skills. They had no skills to defend against a modern factory system imported from abroad hurriedly in a short period. A Luddist response could not be expected. Indeed, the factory system and its routine job and pay were at least initially a desirable alternative to the misery of the village life.

But the awareness of the workers was growing. An industrial peace such as the Shah would have liked to achieve would require appropriate labour organizations such as workers' unions. But the political form of the state was incompatible with the operation of these organizations. The lack of a reformist mediation between labour and capital and the residues of feudal industrial relations produced political oppression in the workplaces.

Political Domination

State-Run Unions
The coup of 1953 decisively crushed the existing unions and ended twelve years of worker unionization.[7] The government then started creating state-run unions whose permitted activities were outlined in the 1959 Labour law (Articles 26–9).

The unions were entitled to conclude collective contracts; to purchase, sell and acquire movable and immovable properties, provided they were not for commercial purposes; to defend the trade rights and interests of their members; to establish co-operative societies to meet the requirements of their members, and to establish and create unemployment funds for the purpose of giving aid and assistance to unemployed workers (Article 27). But the law prohibited them from engaging in political activities and did not recognize the right to strike.[8]

The Labour law was one of the strategies of the post-coup state to exert control over all aspects of political and social life. The best possible condition for the rule of the bourgeoisie, for successful capital accumulation, is the exercise of hegemony in the Gramscian sense, to promote a spurious consensus of the whole community, in particular the working class. The post-coup state in Iran was unable to achieve such a rule, despite the implementation of a number of reform measures such as the White Revolution launched in 1963. The latter was a package of major reform programmes, including land-reform, women's franchise, literacy campaigns and profit-sharing schemes. A strategy of capitalist development required the co-operation of the workforce, their reasonable behaviour and their commitment to a higher productivity level. Thus it was necessary for the state to prevent spontaneous and wild-cat protests and independent workers' organization.

The second role of the unions was ideological. They were to act as mediators and transmit an ideology based upon nationalism, selling the idea of a community founded upon the co-operation of all its members (workers, bosses, state agents) in a society with a unique history and incomparable culture, embodied in the persistent and beloved relationship between the community and its Shah. The term proletariat was denounced by the state ideologues as being no longer appropriate to the Iranian workers; it was only the Western working class which had launched a 'class war'. Similarly, the boss was no longer a '*kārfarma* [employer, capitalist] which is reminiscent of class privileges', but a '*kārāmā* which is appropriate to the hearty cooperation of all groups in the new system of production . . . in the era of [White] Revolution'.[9] This was a form of corporatist ideology of class collaborationism in the sense that it lacked a reformist agreement between the representatives of each part within the institutions of an arbitrating state.

The third function of the unions was to mobilize the workforce for particular purposes, such as pro-regime demonstrations. In 1971 there were reported to be 397 such unions. The number grew to 1,023 by 1978. In 1976 the state amalgamated a number of unions and established the Organization of Iranian Workers, which along with the employers' organization joined the *Rastākhiz* Party, Iran's single party after the Shah abolished all other existing political parties. According to the official figures in 1976, the Organization consisted of 845 syndicates and 20 trade unions with three million workers (Kavousi, 1978, p. 117).

Whether or not the state succeeded in achieving its objectives in setting up such unions is debatable. Some have argued that the state-run unions performed very real functions 'in securing the political and ideological positions of the regime' (Halliday, 1978a, pp. 202–3). But such conclusions are dubious. The fourth function of the syndicates, physical repression, points to the fact that other means failed to secure support for the regime. I shall explain this failure by examining the repressive measures which the state had to adopt in order to control the workers' opposition. These measures may be summarized as the mechanism of union elections and policing the factories. Resort to these policies indicated the failure of the politico-ideological functions of the unions.

The Mechanism of Union Representation

The state could not and did not allow the unions to function in the way set down in the Labour Law. In every election the state would ensure that either its own candidate or the one loyal to its policies was elected. Depending on the circumstances, the methods of these sorts of elections would vary.

First, at times, at best, an election would be held in a workplace where an independent candidate would be elected. However, as a worker in the Teheran Auto car plant described:

> we did have a syndicate, but their tactics were very limited; because they were never given enough power to confront the boss from the workers' viewpoint. For this reason [although] they were in fact formally the workers' representatives, they were in reality the boss's representatives.
>
> Q. Do you think that the representatives consciously refused to work in the workers' interests, or that they were not able to?
> — Well, it depends who you're talking about. There were some who would be bought off pretty quickly; but some were unwittingly on the bosses' side; they even thought they were actually working for the workers' interests . . . On the whole nothing has been done for the workers through the syndicates.

Similar situations were described in such plants as Arasteh and Behshar. The workers would make a tremendous effort to take part in these syndicates, but act in them independently in support of their own class interests. They would utilize any means, official or unofficial, to turn the syndicates, as far as possible, into an independent instrument of class struggle. This was one of the contradictions of the state-run syndicates.

The second possibility was that the workers would take part whole-heartedly in the syndicate elections and get elected; but they then had to work according to the official lines, otherwise they would immediately be dismissed (as in Iran Cars), beaten, framed and arrested (as in Amazon). In the Iran Cars plant in Teheran, a militant worker, Sāmet, had stood for the leadership of the factory syndicate. Since SAVAK was sure that he would win the election, he was barred from entering the factory on the election day in two successive years. For this reason, in the third year, a day before the election, he hid himself at the top of the factory water-reservoir for the night. The next day he was inside the factory, took part in the election and won. Immediately after his victory, however, he was fired. A syndicate member who had held the post for thirteen years and who was a SAVAK agent had reported the case. Various other similar cases were reported after the revolution when documents came to light.

The third method was simply fraud by state agents in producing the results of the polls; this happened, for instance, in the Iran National car factory.

Policing the Factories

The task of policing the factories was performed by the infiltration of secret police agents and the direct operation of SAVAK agents inside the plants as the officers of the *Entezāmāt* or Security Bureau. The insecure position of the state in the militant plants would force the authorities to get their agents elected as leaders of syndicates, in which case they were either recruited employees or direct agents. These syndicate members were the main element of state control within the working class. They played an essential part in mobilizing forces for pro-regime rallies and demonstrations. At the same time, together with privileged employees and foremen, they would set up pressure groups who would enforce political discipline over the factory workers.

The workers would participate in syndicates which were seen to offer the possibility of independence; otherwise they were not under any illusions about the state-run unions. In the winter of 1973 a surprising secret survey conducted by one of the government organizations revealed that only 22.3% of the factory workers were syndicate members, and one-third of them either thought that the syndicate was of no use or else had no idea of its positive functions (Pakdaman, 1980).

The second form of policing was a direct presence of secret police agents, under the guise of such factory institutions as *Hefāzat, Entezāmāt* (Security Bureau), which were the *de facto* branches of SAVAK inside the factories. Each plant had a few direct informers.

> In this factory, the former syndicate members (some of whom were members of *Rastākhiz* Party as well) were also active in security affairs. In the earlier periods when we had the agents of [the Bureau of] Inspection and Information, the members of the *Hefāzat* of the factory (who in fact were the syndicate activists) would report to the inspectors who would take action as they saw fit. [And the workers'] moves and statements would be reported through syndicate activists, *Hefāzat* and Inspectors to the SAVAK which would make its decision accordingly (Pars Metal plant worker).

Entzāmāt and *Hefāzat* were run almost totally by army colonels and officers who were directly linked to SAVAK. They had been set up to protect factories from physical damage resulting from theft or workers' strikes and uprisings. The presence of army colonels in the factories and the hierarchical structure of management had made the factories like barracks. One worker said,

> During the Shah, Iran National [car plant] was a barrack, a garrison . . . there was even a sort of house of detention (*bāzdāshtgāh*); that is [if you did wrong] you had to work in the firm's kitchen (a line worker).

Another worker who became a *shura* leader after the Revolution had this to say:

The head of *Entezāmāt* was a retired employee of the Railway Company, who was very keen to be called Colonel (he was an agent at the same time). The internal manager was a retired army colonel; he used to threaten the lads, used to beat them; he would carry a baton around with him. I always had confrontations with them. One day, they [the gang] attacked me and beat me up good and proper; one of them broke his arm. A number of lads came up and said they supported me; and they asked me to get together everyone on my side and fight back. I refused. There were other workers who wanted to mediate between us to reach a compromise. I didn't accept this either: I wanted to get each of them to confront the manager, one by one . . . The management did not dismiss me, because it was a pretty big event. They were afraid of it causing problems for them. After a while, I received a letter from the director saying that I didn't have any responsibilities there. I went to the Central Office where they said "we aren't firing you, but you must stay in the Sales Department". I was told I didn't have to work, just draw my salary . . .

After the revolution I was elected as a *shura* member . . . I was, for a time, in charge of identifying the SAVAK agents . . . Following the investigation, five employees were found to be agents: the head of *Hefāzat*, the leader of the syndicate, two foremen, and one administrative employee.

In my field research I had access to information available in the plants which I visited. Of the 11 factories which provided data, 10 claimed to have found out the identities of the informers; and in almost all, an army colonel or officer had been active in securing law and order at the factories (see Table 5.2).

The relative autonomy of the *Entezāmāt* officers from the managers may reflect the relative autonomy of the dictatorial state from the bourgeois class (though the whole system was an operation to reproduce the latter's broad interests). As Halliday recognizes, both the mode of control and of inducement to the workers were at times against the interests of the manager and/or owner. In particular, the agents had to be paid by the factory (Halliday, 1978a, p. 205). In contrast with the high salary of *Entezāmāt* officers, minor informers would get an insignificant amount. Available documents indicate that salaries ranged from 1,500 Rls to 3,000 Rls per month in 1973 when the average monthly wage of skilled factory workers was 3,840 Rls (Pakdaman, 1980, p. 23).[10]

The tasks of agents varied according to their position. The white-collar employees would, for instance, monitor correspondence, mail and telephone conversations. The shop-floor agents, on the other hand, would monitor suspicious activities and statements of any kind by the workers. The reports from informers' documents are of the kind, 'Mr So and So usually reads books'; 'there are rumours that the Rouzbeh's (a leader of Tudeh Party, executed by the old regime) statue has been erected in Italy. I heard this from Mr So and So'; 'there are rumours that when the name of Khomeini is called, the workers do *salavāt* [a

Table 5.2
Operation of Secret Police in Selected Plants

Plants	*Ownership*	*No. of agents*	*Position of agents*	*Position of the Entezāmāt officer*
Turkman	State	2	*Entezāmāt,* and trainer	Retired army colonel
Iran Cars	Private (M)	5	Syndicate leader, head of *Entezāmāt*, two foremen; a white-collar worker	Retired army colonel
Metal Works	Private	2	Syndicate member; head of *Hefāzat*	Retired army colonel
Teheran Auto	Private (M)	?	At least one	Army officer
Bloom Helm	Private (M)	2	Syndicate leader; a worker	—
I.T.N.	Joint	4	Four employees	Army colonel
Behshar	Private (M)	(?)	?	Army officer
Amazon	Private	(?)	?	Retired army officer
R.C. Chemicals	Private (M)	(?)	?	?
P.R. Plant	Private	(?)	?	Retired colonel
Alvand	Private	Minor in-former	—	—

(M) = multinational companies

(?) SAVAK agents did exist in the firms, but we are unaware of their number and positions.

demonstration of support]'; 'it is said that Mr X is leftist'. The impact of surveillance would be reinforced by the deliberate tactic of rumour-spreading about the supposed strength and tight control of SAVAK; this was designed to undermine the trust of fellow workers for each other — the trust which is fundamental to organized underground activity.

This at least partly explains the guerrilla-type tendency of socialist organizations before the revolution, firstly in their assumption that 'the workers presume the power of their enemy to be absolute', and secondly that 'their [workers'] own inability to emancipate themselves [is also] absolute'.[11] The presumptions attributed to the workers were those of the leaders of the movement themselves. (Though, undoubtedly, some sections of the workers might have had similar ideas.) However, the desperate introduction of new measures, the policy of stick and carrot, shows the inability of the state to impose the necessary political control. The workers did go on strike. Some estimates mention 20–30 strikes per year after 1973 (Halliday, 1978a,). Leaving the figures aside, the failure of the state strategies to secure the regime and to deactivate the working class by its secret police necessitated the use of military force to counter collective labour action. There are numerous examples of troops encircling the striking plants: Tabriz Tool Making Plant, Tractor Sazi in Tabriz, Pars Metal and Renault are examples in the 1970s.

Conditions of Work: Physical Oppression

As Chapter 3 illustrated, the pace of Iranian industrialization and modernization in the 1960s and 1970s was indeed remarkable. Iranian society underwent an economic and social transformation. But behind this rapid industrial expansion and the fences of modern, multinational factories lay an unobserved oppression. Industrial workers in Iran have had to bear the misery of both traditional work hazards and modern industrial diseases. In all cases the same law applied: 'saving in labour conditions at the expense of the labourers' (Marx, 1977, p. 88).

A set of laws had already laid down regulations on health, safety, and workers' compensations. The laws were supposed to force the employers to provide an 'adequate supply of drinkng water'; to 'maintain on sanitary lines' the work-sites, corridors and warehouses; to dispose of sewage and other factory refuse; to provide showers for the workers in poisonous and dusty works, to provide lockers and clean eating places. The Labour Law itself, through the High Safety Council, was also to inspect new tools and the plans of the newly-established workshops, requiring them to be in accordance with the Safety Regulations. Article 50 allowed for the closure of unsafe working places on the recommendation of the Labour Inspector to the Public Investigation and with the consent of the Ministry of Labour.

So much for the safety laws on paper. Suspecting that the practice varied from the law, a student of the labour movement in the pre-revolutionary period wondered, in practice, how many times such a closure had been carried out, particularly against a multinational company; the actual number of labour inspectors and their qualifications; whether there were any written record of the reports of the Inspectorate, if so, where they were kept and who had access to them; the number of workshops which lacked basic facilities like toilets and washrooms; and the conducting of any investigation of the possible corruption of labour inspectors by the employers (Jalil, 1977, pp. 47–8). Indeed, there have been, *and still are*, enormous discrepancies between the law and reality.[12]

It is difficult to comprehend what conditions are like, and the physical oppression of workers, unless you actually go into a workshop full of fumes, smoke and noise. Conditions of work under both regimes in Iran have been appalling. This is the impression that I got when visiting the modern and multinational firms, not to mention the traditional enterprises. I could only experience the immediate horror; I was not in a position to assess the long-term effects. I could only be *told*, for instance, about the accidents, disabilities and illnesses caused by industrial work.

Industrial Accidents

A survey of the Ministry of Labour indicates that the rate of industrial accidents grew dramatically between 1968 and 1975. The survey points out that within eight years the compensation paid to workers for disability increased from $4.8 million in 1968 to $28 million in 1975 (a 589% increase). The compensation paid to workers for sickness caused by work increased from $7.1 million to $36.5 million respectively in 1968 and 1975 (519%). The compensation paid for malfunctioning in any part of the body increased from $1.2 million in 1968 to $3 million in 1975 (247%) (Larijani, 1974).

It would be naive to rely merely on these figures, and more naive still to assume that the net increase in compensation indicates the regime's liberalism. There have been numerous cases of fraud and corruption where due compensation has not been paid. A worker at the Teheran auto plant is one example:

> At that time, Souren, a SAVAK agent, had been a syndicate leader for thirteen years; and *our* candidate for the membership of the syndicate would be fired, or would be prevented from entering the factory gate by the guards on election days — at that time, I became ill, I had an ulcer. The doctor asked me to pay 300,000 Rls [over £3,000] for the treatment. I then had to sell the carpet I had at home, but I realized that it was not enough. I went to Souren and told him the story, asking for a loan: "five, six or two thousand *toumans*, or whatever you can afford to lend." He said, "I can't afford it." Then we had a head of SAVAK, a colonel, called Mr Ghapanchi, who asked Souren to pay me some money. But Souren said, "there's nothing we can do for you"; then I was kicked out. After a while, when I thought I had no option, I sold my refrigerator and things like that in order to get medical treatment.
> — Weren't you under the Medical Insurance?
> — Yes, I was, but I was still asked to pay above it.

Another worker of the same firm:

> After four months of work here, I got backache, because of heavy work. I spent two months in hospital. After that I was expecting to get better, but I didn't. It took another 3–4 months before I was OK. When I got back to work I realized that I had been refused payment of 3–4 months' overtime. They paid me only three thousand *toumans* on account, which I had already

spent. Because, during the 4 months [of illness] I had spent 14 thousand *toumans* on the doctors and things like that, which I had borrowed from my neighbours.

— Weren't you under Medical Insurance?

— I was, but I wasn't accepted to be treated under the insurance scheme. And, when I would take the prescriptions to the chemist, they would say things like: "we don't have these tablets or those injections". So when I felt that my life was in danger, I had to get private treatment.

Industrial accidents and injuries have been normal everyday occurrences. The documents of the Research Centre of Occupational Health and Safety (RCOHS), a responsible institution which carries out factory inspections, gives the following picture of the industrial accidents in the two months of January and February 1980.

Table 5.3
Industrial Accidents in Two Months

Accidents			Amputations					Minor	
		Frac-	Fin-			Blind-		inju-	
Areas	*Death*	*ture*	*gers*	*Hands*	*Feet*	*ness*	*Burn*	*ries*	*Total*
City of Teheran	7	4	5	4	—	—	3	9	32
Other towns	58	28	31	6	3	3	44	72	245
Total	*65*	*32*	*36*	*10*	*3*	*3*	*47*	*81*	*277*

Other documents in 1979–80 and the first four months of 1980 demonstrate that the Centre recorded an average of twenty industrial accidents each month in Teheran alone.

The figures are, however, misleading and underestimated. They point only to accidents which the RCOHS dealt with, those registered in the Centre. The real rate, as the inspectors themselves confirmed unofficially, was much higher. The Medical Registration Books in two Medical Centres of two plants revealed that each month up to 330 injuries requiring either first aid or leave of absence from work occurred in just one factory.

The figure of the death-toll does not include those indirect and gradual deaths which are the result of industrial diseases; and considering the physical conditions of the workplaces, the rate must be very high. On the whole, it could confidently be estimated that at least two industrial workers are killed every day as the consequence of industrial work.[13]

Chemical Diseases

For an outsider who is visiting the workshops for the first time, even modern ones, the experience is amazing. It is like entering a different

Table 5.4
Attendance of the Workers at the Factory Medical Centre in one month

Causes of attendance	P.R. Plant*	I.T.N.**
Dressing of minor wounds	125	330
Injuries	251	120
Total attendances	686	907
Total workforce	890	735

*During January–February 1981.
**Average of attendance in random days of 1980–81.

Source: My investigations.

world. In a moment you notice that grimy, sweating and curious faces are staring at you through the dark of smoke and fumes, wondering what you are doing there with a brief-case. In a few minutes the workers gather round you. *Everybody* wants to speak out. You are told many things; and they are all grievances, complaints made loudly and angrily.

> This place is full of dust and poisonous chemicals. We work with industrial alcohol here, now we have damaged lungs. And we have pains in our legs. All the moulders have got this pain now. This job is damn heavy, very heavy. Just take a look at these moulders, not one of them's healthy. I've recently had rheumatism, I've got backache.
>
> Q. Don't you go to the doctor?
> A. We do, but our pain is such that even though we get injected or use drugs, it doesn't get better.
> Q. You have been working here on this 12-ton furnace for some nine years; have you had any disease?
> A. Disease?! All of us have got diseases, even mental disease of one kind or another. We've got no doctor, nobody to take our problems seriously. All of us have got something wrong; our hands, feet and so on are either burnt or injured. (Metal Works workers).

In the Amazon factory, I could not manage to stay in the painting shop for more than ten minutes to do interviewing. The air was full of the dust of chemicals. A few workers were wearing only paper masks. The result of a sampling by the OCHS in this workshop showed that the amount of toluene in the atmosphere was 100–500 pmm, whereas the permitted quantity was 150 pmm. Commercial toluene contains benzene.[14] And this is the effect of such conditions on the paint-workers:

> Q. What kinds of problems do you have in this shop?
> A. Bloody paint; my lungs now pain me. I also have footache; that is because of moisture, because of so much water. There are numerous

problems but nobody cares. Even if somebody appears here they always try to postpone action . . . I have been to hospital. I've got sciatica and hearing loss. I've had it for two years. [In the hospital] they said "you've had a defective ear since childhood!" How come two years ago, before coming here, it was OK? In twenty years of work, in some other places it was OK? Now, here, they say it's been like this since childhood!?

In another modern factory in Teheran, I was spontaneously identified to the medical officer responsible as an official of the Ministry of Labour. I was thus allowed to check their documents. I was told the notorious shops were the painting and foam ones. First I talked to the workers of the foam shop.[15]

This material makes it hard to breathe; it causes asthma; I've got a stomach problem at the moment.

We don't feel like having food, I always feel sick. I've been working here for 16 years . . . You know, when I get home from work, my feet ache, and I feel generally out of sorts, I can't eat meals; I've lost my appetite.

Almost all of the workers were protesting. If they had known the extent of their collective tragedy, their voices would have been much louder. The data revealed that of 39 workers in the foam shop, 34 were, or had been, under medical supervision, *all* suffering from lung disease. The remaining 5 workers had not yet been examined. Of the 34 workers, 5 had red marks by their names. These had already been the victims of industrial 'gradual deaths'; their names had not been registered under the category of 'factory victimization', but as natural deaths.

We have had random access to a number of official reports concerning health and safety in the industrial workplaces. Table 5.5 provides the summary of the documents. As it points out, only one factory was reported to be generally normal. But in the Silco plant, for instance, the amount of silica powder, a substance which the workers have to inhale, is present in concentrations which are five times larger than the recommended safety level. In Arak aluminium plant, the concentration of dangerous substances is such that the inspector warns 'We present the results . . . in order that, as soon as possible, a very urgent hygiene measure be carried out, so that the workers will not be forced to do work under such conditions.' In many cases the employers, including those of multinational modern firms, did not provide even drinking water, hot-water showers, changing rooms, dining halls, adequate heat or sufficient light. An independent research project carried out in a number of mostly female-oriented factories in Teheran in 1973 gave the following picture. Owing to the lack of any changing room,

Table 5.5
Conditions of Work in Terms of Chemical Hazards in Selected Firms

Products of firm & date of inspection	Workshops affected	Main dangerous substances	Quantity available in relation to MCA	Effects on workers
Domestic appliances (September 1980)	Painting Insulation	Toluene Benzene C₆H₆ Inhalable fibreglass > 10 micron	2–3 times less than normal	Asthmatic condition, skin diseases, lung diseases. But → skin diseases
Lent factory (January 1980)	All workshops	Asbestos	above	Asbestosis, various forms of lung disease, mainly in the form of pneumoconiosis
Asbestos production (August 1980)	5 workshops	Fibres of asbestos	4 times 3 times 2.5 times 2 times 1.5 times	'' Various kinds of cancers in long-term
Paint making (undated)	1 Processing shop 2 Paint making shop	Carbon monoxide CO	normal	
Motor car production (January 1980)	1 assembly shop	CO. 'Uninhalable air in the hall, due to burning by the workers of wood for heat	above	Dizziness, headache, nausea; unconsciousness; irritating eyes, nose
	2 Welding shop	NxOy, CO	below	Poisoning after long exposure
Car tyres	Main shop	Evaporation of about		Various kinds of lung

Industry (date)	Location	Substance/Hazard	Concentration*	Disease/Effect
		...benzene, toluene, alcohol and ammonia	5-3 times	burning skin, irritant to eyes, nose and throat
Foundry (January 1982)	1 Melting shop 2 Foundry shop	Various kinds of chemical Dust, fumes, high temperature, heat radiation, vibration	above very high	Mainly lung diseases
Chemical processing (May 1980)	All workshops	Spreading of different kinds of gases: F_2, CF_4, CO, CO_2 and many other unidentified substances	Fluorides x 2 Clor — normal	$CO \rightarrow$ irritant to eyes and skin. Fluorides $\rightarrow$ irritant to eyes, skin, nose, throat; dizziness, burns to skin; stomach pains
Chemical products (August, September 1981)	1 Most shops 2 Marynite shop	CO, CO_2 spread over the shops and on the objects Chlorine gas Asbestos	above below above	Initially headache, irritated eyes, nose; poisoning in long-term Lung disease: pneumoconiosis
Brick making (December 1979)	Whole work-place Furnace	Dust Furnace radiation worker without special glasses	above, esp. in summer	Can cause silicosis Cataracts
Silica powder (November 1981)	3 workshops	Inhalable silica dust (quartz) SiO_2 " " " " " "	5 times 10 times	Chest, lung diseases (Silicosis) " " " " " "

*Maximum Concentrations Allowed.

Source: Various reports of Factory Health and Safety Inspectorate in Iran; Kinnersley, 1979; Gardner and Taylor, 1975, pp. 78–97.

women have to change their clothes in the workshop screened by a *chador*, or have to put on the uniform over their normal dresses. The workers of these factories which are provided with some sort of dining halls, have to pay 10–15 Rials; and those without dining halls have to bring lunch with them. However, since there are not any suitable places to heat the food, the workers usually have to bring bread and cheese . . . In the winter they did not have any heaters, so the workers had to have their lunch around the machines. (Sanavandi, 1974, pp. 45–6)

The factory inspectors could offer more accurate and harsher reports, provided that they were allowed to. Their reports have been censored.

There have been so few industrial safety experts that many minor cases have virtually been ignored, or accounted for as the acceptable facts of factory life. In 1980–81, there were only 14 personnel employed in industrial hygiene and safety for some 330,000 large- and small-scale industrial units. Apart from workshop inspection, still fewer investigations are conducted on the affected workers themselves. I came across only two reports for the period following the Revolution. The reports were concerned with the effect of chemicals upon the workers' health: reports on the concentration of lead in the workers' blood in two factories. The results, kept secret from the workers themselves, were not surprising: in one factory, the blood of over 60% of the workers contained lead at a higher concentration than the safety level; in another, the rate was over 70%. As Kinnersley (1979, pp. 157–8) states, 40 micg/100cc has been considered as the safety level, above which level the poisoning of the body begins (depending on the personal threshold which varies in different people).

Table 5.6
Samples of Blood Tests of the Industrial Workers

Chemical Plant (A) August 1980		Chemical Plant (B) August 1981	
No. of workers	*Lead micg/100cc blood*	*No. of workers*	*Lead micg/100cc blood*
19	40	2	45
1	30	1	55
11	45	6	60
2	35	3	65
13	50	9	70
17	55	5	75
3	60	10	To be retested
9	—		

Source: My field investigation.

Noise

The result of any investigation into industrial noise has also been kept secret. Thus the right of negotiation by the labourers over such work conditions continues to be out of the question. The overwhelming majority of the factories inspected (Table 5.7) had terrible noise well above the safety level (see the footnote to the Table). The conditions in the modern, multinational companies were as bad as the domestic firms. Factories exist where noise reaches up to 110 dB (the sound of an earth-moving machine). The effect of an increase in the number of dB over the safety level is progressive. 'Each increase of 3 dB on the scale represents a *doubling* of sound intensity — so 93 decibels is not 'just over 90' (Kinnersley, 1979, p. 49). An official expert reported after the inspection of a large car factory Benz Khavar (Mercedes Benz):

> In this large industrial unit, owing to the lack of any reasonable planning, the level of noise in most parts was high, and fundamental problems of hygiene and safety have not been taken into account: in fact, the exploitation of labour power and higher profit were the only objectives. In most of the work sites noise is so high that it is impossible to bear even for a few moments.

Following a hearing test of a sample of workers in that firm the results revealed that 46% of the workforce suffered from occupational deafness; 9% from 'poisonous or nervous deafness' (i.e. neural deafness); 3% from conductive hearing loss; 2% from 'pure sensory H(earing) L(oss)' (i.e. sensory-neural hearing loss), and 4% from miscellaneous hearing loss. In all, some two-thirds of the workers in that firm had a high degree of hearing impairment. The above reports seem to underestimate the actual conditions. The head of the Noise Department of the Centre (RCOHS), and the only expert in the field, stated to me that 'over 70% of the workers are suffering from occupational deafness'. 'What is the solution?' I asked. 'In my view,' he answered, 'all industries must be demolished and reconstructed again; because all of the plants were [set up] on the basis of capitalism and exploitation. The issue of workers' [health] was virtually out of the question.'[16]

Other Hazards

Investigations into other forms of work hazards have rarely been carried out. You rarely come across a reference to light, for instance. In three reports which I did see, the light was found to be substantially inadequate in each plant, ranging from half to as low as one-fifth of the required level (in Mazyar, Teheran Auto, KW firms). Employers may argue about the impossibility of removing chemical hazards or smells; what justification can they give for insufficient light? A very irritating smell was one of the hazards which was unquantifiable. It was probably the major sensory irritant in a chemical or leather workshop. All such working conditions and physical oppression have been going on for a long time, and are continuing. The fatal consequences of this long-term exploitation are only now becoming apparent.

Table 5.7
Measured Levels of Noise in Selected Plants*

Factory	Date of inspection	Average sound in decibels (dB)
Spinning factory	Feb 1981	90–97 dB
Chewing-gum factory	Feb 1982	95–105
Car plant	Jan 1980	Above the safety level
Dairy firm	Sept 1981	Above the safety level
Silicon factory	Oct 1981	Above the safety level
Tyre plant	Aug 1981	85–100
Foundry plant	Dec 1981	90–105
Brick-making factory	Nov 1979	Above the safety level
Aluminium manufacturing plant	May 1980	90–110 dB
Steel processing factory	June 1981	86–102 average 4 shops
Car factory	May 1981	Far above the safety level
Amazon Domestic Appliances	Sept 1980	75–85

*The official safety level in most factories is 90 dB. P Kinnersley, however, suggests the level to be 80 dB, for 'hearing damage begins here' (p. 50). In Holland the recommended limit is 80 dB. The safety level is also determined by the balance of forces of capital and labour; as Kinnersley writes, ' "Safety-levels" for noise in industry are a compromise between what's good for you and what's good for business' (p. 54).

Source: My field research.

The Function of the RCOHS
The RCOHS was set up with funds from the ILO. Its real function during the time of the Shah, according to one of the anti-clerical principals, was 'just a show, a place for showing porn-films'. In the post-revolutionary period, its functions, even though it may not show porno-films, have not changed dramatically.

In 1963, the Ministry of Labour had a staff of about 35 inspectors, to check on more than 18,000 workshops and plants. The Plan Organization calculated that two visits a year to each plant would require at least 160 inspectors in 1963 and 200 would be needed by 1968 (Department of Labour of the US, p. 34).

As noted, in 1981, the total personnel of the department of occupational hygiene and safety were 14 — to check on some 330,000 large- and small-scale manufacturing units. In this year there was only one single noise (hearing) specialist, and one for chemical hazards.

There were very few doctors in factories; fewer than ten large plants were said to have medical staff. The reason was not so much the shortage of doctors *per se*, as a reluctance on the part of state and employers to pay them. It is not surprising that the total of annual health examinations does not exceed 12–15, according to the officials of the Centre.

Tough control was (and indeed is being) imposed upon both the specialists preparing their reports, and upon the public, in particular the working class, by denying them access to information. Pressure from below (the threat of workers' rebellion) on the one hand, and the logic of economizing on the costs of production, on the other, make the bourgeoisie and the state tell lies about the health and lives of the labourers and force their technical experts to do the same.

> One of our colleagues in his reports on a factory had written: "In this workshop the concentration of dust is very high, and the atmosphere is *unbearable*." Other colleagues recommended him not to use terms like "unbearable", because the higher officials do not like them, especially as the reports may fall into the hands of "nasty" people (an official in the Centre).

The example points to the *political* significance of the secrecy of information. Meanwhile obvious lies were also encouraged for economic reasons, like keeping the wages of labourers low.

> Factory inspectors tend to use terms like "hard labour", less because this phrase in a report would entitle the workers to be paid the "benefit of work hardship". Of course one must tell the truth; but in this situation it is indeed difficult to pay benefit of work hardship, and such reports could be an excuse for the workers to put the factories on strike; that is why it is taken into consideration (an official in the Centre).

Considering the industry-wide bad conditions of work, including the unpaid hard and dangerous work, it follows that the workers were defrauded.

The issue, however, is more political than economic: the workers are denied their right to have access to information about their bodies and environment. Such a denial of rights is sanctioned by the Labour Law (Article 53).[17] The workers must therefore be encouraged to demand that their workplaces be inspected regularly; and more importantly, to demand to have access to the results of such examinations.

Not only the labour force, but also any other unauthorized citizen is denied the right of access to such information. My request to study the reports of the inspectorates was rejected outright by the general director who initially referred me to the above Article of the Labour Law. My insistence, however, forced him to tell the truth. 'We cannot trust you or anybody like you to get these secrets; they may, somehow, be passed on to the workers, in this way putting all the factories of Teheran on strike.'

Notes

1. See Marx, 1977, p. 382; and 1979, pp. 449–50.
2. Official documents such as the reports of the Institute of Research and Hygiene of the Industrial Labour Force, Ministry of Labour, emphasize this.
3. For instance in Iran car plants; (my interview with the workers), and in textile factories (workers interviewed in a TV programme, spring 1980, Teheran).
4. For an historical study of control, see Edwards, 1979.
5. Excluding oil, communications, mining, railways and utilities.
6. 'In 1976 it took 45 hours to assemble a GM Chevrolet in Iran whilst the same process could be performed in 25 hours in West Germany', in Halliday, 1978a, p. 158.
7. Some accounts of trade unionism in Iran may be found in: Halliday, 1978; Abrahamian in Bonine and Keddie, 1981; and Abrahamian, 1982. A detailed documentary history is provided in Chaqueri, 1978, and Lajevardi, 1985.
8. For a review of the Labour Law, see Jalil, 1977.
9. Resolutions of the 18th National Conference of Labour 26–29 Ordibehesht, 1977, in Kavousi, 1976, p. 164, Article 1.
10. The approximate rate of exchange at the time was $1 = 70 Rls.
11. A pioneer of the guerrilla movement, Amir Parviz Pouyan (1975) in Ghotbi, 1978, p. 72.
12. No official (reliable) report has ever been published on the conditions of industrial work under both regimes. Data do exist, but are kept secretly. The actual secrecy has been supported by law (Article 53 of the Labour Law). Almost all analyses below will be carried out on the basis of our field research: unofficial inspection in a certain number of plants; visiting the hospital for industrial workers; and access to the official reports of investigations of workplaces; investigations of the Research Centre of Occupational Health and Safety (Ministry of Labour); and the Centre of Medical Documents of Ministry of Public Health.
13. The records of industrial accidents of only one single police station in Teheran (Azadi Avenue) during 1980 (1359) revealed 32 cases of industrial accidents of which 29 were death records. The death casualty rate among the construction workers (including those in factories) was the highest, about 30%.
14. Benzene is a substance in paints, lacquers, varnishes and it is dangerous. 'Inhaling a large dose of benzene will make you unconscious and soon kill you; smaller amounts make you feel ill, confused and disoriented. Prolonged exposure is likely to damage your bone marrow' (Kinnersley, 1979, pp. 166, 343).
15. Foam which is used as a material for insulation and paints consists of a chemical substance called toluene di-isocyanate (TDI). It is liquid, highly toxic and highly inflammable; it irritates eyes, nose and throat; small concentrations can cause permanent asthmatic conditions and dermatitis (Kinnersley, 1979, p. 378).
16. In a very noisy factory where it was impossible to record the interviews, I noticed a worker on a noisy machine talking to himself. When I asked the reason, I was told by another lad, 'He's gone mad, because of the noise.'
17. 'Labour inspectors have no right, even after leaving their jobs, to divulge any commercial and technical secrets they may have learnt in the course of their work' Article 53.

6. The Industrial Working Class in the Revolution

The February Revolution of 1979 had widespread popular support. A section of the bourgeoisie (notably the bazaar merchants), a range of urban traditional and new petty-bourgeoisie (tradesmen, small producers and civil servants), the newly proletarianized masses (including the migrant poor) and the richer working class (including the relatively well-paid oil workers) all wanted to get rid of the Shah.

The Revolution did not, however, take a classical bourgeois democratic form, primarily because of the lack of strong peasant participation to demand the overthrow of feudal socio-economic relations (as happened in the French Revolution of 1789, almost all European Revolutions except those of 1848 and 1871 and the Russian Revolution). The increasing rate of the accumulation process, in particular after the land reform of 1962, the rise in the price of oil and an overall penetration of the countryside by the laws of capital accumulation, had reduced the rationale for a bourgeois democratic revolution. Instead, as we saw in Chapter 4, a semi-proletariat had been created with different demands and aspirations.

No account of the role of the working class in the revolutionary process has so far appeared. What has emerged sporadically is limited to praising the working class's determinant role in the anti-Pahlavi struggle rather than offering any critical analysis of its actual involvement and strategies, or strengths and weaknesses.[1]

Political Events from 1978 to February 1979

The working class entered the scene of struggle in the second half of summer 1978. Within the next five or six months up to February, the strike movement reached its peak, making 'all wheels stand still' (Lenin on strikes). Various strata of the urban population — intellectuals, students, lawyers, teachers, other professionals, small traders, bazaar merchants, craftsmen, the clergy and the migrant masses — had already taken part in street demonstrations that had started ten months before.

The contradictions and limitations of capitalist development in Iran, which were partly determined by global economic trends, revealed themselves in a number of ways: the end of economic boom of the mid-1970s, the revision of the Fifth Development Plan and the start of the recession in early 1977. Inflation raised the prices of food and housing and eroded the income of the lower classes (Walton, 1980).

This was happening in the context of a peculiar political situation and state form which made society ripe for a radical transformation. The contradictions of the Shah's capitalist state revealed themselves in unbearable repression, structural corruption and the underdevelopment of political relations and institutions in relation to the rapid accumulation and socio-economic change which had developed new social classes (working class and the new middle class) with respective socio-political aspirations. These political aspirations came into direct conflict with the dictatorship. The combination of economic conditions and political repression acted as an impetus to push the masses on to the streets.

The Beginnings

We made it clear in Chapter 5 that the working class was oppressed and struggling at the point of production. A new wave of strikes, which corresponded to the initial phase of struggle began in the spring of 1978. In March workers at Azmayesh plant in Teheran went on strike, protesting against a management plan to make three hundred workers redundant. In the same month, some six hundred gardeners employed by the oil industry stopped work demanding a pay-rise. In April, 2,000 workers in the brick-making industry in Tabriz came out, demanding better conditions and welfare. As time went on, the number of strikes increased.

> It is often enough for one factory to strike, for strikes to begin immediately in a large number of factories. What a great moral influence strikes have, how they affect workers who see that their comrades have ceased to be slaves and, if only for the time being, have become people on an equal footing with the rich (Lenin, 1978, pp. 62–3).

Until August, the form of demands was economic, though we should not ignore their associated political content. In the period after September there was a progressive increase in the numbers striking; the period also marked a turning point in the nature and the forms of the demands that were made (see Table 6.1). According to the available data, in recorded strikes (fewer than the real number) at least some 35,000 workers at different factories stopped work in September, putting forward both economic and political demands, organizing demonstrations and releasing resolutions.

About 60% of the demands made in September were economic (for pay-rises, improved welfare, extra holidays, implementation of job classification) and the remainder were directly or indirectly political: about control over the funds and financial affairs, the discrimination between men and women workers; calling for the dissolution of the yellow syndicates and the establishment of a new form of workplace organization and the dissolution of the Workers' Organization of the Rastakhiz Party and of the *Hefázat* and the expulsion of their agents (secret police); change or expulsion of management, expulsion of foreign experts and protest against interference by military forces in workplace affairs.

The rebellions in industrial workplaces were a reflection of socio-political developments in society as a whole. This continued to be so until the workers began demanding workers' control. In terms of militancy, the workers were still lagging behind the other groups. On 5 September (a religious holiday) millions had taken to the streets, throughout the country, in a peaceful demonstration; and two days later, on Bloody Friday in Teheran, the street battles against the army had left hundreds of dead bodies on the streets.

A few points must be made on the question of militancy. We must draw a qualitative distinction between the nature and forms of the working-class struggle and the struggle of the other masses. The working class is *not* simply an aggregate of individuals, and the militancy of the class is not necessarily the same as that of the individuals of that class. 'People act one way as individual atoms in the social fabric; they often act quite differently as part of a class collectively' (Draper, 1978b, p. 40). Working-class militancy and effective struggle do not have to take the form of bloody street confrontations. Militancy in the factory at the point of production may be more appropriate as well as effective.

October and After: The Escalation of Strikes
The revolutionary movement which had aimed to overthrow the Pahlavi regime, and which, following Bloody Friday, had forced the regime to declare Martial Law, assumed a new momentum in October. When 40,000 oil-workers, 40,000 steel-workers, 30,000 railway-workers had put down their tools within less than three weeks, the dynamism of the revolutionary process changed radically. Workers in hundreds of plants and companies were rapidly adding to the strike movement which spread to many different sectors of the economy: the state sector, industry and services. Given the military rule, the pace of work stoppages in this period was indeed surprising: according to recorded reports, on 6 October alone railway-workers in Zahedan, 40,000 steel-workers in Isfahan, workers in the copper-mines of Sar Cheshmeh and Rafsanjan, at Abadan Petrochemical, at Isfahan Post and Telegraph Company and all the branches of the Bank of Shahrier went on strike (Ayandegan, 16 January 1979, 1357/10/26). The day after was the same: all the refineries, the Royal Air Services, the Iranit factory in Ray, the customs officers in Jolfa, the Department of Navigation and Port Affairs of Bandar Shahpour, Tractor Sazi in Tabriz, radio and TV stations in Rezayeh, 80 industrial units in Isfahan, a steel-mill in Bafgh, employees of the judiciary through-out the country and employees of the Finance Department in Maragheh joined in. The next day it was the turn of Zamyad plant in Teheran,

General Motors, the Plan and Budget Organization and the railway-workers in Zahedan (again). The next day (11 October 1978) the largest daily newspapers went on strike. The Canada Dry factory, the ports and shipyards in Khorramshahr, the Iran Kaveh plant, the fisheries of Bandar Pahlavi, Minoo factory, Vian Shre plant, Gher Ghere-i Ziba, *all* workers in Gilan province, 2,000 brick-makers in Tabriz, oil-workers in Abadan and Ahwaz, in the pipe plant and Machin Sazi in Saveh, 40,000 workers of Behshar Industrial Group throughout the country, bus-drivers in Rezay and communication workers in Kermashah joined the strike in rapid succession (Ayandegan, 20 January 1979). With every day, there were new strikes. Martial law failed to crack down on the revolutionary movement. On 30 December, Bakhtiar, a remnant of Mosadegh's National Front, accepted the Shah's offer to form a government. By the time the Bakhtiar cabinet was formed, almost all the key economic sectors were idle: oil, communications, transport, public services, banks, customs and even the actors who dubbed cinema films and TV programmes.

The inactivity of key sectors tended to paralyse social and economic activities.[2] The Bakhtiar cabinet acted the same role in Iran that Mrs Aquino was to do in The Philippines, but it was too late, and strong religious leadership had been formed by Khomeini. During Bakhtiar's period of office, the general strike gained a novel dimension. It spread from wage-labouring sectors to the independent ones: at this time, almost all the shops in Teheran and other towns were shut (*Ayandegan*, 1357/10/21).

The Oil Strike

The oil strike was of particular domestic and international significance. While the regime could tolerate the massive street demonstrations of the religious festival on Fitre Day, the struggle of the oil-workers was intolerable to it. Industries such as oil and communications were the most strategic economic sectors. It would, however, have been wrong to concentrate merely on these sectors on the grounds that they would automatically paralyse the rest of the economy. The organization of strikes by the oil-workers could continue only in the context of a total revolutionary movement. And, in turn, such a movement could defeat the regime only with the support of the oil-workers.

Following a call to strike on 15 October in the Abadan refinery, troops were called into the workplace, arresting seventy workers and the leader of the union of the Teheran Oil Refinery Workers. After this, the workers in Lavan, Bahrakan, Ahwaz, and other oil-fields stopped work. Negotiations with the Finance Minister, M Ansari, broke down, and on 2 October the following demands were formulated by the strike committee.
1. End martial law;
2. full solidarity and co-operation with striking teachers;
3. unconditional release of all political prisoners;
4. Iranization of the oil industry;

5. all communications to be in the Persian language;
6. all foreign employees to leave the country;
7. an end to discrimination against women staff employees and workers;
8. the implementation of a law recently passed by both houses of parliament dealing with the housing of all workers and staff employees;
9. support for the demands of the production workers, including the dissolution of SAVAK;
10. punishment of corrupt high government officials and ministers;
11. reduced manning schedule for offshore drilling crews.

Following the issue of the demands, the production and export of oil halted; their resumption was dependent on the fulfilment of the demands. Production declined from 5,700,000 barrels a day in late October to 1,800,000, and then to nil in November (*Kayhan*, 6 January 1979). The oil strike had an international impact which gave the workers a peculiar social and economic power; 'the social power which', as one writer put it, 'stems from their being organized by capital into an international class' (Turner, 1980, p. 272). The international impact of the strike was such that, from the other side of the world, Sweezy and Magdoff wrote,

> There have been few spectacles in recent history so inspiring and heart-warming as that of 70,000 oil workers, far and away the best paid and most privileged segment of the working class, bringing to a complete halt the huge production and refining complex which is the Iranian Oil Industry, and doing it not for better pay or special privileges, but in support of the quintessentially *political* demand of the whole Iranian people that the Shah and all he stands for must go (1979, p. 17).

The oil-workers caused a 10% drop in world consumption of oil by non-OPEC and non-socialist countries. Domestically there was a 42% drop in industrial production in the second half of 1978 and a drop in the state's income of 21.4% (from that in the previous year).

One result of the revolutionary crisis was a further economic crisis whose symptoms had already started to appear in the second half of 1978. After the insurrection, the crisis showed itself in industrial recession, the flight of the industrialists, shortages of raw material, the nationalization of the banks and a number of industries and mass unemployment. The next chapter will deal with the new working-class movement which the crisis produced.

The Revolutionary Crisis and the Metamorphosis of Demands

One of the interesting features of the working-class struggle was the transformation of economic demands into political ones. Like the development between February and October 1917 in Russia, the demand transformation among the Iranian working class attested that it is very hard to separate in practice these two forms of struggle, in particular in a critical revolutionary situation. Since the terms are usually misconceived, let us look at what Marx and Lenin had to say on the issue.

Marx and Lenin on Economic and Political Struggles

> Every movement in which the working class comes out as a *class* against the ruling classes and tries to coerce them by pressure from without, is a political movement. For instance, the attempt in a particular factory or even in a particular trade to force a shorter working day out of individual capitalists by strikes etc., is a purely economic movement. On the other hand, the movement to force through an eight-hour law etc. is a *political* movement. And in this way, out of 24 separate economic movements of the workers there grows up everywhere a *political* movement, that is to say, a movement of the class with the object of enforcing its interests in a general form, in a form possessing general, socially coercive force. While these movements presuppose a certain degree of previous organization, they are in turn equally a means of developing this organization (Marx, Engels and Lenin, 1974, p. 59).

We may conclude from the statement, first, that the concept of class struggle is equal to political struggle (the struggle for conquest of political power). The second conclusion is that political struggle stems from, or rests upon economic struggle (that is, the struggle of the workers of an individual factory against the individual capitalist). Here, thus, there seems a tendency to treat the three terms — economic struggle, political struggle and struggle for socialism (or struggle for setting up an alternative socio-economic structure) — as the expression of one and the same movement.

This particular piece of Marx's writing refers to the activities of the First International within which and alongside the different sectarian political tendencies there also existed a 'real working-class movement' like the English Chartist movement which was itself the product of the long process of the evolution of the English working class since the second half of the 18th Century. Yet, the post-International developments, in particular the bourgeois tendency of the leadership within the English labour movement, would encourage Marx to argue for the necessity of a *political* organization of the working class alongside the trade unions. However, the exact relationship between the two remains ambiguous (see Draper, 1978b, pp. 115–46). These political developments were occurring at a period when industrial capitalism was still in its initial stages and lacked the material basis to develop a hegemonic capitalist state, which it would require explicitly political struggle to oppose.[3]

Lenin's definition of economic struggle is similar to that of Marx: 'when the workers of a single factory or of a single branch of industry engage in struggle against their employer or employers'. On the other hand, political struggle according to him is when all the foremost representatives of the entire working class of the whole country are conscious of themselves as a single working class and launch a struggle that is directed not against individual employers, but against the *entire class* of capitalists and against the government that supports that class (Lenin, 1960, pp. 215–20).

While we can see a resemblance between the views of Marx and Lenin in the two concepts of economic and political struggles, there are differences between them as to the transformation from the former to the latter. Lenin does not hold a single theory on this issue; Lenin the practical revolutionary took different stands in different circumstances.

Before he wrote *What Is To Be Done?* he argued that 'every economic struggle necessarily becomes a political struggle' (1960a, p. 213). In the years around the turn of the century, a number of Russian Social Democrats (Economists) concentrated their agitation almost entirely around the immediate, limited, and basically economic demands of the working class. As a response, Lenin wrote the polemic of *What Is To Be Done?* as part of the internal debate. In this pamphlet he argues,

> There is much talk of spontaneity. But the *spontaneous* development of the working-class movement leads to its subordination to bourgeois ideology . . . for the spontaneous working-class movement is trade unionism . . . and trade unionism means the ideological enslavement of the workers by the bourgeoisie (Lenin, 1973a, p. 32).

But the logic of political development during the revolutionary process of 1905 (and 1917) and the momentum and form of the proletarian political struggle led Lenin to accept that

> The economic struggle, the struggle for immediate and direct improvement of conditions, is alone capable of rousing the most backward strata of the exploited masses, gives them a real education and transforms them — during a revolutionary period — into an army of political fighters, within the space of a few months (Lenin, 1973b, p. 242).

Under the same logic, he praised the rise of the spontaneous strike movement (1978, pp. 157–61), and urged the party members to work within the non-party bourgeois workers' organizations (1973b, pp. 169–76).

The Historicity of Economic and Political Struggles

Before dealing with the concrete case of Iran, I shall make a few theoretical points concerning the formal and realistic approaches to the issues of economic and political struggle. In so doing, I shall attempt to present my understanding of Marx's and Lenin's conception of economic and political struggles.

The nature of the demands in any strike movement reflects the particular stage of its maturity. I shall assume that the making of political

83

demands represents a more advanced stage of a labour movement than the making of economic demands. The concepts of political-economic demands and struggles are often defined rather descriptively: economic demands are those couched in an economic form, such as those concerned with pay-rises and better working conditions, and political demands in a political form (change in a law or the right to vote). I would suggest, however, that we need to go further: the value of any workers' demands (and organizations) is determined not simply by examining the demands themselves but by analyzing them in the historical context in which they are advanced.

In general, an economic struggle may be defined as any struggle in any form which is waged for limited and immediate goals. According to this definition, therefore, a purely economic demand, such as for a pay-rise, may well be part of a political struggle, when it is advanced *in order* to oppose the state/capital by inflicting economic pressure in a situation where the state/capital is unable to fulfil that demand. Similarly, an advanced and formally political action might be entirely economic and trade unionist. The opposition mounted by the National Graphical Association (NGA) in Britain against the government law of secondary picketing provides a typical case of this, especially when account is taken of the subsequent contempt of court decision in November 1983. In spite of its political form, the objective of the NGA was immediate and limited to the defence of specific rights. The question of how an economic struggle becomes elevated to a political struggle is a complex one. Any strike movement based on economic demands is limited and may fail to realize its full historical potential. The foundation of Lenin's polemic as to why economic struggle fails to elevate itself to a political struggle is based upon the assumptions that a) in normal conditions, it is the dynamism of capital accumulation that determines the character of socio-political developments; b) that capital would be *able* to fulfil any economic demands made by the working class and thus possesses an unlimited power of manoeuvre to defuse the political content of any economic struggle, and c) that, in this way it institutionalizes and integrates class conflicts into the fabric of the state.

A basic problem with these assumptions is the way in which they have been generalized, not solely by Lenin, but also by Leninists. In reality, in any particular society and at a given moment in its historical development, the power of capital to manoeuvre is determined by its own strength and the strength of the opposition. So the power of manoeuvre of capital in Iran differs from that in, say, Japan. In the Iranian case before the revolution, two specific periods could be distinguished: before the revolutionary crisis economic demands were harshly resisted by the state; but after that period, the state was prepared to negotiate and concede economic demands. At this period, however, a mere emphasis on the very same demands would have failed to realize its potential and they had to be transformed into totally political demands.

The Iranian Experience

The diagram below, the result of 115 labour reports and resolutions, demonstrates the trend of economic-political demand transformation, from May 1978 to January 1979. By January some 85% of the demands, in form and essence, were political — that is, for going on strike to support strikers in other factories, for freedom of political prisoners, end to martial law, abolition of colonial contracts, and the overthrow of the Pahlavi regime.

Figure 6.1
The Trend of Political Demand-Making

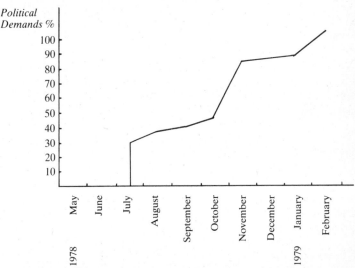

In October and before, some 55% of the demands were still in an economic form (pay-rises, welfare and extra holidays). These demands may be argued to have the aim not solely of obtaining immediate and limited concessions, but also of inflicting economic pressure to deepen the crisis. Such a tactic was certainly adopted in the metal plant, as an activist described:

> In '57 (1978), we decided to go on strike, as the *Imam* had recommended. In fact, we used our year-end bonus as an excuse; you know, we would usually get our bonus in the second half of the year. So we used that as an excuse. Martial Law soldiers poured into here. They took some of the workers away in their cars. The rest of the workers said nothing and got back to work..The Martial Law people, meanwhile, asked what was our grievance: "Why do you do such things?" We said, "Nothing's up with us — we just want our bonuses, management don't respond." We shut down this plant later on when the situation was getting tense.

Table 6.1
The Trend of Demand-Making, May 1978 to February 1979*

| | 1978 | | | | | | | | 1979 | | | |
	May	June	July	Aug	Sept	Oct	Nov	Dec	Jan	Feb	Total	%
Economic Demands												
1. Pay rise	2	2		2	10	14	1		1		34	29.8
2. Welfare** †	1	1	5	2	14	37	3		1		65	57.0
3. Extra holidays			1	2	3	2	1		1		10	8.7
4. Perfect implementation of job classification scheme				1	2	7	1				11	9.6
5. Delayed wages					1	1			3		5	4.3
Radical demands (indirect political)												
6. Control over funds, finance and profit-sharing scheme			1		3	2			2		8	5.5
7. End to discrimination between workers, respect for workers				1	1	2					4	2.7
8. Five days work, 40 hours week					2	2			1		5	3.4
9. Protest against lay-offs, demand for their return				1	1	2			4		8	5.5
10. Dissolution of yellow syndicate, formation of new organizations††			2		3	2			2		9	6.2
11. Abolition of WO & *Hefāzat*, expulsion and trial of those responsible					3	3	1		1		8	5.5
12. Abolition of penalties and disciplinary measures						1	2		1		4	2.7
Political demands												
13. Change in management, stop employing new managers				1	5	11					17	11.7

No.	Demand										Total	%
16.	Solidarity with other workers & protest against arresting workers	1		4	5		6				13	8.9
17.	Freedom of political prisoners, return of the exiled			5	4		2	1			12	8.2
18.	Trial of those responsible for massacre of revolutionaries			1	1		2			4		2.7
19.	End to censorship, freedom of expression and political parties			2	3	3			8			5.5
20.	End to martial law			9	5		3		14			9.6
21.	Abolition of colonial contracts, boycotting foreign goods				3		1	1	8			5.5
22.	Dissolution of parliament, SAVAK & Bakhtiar government				1		3	1	5			3.4
23.	Downfall of Pahlavi regime								8			
24.	Other‡											100

Proportion of economic/political demands

May 100% econ.	June 100% econ.	July 70% econ.; 30% pol.	Aug. 63.5% econ.	Sept. 60% econ.
Oct. 55% econ.	Nov. 17.5% econ.; 82.5% pol.	Jan. 14.8% econ.; 85.5% pol.	Feb. 100% pol.	

*This table has been compiled on the basis of 115 labour reports or resolutions.

**No *new* strike or protest incident was reported, probably indicating all units to be on strike.

†Welfare = including housing allowances; medical services; food, travel and child benefits; loan and conditions of work.

††WO = Workers' Organization, state-controlled, affiliated to Rastakhiz Party. *Hefāzat* = Security Bureau, factory secret police office.

‡Others including: 'No one is to be exploited by the rich; workers' participation in the Revolutionary Council (new government) demanded by 17,000 shipyard workers and associated companies; workers' situation must be prime concern of next government; new labour law prepared by the workers themselves; and establishment of the rule of the masses.

A member of the factory committee of the Arj factory also had the same idea.

> We decided to launch a political strike, that is, to transform the economic strike into a political one. We proposed it to our lads who we knew well . . . But those who ate out of the boss's hand just neutralized it. In fact, they spread rumours that "they (the strikers) want to stop us getting our wages", and such like (my interviews).

At the initial stages of the strike movement, the reaction of the state was to resort to the classical tactic of stick and carrot, reform combined with repression. In August, for instance, the government had conceded on certain issues: the payment of unemployment benefit, for the first time in working-class history; the extension of annual holidays by three days; full compensation for early retirement. On the other hand, the mounting strike pressure forced the state in September to resort to disciplinary measures. On 11 September, new regulations were issued warning workers 'not to leave the workshop without permission; to show proper conduct; to obey orders; to respect the managers' (*Khabar-i Kargar*, no. 2). Such measures could hardly be taken seriously by the workers. The state's strategy at this point was to stop political demands by making economic concessions. Thus, in six months, the wages of all workers rose on average by 25%. Some sectors, such as metal and construction, obtained a 60% pay-rise (Bank Markazi Iran, 1979, p. 25). The pay-rise was combined with payment of other benefits such as housing, child benefit and overtime.

After September, the confrontation between the masses and the regime reached a point where economic pressure was no longer enough; the workers did not stop there. Promises by the Labour Minister of the Bakhtiar government for a radical change in the Labour Law and the establishment of democratic workers' unions were totally ignored by the workers. Demands tended progressively to assume a political character.

The employees of a steel complex went on strike initially for better welfare provisions. On 7 October, they advanced new demands for housing allowances, an end to strict military regulations and a change of management. Following the stoppage of work, military forces occupied the plant, as a result of which the ending of the strike was made conditional on more demands. For a short period, when the soldiers were occupying the plant, the workers were forced to resume work. Circulating leaflets, they informed people:

> come and see that we are working under the shadow of tanks, cannon, rifles and bayonets . . . entering the factory premises is like stepping into a concentration camp . . . it is by the force of rifles and bayonets that we are made to work (in *Khabar-i Kargar*, no. 2).

Eventually, making certain political demands, the whole steel industry downed tools on 13 January.

As long as the regime still had some sort of power of manoeuvre, the only response to political strikes was the use of military force. After political demands had been made by the oil-workers, when negotiations with the government failed, 1,700 delegates from various workplaces staged a mass meeting in the Abadan refinery in front of military forces, deciding to stay all the night in the Administration Department. Tanks and armoured vehicles took position. As the delegates refused to leave there, a bloody confrontation ensued in which two were killed and eleven wounded (*Le Monde*, 16 November 1978). Similar military actions were carried out in Tractor Sazi, Machin Sazi and Pars Metal plants as they started anti-regime strikes.

Internal Political Struggle

The domain of political struggle is not limited merely to those actions carried out against the laws and values of a capitalist order at a societal level; it also characterizes certain types of action and demands which are advanced at the point of production. These are what I would call internal political struggles and they form a part of the demands made by the Iranian factory workers in the revolutionary period.

To clarify the issue, I shall look at an abstract workplace *per se*, without an historical and politico-economic context. Marx argued that 'all directly social or communal labour on a large scale' requires a 'directing authority' to co-ordinate the movements of the individuals. But under capitalist production the co-ordination assumes a particular form. For it has to operate in accordance with the vital requirement of capitalist production, the maximum extraction of surplus-value. In these circumstances,

> the control exercised by the capitalist is not a special function arising from the notion of social labour process, and peculiar to that process, but it is at the same time a function of exploitation of social labour process, and is consequently conditioned by the unavoidable antagonism between the exploiter and the raw material of his exploitation (Marx, 1979, pp. 449–50).

One must now examine how the function of control (distinct from the function of co-ordination) must be exercised, so that — despite the workers' opposition within the antagonistic production process — the maximization of profit, the driving force of capitalist production, is guaranteed.

Marx argues that capital has to transform the social relations within the production process, in accordance with the logic of surplus-value extraction, thus establishing a 'despotic direction' (Marx, 1979, p. 450). As the production process becomes more complex, and the labour force becomes more and more concentrated, despotism takes novel forms. New strata of wage-earners occupy new positions and perform the functions of social control (foremen, supervisors, heads of department and so on). The establishment of a social division of labour (distinct from, but parallel to, the technical division of labour) lays down the basis for the structuring of control: hierarchy and relations of power at the point of production appear to be the natural and normal structure of the workplace; so that the laws, value and rights of the agents are defined and legitimized. In the more advanced form of labour processes, power and authority tend to be objectified by the diktat of automation. There is a tendency towards a reduction in human medium power; it is replaced by a reified control, especially when the deskilling of supervisors and middlemen and 'Taylorization of intellectual work' tend to prevail (Cooley in Levidow, 1981).

The production process thus comprises two kinds of technical and social (authority) relations. Similarly it is the arena of two forms of struggles: economic struggle in the sense of 'effort bargain, that is, the more monetary reward for labour expended or reward for effort' (Burawoy, 1982); and political struggle in the sense of struggle against the established laws, rights and power relations at the point of production. Struggles for control over funds and investments; the abolition of disciplinary measures, and the abolition of the yellow syndicates should all be assessed as political struggles. They question established values and laws, and in a word, class relations.

Moving from the abstract to the concrete level, we hold that if the internal struggles (at the point of production) are waged not as mediation for a broader class struggle but for their own sake, for immediate ends, they still remain at the level of a 'trade union struggle' in the Leninist sense. In the specific sense of Iran, I would suggest that these radical demands had political connotations since they were advanced in order to put pressure upon the vulnerable position of the Shah's state.

Spontaneous or Conscious Struggle?

One of the most important aspects of any revolutionary struggle is the question of whether it is spontaneous or conscious. Let us clarify these two concepts. For Lenin, the fact that an action is spontaneous does not imply that it is unplanned, without leadership and mechanical. Rather, it signifies a low level of struggle, 'a class struggle in embryo', waged by the workers who can recognize the irreconcilable antagonism between themselves and their employers, but not that between themselves and 'the whole of the modern political and social system': awareness of the latter is characteristic only of social democratic consciousness (Lenin, 1973, p. 36). In this sense, a conscious struggle is one which is led by a conscious element, that is, a social democratic party. In a Leninist sense the strike movement in Iran was certainly a spontaneous movement. However, such a simple characterization cannot help us to perceive the real attributes, complexity and variety of the working-class organization of struggle.

Organization

My study of the strike movement suggests that any collective action was carefully thought out, planned and put into practice. The strike leaders would decide what form of action to take, what kinds of demands to put forward and what tactics to adopt to foil secret police counter-measures. In the early months of the revolutionary upsurge, decisions had to be made in the secret cells which had spontaneously blossomed over the years. The plans would be conveyed to the mass of the workers through trusted connections or through spreading rumours, getting the message across through everybody and, at the same time, nobody. A leader of Arj plant strike explained:

> Before the Revolution, we were [members of] the syndicate. We would demonstrate inside, and at times would do so out of the factory. In order to plan effectively, and co-ordinate, the syndicate decided to set up a committee for the co-ordination of demonstrations . . . the committee, of course, was secret. We would inform the other workshops, asking them to join in demonstrations . . . This syndicate intended to bring all workers of this area out on to the streets . . . [Anyway] we set it up, in order to prevent others from interfering [in our affairs], and from probably changing the direction of our activities.
>
> Q. How would the strikes get started?
> A. The plans would be made secretly, of course.
> Q. Were there any workers who would carry out underground activities in the factory?
> A. Of course, undoubtedly. One would inform another; he would inform the next, and so on. In this way the strike would get started.

In Caterpillar plant, another strike leader described his experience:

> We were a group of workers and employees who knew each other well through our participation in various revolutionary activities for at least 7–8 years; and because we were of similar mind about the social problems. In earlier times, we were rather suspicious of each other. For instance, I was suspicious of this friend of mine, Mr Kamali, because of something which happened to him: [he was arrested] and got just two months! Considering the way things were at that time, we thought he should have been given more than two months. I and another comrade decided to test him, to see whether or not he was a SAVAK agent . . . Mr Kamali thought of me in the same way. However, we did get to know each other. We made contact in this way: I gave him a book by Mr Khomeini. With that beard and every-thing, I thought he might be religious. Anyway, we were to get closer . . . We managed to form a secret nucleus . . . this nucleus would engage in all sorts of political activity here, as far as it could. I would also always intervene

in the other workplaces. If necessary, it would organize in other factories . . . or it would distribute workers' literatures countrywide (in A Ghotbi, 1979, pp. 94, 105).

When the revolutionary crisis became more acute, spontaneous committees tended to surface. The crucial decisions would be taken in organized mass meetings and elections would be held to set up the committees. Where a radical syndicate existed, it would revive its activities to organize strikes and other forms of protest.

The committees often assumed total responsibility for the workplace. In the oil industry, for instance, a committee was responsible for the day-to-day operation of the whole industry. It enjoyed a great deal of power to manoeuvre, and had such a flexibility that it could often neutralize the counter-measures of the military to crush the strike. It would summon delegates from the different parts of the industry for a meeting to release instructions within 'the half hour, before the troops could come and drive us away'.[4]

Leadership

Who were the organizers of the strikes? Did they belong to any particular political or religious organization? An accurate examination of the issue requires detailed empirical research which has not yet been conducted by anyone. Yet it could be argued in general that one of the main features of the strike movement was that its grass-roots organizational leadership was within the workplace, and not from outside organizations such as political parties, unions or religious institutions.

Our study of the socio-political conditions in the pre-revolutionary factories (Chapter 5) showed that any organic connection between the workers and the political opposition was unlikely. In terms of their broad ideological and political backgrounds, the leaders of strikes may be divided into three categories. First, there were those who seemed to be influenced specifically by left-wing ideas (a few leaders in the Caterpillar plant, the oil industry, or the industries in the Caspian Sea area). The second group, who came from religious circles, would convey the instructions of the religious leaders through distributing their leaflets; a number of activists in the Leyland Motor and the Iran-Transformer plants fell in this category. And thirdly, there were the secular activists with trade unionist tendencies, such as the strike leaders of the Zagross factory in Teheran. Thus, whatever forms of struggle were waged, and whatever forms of consciousness were developed, almost all originated on the factory floors. Outside influences were felt in the later stages of the revolutionary process: the activities among the working class of left-wing groups, students and, later, the *mullas*, became widespread only during the Bakhtiar government, when the condition for open political agitation were realized.

Independent Actions

Until the uprising most workplaces were shut down and there was no opportunity to observe the ability or otherwise of the workers to run the production process. It would have to be tested afterwards. Yet the oil and railway workers who were recommended to resume work by the Committee for Coordination and Investigation of Strikes (CCIS), Khomeini's special committee to investigate the strikes, demonstrated that ability despite the expulsion, in the oil industry, of some eight hundred foreign experts (Nore and Turner, 1980, p. 280).

The political involvement of the workers within a few months of the revolutionary upsurge, their engagement in discussions, plannings, organization and confrontations with the army pushed the most backward sections of the working class into the struggle. They advanced the internal struggles within workplaces not simply for immediate ends but to alter the existing political order. The working class gained a political consciousness and a sense of anti-imperialism. It was not, however, a socialist consciousness in the sense of struggle against a bourgeois state *per se*, with the prospects, however vague they may be, of an alternative socio-economic order. While the workers indeed controlled all revolutionary activities within the workplaces, they did not and could not exert their leadership upon the mass movement as a whole. This leadership was with someone else: Khomeini and the clergy associated with him. The revolutionary bourgeoisie could move only under the shadow of the latter.

Despite its inability to exert a hegemony over the whole mass movement, the working class in its fight against the Shah's regime was independent, that is, its decisions on how to advance its struggle were not led or controlled by any external force. Where the imposition of order by an external authority occurred, conflicts and tensions were inevitable. The Railway Strike Committee refused a number of times to resume work and carry fuel for the 'consumption of the people' as the CCIS, Khomeini's representatives, requested. The workers had already rebuffed the same request made by the Shah's regime, arguing that it was 'a plot to use the trains for transporting military goods and equipments' (*Kayhan*, 8 and 10 January 1979). They agreed to the request coming from the Committee only when the authenticity of the request had been demonstrated. In another development the Customs workers declared that they would be prepared to release only vital goods: food, medicines, medical-stuffs, papers, typewriters, heaters, and so on. They also made it clear that they would refuse to release the goods belonging to embassies of the USA, Britain and Israel. Meanwhile the workers rebuffed the Ayatollah Shariatmadari's request to permit the import of food on the grounds that the state would misuse the opportunity to import armaments under the guise of food. The Oil Strike Committee accepted the request of the CCIS to resume production for domestic consumption only after long debate, negotiations and assurances.

The Strike Committee of the oil industry possessed a high degree of independence and authority, and seemed to Khomeini and his allies a parallel organ of power. Differences of interests and conflicts came to the surface before the insurrection and before the Shah had departed. The confrontation culminated when, some three weeks before the insurrection, the leader of the oil strikers resigned as a gesture of protest against 'the dogmatic reactionary clergy', and against 'the new form of repression under the guise of religion'. His immediate concern, according to his open letter 'to the masses of Iran', related to the 'existing repression . . . and arbitrary interferences by the Especial Envoy (of Khomeini) in the duties and responsibilities of the Committee of the Strikers' representatives'.[5] Bitter confrontations occurred immediately after the insurrection when the strike leaders were arrested by the new regime, and charged as counter-revolutionaries.

The Weaknesses

The fact that the oil strikers' leader protested in such a manner should be viewed as an indication of his awareness of the nature of the *ancien régime* as well as the prospects for the revolutionary one. However, the very fact that he did resign exemplified the general handicap of the whole working-class movement.

The Lack of a Co-ordinating Organ
In Russia, in 1917, within only three days of the rebellion of working-class women on 23 February, the Soviet of Petrograd was formed and became the organ of a later revolutionary upsurge until October. In October the Central Council of Factory Committees was founded. This Committee had the task of co-ordinating all the factory committees which sprang up immediately after the abdication of the Tsar.

In Iran, although the *de facto* strike committees mushroomed within the workplaces after the Shah's departure, no effective initiatives were taken by the workers to unify and co-ordinate the committees; no central strike fund was established. Two days after the Shah's departure, in January, Ayatollah Taleghani, a liberal, popular clergyman, and not the workers, instructed that each industry, group and organization should set up a strong central organ for organizational purposes; so that 'each organization should have only one single central nucleus to carry out the task of decision-making'; and that 'a unified nucleus and organization must be set up to encompass [industrial and commercial] trades, workers and administrative organizations' (*Ayandegan*, 17 January 1979).

Despite these initiatives, no further practical steps were taken to co-ordinate strike committees by industry or trade. This failure by the working class needs explanation.

The factory system in Iran, because of the geographical dispersion and administrative independence of each unit, would, in practice, make it difficult to unite all the strike committees. A close consideration of the strike movement shows a correlation between successful and militant committees and the high concentration of the workforce in a single industrial unit. To organize 70,000 oil-workers is much easier than organizing 20,000 workers in 200 factories, say, in Teheran alone. Organization and co-ordination of strikes in oil, steel, railway and telecommunications were more coherent, and the demands of the workforce more radical. For, in addition to their strategic position in the economy, and relatively high concentration of labour in these sectors, the organization and composition of the labour process objectively contributed to the unity of the workers.

There is no evidence to demonstrate any organized labour struggle, in the form of strike committees, in small-scale workshops. While the employees did take part in the struggle, they did it not as a unified class force, but as an oppressed mass. The reason for that must be sought in, i) the particular form of the organization of production and limited concentration of labour; ii) the direct control on the part of the employer, iii) the paternalistic relationship between labour and capital, and iv) the administrative independence of each of these small units.[6]

The existence of workers' unions could act as a positive force to widen workers' interests beyond the limited sphere of factory to that of industry or trade. Moreover, workers' unions would have acted as organizations to co-ordinate the dispersed strike committees. Iranian workers, however, lacked any trade or industrial unions. The most important limitation, however, was the absence of an effective political force committed to organizing the working class for the strategic objective of socialist construction.

No regional, nor, of course, national co-ordination committee was formed. This vacuum encouraged the alternative power bloc, the Khomeini group, to take the initiative. Their immediate move was the creation on 20 January of the CCIS composed of three religious liberals: Bazargan, Y Sahabi, Moinfar, and two clergymen: Bahonar and Rafsanjani. The main tasks of the Committee were declared to be to 'call off those strikes which jeopardize the work of the main industries involved in the production of people's urgent needs, and those threatening the country's survival'. The CCIS succeeded, by 30 January, some three weeks before the insurrection, in persuading 118 production units, and a few public services, to resume work. The operation of these industries and services was argued by the CCIS to be essential for the success of the revolution. We are unaware of the reaction of the workers in these units to the request of the CCIS; yet, we know that the tendency of the workers in such critical sectors as oil, railways and telecommunications was to maintain their control over their own movement.

The Rudiments of Soviets?

The absence of a unified co-ordinating body in the labour movement made any prospect of forming an independent workers' council or soviet doubtful. Such proletarian organizations would have connected the dynamism of the struggle at the workplace to the day-to-day requirements and demands of the mass movement outside the points of production. The revolutionary crisis had furnished the material basis for such organizations; and their organizational and functional forms were present in embryo. Strike committees and experts of the Isfahan steel-mill negotiated with the railway-workers, requesting the latter to carry the coal they required from Kirman, to keep the plant boilers warm. A similar agreement was reached between the oil-workers and the railway-workers to carry the fuel necessary for domestic consumption when all other production was at a standstill. These kinds of proletarian co-operation were a rather rudimentary form of working-class social administration.

On the other hand, during the later weeks, popular organs in the form of district and city councils started blossoming. In December and February people took control of a number of cities and towns, in particular in the northern Azeri and Caspian Sea provinces, including Zanjan, Orumieh, Salmas, Ardabil, Maragheh and Ajabsheer. In a number of northern areas people formed *shuras* (councils) in order to administer their day-to-day affairs. In the towns of Sāri and Amol a solidarity council was formed. It was composed of representatives of 27 industrial groups and trades, including teachers, traders and state employees (*Ayandeghan*, 16 January 1979). Within cities such as Teheran, various forms of neighbourhood councils were spontaneously set up, and aimed to fulfil the basic needs of the people, including the 'supply of foodstuffs and consumable goods; the just distribution of fuel and petrol; the administration of law and order; refuse collection, public hygiene and the like.' The councils were also committed to cultural and political activities: the

> identification and expression of sympathy with the families of revolutionary victims; production, duplication and distribution of political leaflets and tracts; dispute settlement between the people of the locality; the co-ordination of demonstrations and other forms of political struggle (*Kayhan*, 10 January 1979).

However, there is no evidence to suggest an organizational link between the working classes and the neighbourhood popular *shuras*. Perhaps the more notable of the popular organizations were the political organs within the armed forces; in the Air Force one took shape under the name of *Shuray-e Homafaran* (Council of Air Force Servicemen). However, any organizational link between the latter and the district or strike committees was almost non-existent. In this situation the emergence of a mass organization of alternative power could hardly be expected. Yet a peculiar form of workers' organization did emerge after the insurrection.

These organizations, factory *shuras*, persisted and fought a difficult battle for survival, as we shall see in the next chapter.

Notes

1. The existing literature suffers from misunderstanding and inadequate sources. See, for instance, Abrahamian in Bonine and Keddie, 1981 and Zabih, 1982. A detailed, though short, account of the oil-workers' strike by Terisa Turner, based on an interview with one of the strike leaders, is an exception; see Turner in Nore and Turner, 1980.

2. *Kayhan* newspaper reported on 6 January 1979 that

> the shortage of fuel (resulting from strike in oil industry) has made the Ministry of Agriculture idle. The Municipality is already closed as the refuse collectors are unable to move. All the offices of the Department of Registration have been closed down, owing to the lack of fuel and petrol.

3. For the development of revisionism and reformism in the European labour movement, see Richards, 1979.

4. An account by an oil-worker in Nore and Turner, 1980, p. 300.

5. At the end of his statement he warned, 'Those who think that we have reached the end of the road, and that victory is at hand, have not "recognized the nature of American Imperialism"; they do not know the great strategic and economic interests of Imperialism in Iran; and that the enemy has just been wounded but not eliminated. Imperialism still controls the whole axes of power, the axes which require just a little amendment to be functional again' (the statement of M J Khatami, published by *Ayandegan*, 2 February 1979).

6. It is interesting to note that in Petrograd in 1917 about 68% of total enterprises had more than 1,000 workers each (Smith, 1980, p. 16).

Chronology of Pre-Revolutionary Events

May 1977:   The protest of the intelligentsia surfaces in the form of open letters to the Court.

June–August 1977:   The protest of shanty-town dwellers against slum clearance; 50,000 demonstrate.

January 1978:   Violent confrontation between theology students and police in holy city of Qum. It was over a slanderous article about Khomeini who was in exile in Iraq.

18 February 1978:   Mass demonstration and riot in Tabriz, the capital of Azerbaijan.

March 1978:   Spread of mass demonstrations in other urban areas.

August 1978:   The first wave of industrial strikes.

27 August 1978:   Labour Law was revised: payment of unemployment benefits; extension of annual holidays by 3 days; early retirement with full payment.

September 1978:   Mass demonstrations continue in Teheran.

7 September 1978:   Martial Law is declared in Teheran and 11 other major cities.

8 September 1978:   Black Friday: hundreds of protestors are killed in Teheran.

9 September 1978:   Strike at Teheran Oil refinery.

11 September 1978:   Publication of a Labour Disciplinary Act.

September 1978 onwards: Spread of strikes to other oil refineries and factories.

6 November 1978:   Shah appoints a military government; General Azhari's cabinet is formed.

10–11 December 1978:   Millions of people demonstrate against the Shah's regime. Soldiers in many areas join the marches.

31 December 1978:   The cabinet of General Azhari collapses as Bakhtiar agrees to form a new civilian government. This is followed by a general strike which brings the whole economy to a halt.

16 January 1979:   Shah leaves the country; the Iran Workers' Organization affiliated to the Rastākhiz Party is abolished.

20 January 1979:   Formation of the Committee for Co-ordination and Investigation of Strikes; members include Bazargan, Y. Sahabi, A. Moinfar, J. Bahonar and Rafsanjani.

21 January 1979:   Bazargan calls upon the workers of the oil

	industry, the customs and ports to step up production and services.
30 January 1979:	On the recommendation of the Committee, 118 production units start work.
1 February 1979:	Khomeini returns to Iran from Paris.
5 February 1979:	Khomeini appoints Bazargan as Prime Minister of his provisional government.
9 February 1979:	The Javidan Guard (Imperial Guard) attacks the barracks of the mutinous airforce technicians in Teheran.
10–11 February 1979:	Two days of insurrection.
11 February 1979:	The Shah's regime is overthrown; Bakhtiar escapes; jubilant armed youths take over control of the streets. The victory of the Islamic Revolution is declared.
13 February 1979:	Khomeini orders workers to return to work.

7. The *Shuras*: The Emergence, Structure and Struggles

The *shuras*, or factory committees (or councils) were a particular form of workers' organization that emerged in Iranian industry following the overthrow of the Shah's dictatorship in 1979. They were shop-floor organizations whose elected executive committee represented all the employees of a factory (blue- and white-collar) and/or an industrial group, irrespective of their trade, skill or sex. Their major concern was to achieve workers' control.

The *shura's* concern for offensive control was what differentiated the *shuras* from a shop-steward movement. But the *shuras* also differed from syndicalism, which fought a political battle to change the social structure through industrial activities. The *shuras* lacked a clear political objective. Unlike the factory committees of the Russian Revolution of 1917, the *shuras* were not influenced by the outside left political tendencies and did not act as a vehicle for social change. They restricted themselves to demanding workers' control and the transformation of power relations in the industrial arena.

Four Periods of Struggle

The dynamics of political development after the Revolution were rapid, unexpected, complex and contradictory. In this study we shall divide the post-revolutionary workers' struggle into four periods. Each period is characterized by different positions of, and relationships between, labour, capital and the state.

The First Period
This covers the period between the February 1979 insurrection and the first wave of political pressurization in August 1979; it was characterized by control from below. The significance of these few months lies in a) the continuation of the revolutionary struggle by the working class after the revolution, waging a struggle independent from, and at times directly against, the leaders of the revolution; b) the crisis of legitimacy of capitalist relations; c) the instability of the new state; and thus, d) the creation

of an objective situation for workers' control, through the organization of the *shuras*.

In the months leading up to the insurrection workers had shut down almost all industrial establishments. While these two to three months of strikes had had a tremendous political effect on the workers, they still did not have any experience of self-organization at work. After the flight of the owners and senior managers, there was a power vacuum in most of the factories. On the other hand, the workers developed a strong sense of possession of the factory, and hence a feeling of commitment to and responsibility for it as part of the people's wealth. During this period, workers managed and ran the factories themselves. The Bazargan government expressed early and direct opposition to the *shuras*, claiming that the triumph of the revolution had eliminated their tasks. Towards the end of this period Bazargan reintroduced the one-man management system with liberal professional managers.

This period ends with the first wave of extensive repression in August 1979, coming mainly from the ruling clergy: left-wing organizations were attacked and their headquarters ransacked; the government banned progressive newspapers, monopolized the official media, and launched extensive military attacks on Kurdistan. These events were followed by increasing attacks on the labour movement and the purging of antagonistic *shuras* and individual workers.

The Second Period
September 1979 to June–July 1981 was marked in labour relations by a) a systematic return of management from above; b) the consequent gradual demise of the *shuras* as effective organs of workers' control; and c) a necessary shift from offensive to defensive struggle.

The Bazargan government appointed liberal managers to pursue further the strategy of one-man management. This was strongly opposed by the workers. Immediately after the hostage crisis erupted, the struggle in the factories escalated. These struggles, together with the post-Bazargan government's (Rajaii's cabinet) intention to implement an Islamic corporatism, led to the ratification of the constitution of the *Islamic shuras*. Meanwhile, the inter-state conflicts between the liberals and pro-Khomeini clergy increased. Thus this period saw the gradual establishment of the Islamic Association (IA) (*Anjaman-i Eslami*) in the factories under the ruling clergy organized in the Islamic Republican Party (IRP). The Associations were the vehicle for the consolidation of the clergy's power in the workplaces in opposition to both liberal managers and the independent *shuras*. Towards the end of this period, the *maktabi* (the Islamic) management, as a part of the same strategy to consolidate the power of the clergy, gradually replaced the liberal management as the conflicts between different wings of the government intensified (Bayat, 1983). Liberal managements were losing ground in the workplaces, and hence an alternative management based on force and ideology (religion) gradually became dominant. The Islamic Management, with the co-operation of strengthened IAs, started a harsh campaign against the independent *shuras*. At a political level, the conflict was between the Islamic fundamentalists and President Bani' Sadr and the liberals and was around the issue of maktabism (emphasis on ideological values) *versus* specialism.

The liquidation of the independent *shuras* was stepped up after the second wave of suppression during the closure of the universities. Among the *shuras* closed were those of the Tool-making Factory, Lift-Track, Pompiran and Kompidro in Tabriz; the Union of Workers' *Shuras* of Gilan (with 300,000 workers); the Union of Workers' *Shuras* of Western Teheran; those of the oil industry in Ahwaz and the railway-workers. *Khane-i Kargar* (Labour House), previously a free headquarters for workers' assemblies, became the centre of pro-IRP *shuras* and Islamic Associations.

The Third Period
This lasted from the June Days of 1981, following the dismissal of President Bani' Sadr and the mass execution of the opposition forces until mid-1982. The clergy, those followers of the political form of *valayat-i faghih* organized in the IRP, now gained total state power and campaigned against all the opposition, from the liberals to the far left. The period was characterized by a) the domination of both the *maktabi* management and the Islamic Associations as the real power-holders in the factories; b) militarization of the factories and attacks on the real and formal wages of the workers; and c) an official ban on the formation of even the pro-government *shuras* for the time being.

The Fourth Period
This coincided with the emergence of the rift between the two major factions of the ruling clergy known as *Imam's line* — the followers of Khomeini's project of *Valayat-i faghih* (Islamic rule); and *Hojjatieh*, more fundamentalist and non-pragmatic elements. In the sphere of industrial relations it is characterized by the mounting conflict between the managements (including the Islamic ones) and the powerful Islamic Associations. From the viewpoint of the far-sighted and rational elements of IRP, the historical mission of the IAs to undermine both the liberal managements and the independent *shuras*, had been completed. They (the IAs) were then encouraged to limit their activities to only cultural and social issues — to retreat from their position of power in the workplaces, and from interfering in management authority — a matter that IAs could hardly accept.[1]

A Brief Outline of the Workers' Struggles After the Revolution

The Period of Control from Below
Immediately after Khomeini's order to return to work on 15 February 1979, and despite his threats, a new wave of workers' struggles sprang up.

This industrial unrest was fuelled by the radical transformation in the workers' consciousness that had occurred in the course of the Revolution, and the particular situation after the insurrection.

In the very first month after the Provisional Government (PG) came to power in February, at least some 50,000 workers went on strikes, demonstrations, sit-ins, or launched other forms of struggle. In the five months following, it was the same story. The workers' demands could be divided into two broad categories of economic and radical demands. The economic demands were mainly for the payment of delayed wages and against lock-outs and lay-offs. Capital tended to move from the productive into the trade sector, where it could be secure from the danger of wild confiscation, and the 'interferences of irresponsible officials'. Most of the bankrupted and locked-out units were owned by private capital. The Provisional Government provided some Rls 85 billion credit for industry in 1979 in an attempt to salvage it from the crisis. Private capital used only Rls 25 billion. Against such a background, the PG was forced to nationalize and to supervise at least some 483 production units. The same objective economic conditions which forced the workers to defend their already existing rights and advantages were the basis for an offensive battle. The workers questioned the fundamental rights of capital, which was in disarray.

In the economic battle, direct and indirect demands for a pay-rise were the major issue. Together they formed over 40% of the total economic demands (see Table 7.1). The wage battles were despite a wage-increase, during the revolutionary process, of 25%. According to official figures, the index of the per capita wage and benefits in 1979 showed a 53% rise in comparison with the same period in the previous year (Bank Markazi, 1979). The minimum wage-level grew from Rls 215 per day for unskilled labourers to Rls 567 in that year. The wage battle did not stop; the rising rate of inflation undermined real wages. The struggle culminated in April when the workers demanded the year-end bonus.

Lack of workers' unions led to a considerable variation in pay-rises as each unit struggled individually. The industries which had a relatively large workforce, such as the oil industry and the factory-workers of the province of Gilan (in the Caspian Sea area) who for some time were organized under the co-ordination of the Factory *Shuras* of the Gilan Province, were exceptions. Differentials in pay continued after the revolution: between the manual workers of a single factory, between the manual and the intellectual workforce, and between different factories in the same industry.

The fight against wage differentiation was one of the major struggles in which the *shuras* in this period were engaged. In the absence of a union of factory *shuras*, it was hard to fight for and succeed in narrowing the inter-factory wage variations. The gap provided one material ground for the division of the working class (see, for instance, the pay differential in two factories of Fanoos and Metal Works, Table 3.6).

Table 7.1
The Trend of Demand-Making, February 1979 to February 1980

	1	2	3	4	5	Total 5 months	% 5 months	6	7	8	9	10	11	12
Economic Demands														
1 Delayed wages	26	15	9	13	14	77	17.8	1	1	3	2	2	—	2
2 Against lock-outs, lay-offs, return to work	24	24	13	11	14	86	20.0							1
3 Formation of genuine unions	5	6	5	1		17	4.0		1					
4 Pay-rise, overtime bonus, against wage-cuts	5	11	14	21	20	71	16.3	6	2	2		1	1	1
5 Implementation of profit sharing scheme	4	7	1	3	2	17	4.0	1		1		3		3
6 Repayment of taxes and fines	6	3	3	1		13	3.0							
7 Permanent employment		4	2	4	9	19	4.3	1	1		2	1		
8 Eight-hour day		3	1	2	7	13	3.0	1	1			2		
9 Equal wage for men and women	1				2	3	0.6							
10 Various benefits*	16	18	18	30	32	114	26.3	7	5	2	3	8		2
Total economic demands	87	91	66	85	102	431	100.0	17	11	8	7	17	1	9
Radical Demands														
1 Dissolution of Hefâzat, Especial Force, expulsion of counter-revolutionaries, trial of SAVAK agents and capitalists	3	4	4	1	6	18	8.3	3	2			2		
2 Struggle for formation or recognition of *shuras*	11	9	4	4	2	29	13.4				1	3		

3 Persecution, expulsion of managers, foremen, bosses appointed before or after Revn.; appointment of new management	3	13	5	12	10	43	20.0	1	1		1	2	2	1
4 Control over production or distribution; management of the units; right to intervene in all affairs of units	2	6	4	4	6	22	10.2	2	—	—	—	2		3
5 Control over contracts; over distribution of Especial Benefit	3	5		1	2	11	5.1				1			1
6 Control over hire and fire	1	4				5	2.3							
7 Nationalization or confiscation of capital	1	3	3	3	2	12	5.6						2	1
8 Against censorship, mistreatment, discrimination & sacking militant workers	3	3	2	11	10	29	13.4				3	4		2
9 Against conciliationist *shuras*		3	1		2	6	2.7		1	1		1	1	
10 Right to assemble & strike	1	4	1	1		7	3.2							
11 New labour law	2	3	2			7	3.2					1		
12 Forty-hour week	5	6	2	4	9	26	12.0	2	1	3	1	1	2	
Total Radical Demands	*35*	*63*	*28*	*40*	*49*	*215*	*100.0*	*9*	*5*	*4*	*7*	*16*	*7*	*10*
Number of units involved	*63*	*58*	*47*	*52*	*67*	*287*	—	*14*	*5*	*7*	*8*	*12*	*3*	*9*

*Including housing allowances, child benefits, consuming co-operatives, job classification, other bonuses, extra holidays, etc.

1. February–March 1979
2. March–April 1979
3. April–May 1979
4. May–June 1979
5. June–July 1979
6. July–August 1979
7. August–September 1979
8. September–October 1979
9. October–November 1979
10. November–December 1979
11. December 1979–January 1980
12. January–February 1980

Table 7.2
Wage Differentiations Between Manual and White-Collar Workers: February–May 1981

Monthly earnings (Rls)	Metal Works Manual %	Metal Works White-collar %	Engineers Managers %	Amazon Warehouse Manual %	Amazon Warehouse White-collar %	P.R. Plant Manual %	P.R. Plant White-collar %
Under 12,000	1.9	21.1	—				
12,000–20,000	46.6	38.8	—				
20,000–30,000	39.3	14.1	—				
30,000–35,000	3.9		—				
35,000–45,000	4.1	16.0	—				
45,000–55,000	1.0		—				
55,000–65,000	1.4		20.0				
65,000–80,000	1.0	6.0	40.0				
85,000–95,000	0.5						
100,000–150,000	—	—	33.3				
260,000	—	—	6.6				
Total	100.0	100.0	100.0				
	No. = 557	No. = 85	No. = 15	1,888	400	795	95
Average wage Rls/monthly				31,000	59,000	90,000*	107,000*

*Total income including all benefits, overtime and piecework bonuses.

Serious attempts were made to narrow the gap in pay for manual and intellectual work through, on the one hand, increasing the formal wages of the low-paid by the *shuras* and, on the other hand, decreasing the income of highly-paid employees in both the *shuras* and by the government. Despite these efforts, highly-skilled experts still enjoyed relatively high salaries (see Table 7.2).

Narrowing the pay gap between manual and intellectual labour provides a material basis for immediate solidarity between the two as against the employers (be they private or state). This tendency could be unequivocally observed in such plants as Metal Works and Fanoos plants. In the PR Plant the gap remained, as did the political rift, between the two strata.

Table 7.2 indicates the extent of wage parity between the manual labourers and white-collar workers. Although equal pay can be the source of an immediate feeling of common identity, cultural and ideological divisions do not necessarily wither away. I would suggest that the *shuras* could and did play a significant role as a medium of strategic solidarity and identity.

Period of Management from Above
The general radical labour struggle ceased in the subsequent periods. This general downturn was manifested in various ways.

Quantitatively, there was a decline in industrial incidents. More specifically, labour unrest dropped from 287 incidents within the first five months following the insurrection to 58 during the subsequent seven months (see notes on Table 7.1). The downturn continued in the third period at a rather higher rate. The number of industrial incidents (strikes, sit-ins) fell from 366 in 1979–80 to 180 in 1980–81, and to 89 during 1981–2 (see Table 7.3). Three reasons were behind this trend. Firstly, some of the demands concerning wage-increases, return to work and the expulsion of elements of the previous regime had been fulfilled. Secondly, as soon as the new state consolidated itself, a national campaign of intimidation and harassment began after the invasion of Kurdistan. This policy forced labour into a defensive and cautious position. And thirdly, with the gradual re-implementation of the government strategy of management from above, the contradictions of workers' control began to appear.

The overall crisis transformed offensive struggles and demands into defensive ones, and the radical demands turned to immediate economic ones — mostly in response to the regime's new offensives against labour. Whereas previously the *shura* had been in control of the workplace, it now had to be under the control of a management supported by the Revolutionary Council. Simply speaking, the struggles in the second period for Special Profit, for instance, meant that the *shura* was no longer in control of the financial office, calculating the profit and allocating it among the rank and file. All this, however, does not imply a total collapse of the labour movement. Despite the decline in labour militancy, the defensive struggles continued in response to the accelerating rate of repressive measures which the state adopted against labour which culminated in the inception of war with Iraq and following the June Days of 1981.

Table 7.3
The Breakdown of Industrial Incidents in 1979–82*

Industries	1979-80	1980-81	1981-82	1984-85	Total
Metal, steel, oil	85	84	47		216
Textile & leather	45	34	13		92
Paper & wood	14	3	—		17
Food processing	20	12	5		37
Construction	91	19	4		114
Mining	5	—	1		6
Transport & communications	19	10	7		36
Miscellaneous	87	18	5		110
Total	*366*	*180*	*82*	*200*	*828*

*Including various forms of strikes, sit-ins and occupations of the plants (see Table 10.2).

Sources: Labour reports in various issues of *Kar*, *Paykar*, *Dawlat va Enghelāb* and *Rah-i Kargar* Nos. 8 and 14, 1984, 1985.

At least three major waves of workers' struggle have to be mentioned in these two periods. The first was at the time of the Embassy seizure, when the workers, capitalizing on the anti-imperialist rhetoric of the state, launched a new offensive against state managers, demanding more authority over workplace affairs and expropriation of joint-venture enterprises. The second wave spread in the winter of 1980–81 as a widespread reaction against the state's policy of abolishing the profit-sharing scheme. The policy went ahead in spite of resistance. And the third wave surfaced again as a defensive response to further state offensives to cut back the significant perks of the car-industry workers. Here too resistance was useless. But militancy continued in various covert forms which forced industry into a crisis of productivity in 1982 and 1983. The details of these battles and their impact on the industrial crisis are presented in Chapter 10.

Active workers' struggles revived once more in 1984–85 when 200 industrial incidents were reported to have occurred over pay-rises, delayed wages, overtime pay and benefits. Of these incidents 90 were illegal strikes, and in 65% of all cases workers won their cases. Involved in major strikes were Shahrood Coal Mines, Haft Tappeh Sugar Plantation,

Tobacco Industry, and the Canada Dry plant; but the most important strike was that of 27,000 construction workers of the Esfahan steel mill who were out for 15 days. On 10 December 1984 the strikers forced the government to retreat from its plan to lay-off or replace the construction workers (*Rāh-i Kargar*, 1985).

The Emergence of the *Shuras*

The factory committees were organizational forms of working-class reaction to the inability of capitalism to fulfil the workers' demands at a time of crisis. In a revolutionary situation, where there is an absence of normal control on the part of the state, the labour-capital relationship becomes highly tense: the accumulation rate of capital is undermined and its control becomes shaky, while labour, in terms of ideology and militancy, becomes unprecedentedly radical.

Three days after the insurrection of 14 February 1979, Khomeini ordered all workers to return to work. For him and for the engineers of the new society, the historical task of strikes had been ended; a return to work was crucial to consolidate the new order. The resistance of the oil-workers would force Khomeini to resort to threats.

> Any disobedience from, and sabotage of the implementation of the plans of the Provisional Government would be regarded as opposition against the genuine Islamic Revolution. The provocateurs and agents will be introduced to people as counter-revolutionary elements, so that the nation itself will decide about them, as they did about the counter-revolutionary regime of the Shah (*Ettelāāt*, 15 March 1979).

Any attempt to reproduce the old order could lead only to the escalation of a new crisis. The workers did return to work: the CCIS succeeded in convincing strikers in at least 118 production units to resume operations. On their return, however, the workers faced three problems. Firstly, construction or contract works and the like had already been paralysed during the escalation of the strike movement. The owners had made losses, given up the business and fled the country. The capitalists had not left behind anything worth appropriation by the workers. The workers in these sectors formed a considerable proportion of the post-revolutionary unemployed. The second type was a group of industries whose owners and managers, after taking large loans from the banks, had fled the country. For the workers that meant re-operating, running and controlling the plants. But for the Provisional Government it meant the burden of nationalizing such industries, along with the bankrupted banks and insurance companies. At least 483 production units were nationalized under the umbrella of the state-controlled Organization of Nationalized Industries of Iran (ONII) (Bank Markazi Iran, 1981). The third group of problems were in basically small-scale profitable and private industries of indigenous capital whose owners remained in the country, declaring their support for the Revolution.[2] Some of these industries became the battleground for capital-labour confrontations when the workers returned. As we shall see, the *shuras* emerged in both groups of industries — those with and without owners or top managers. Many accounts see the *shuras* as a means of filling the vacuum in the absence of management, or of saving jobs. What is missing in this approach is consideration of two essential issues: the inability of capitalist rationale to meet quite normal demands of the labourers in a revolutionary situation; and the ideological transformation among the workers.

To illustrate the first issue, it is interesting to note that in some units workers' control was demanded and later implemented primarily through a demand for the payment of delayed wages. (Though we should admit that, in such cases, workers' control was initially adopted as a solution to an immediate problem, not as control for itself.) For the workers who returned to work after months of stoppage, the most immediate necessity would have been the payment of wages for those months. The manager would argue, 'You have not produced anything during the strike period, what should I pay you for?' The worker would respond, 'That is true; we did not produce; we didn't, precisely because we wanted to overthrow the regime. We have been subsisting on loans; we went under the risk of arrest and even death; is this the reward?' Direct action became the only solution. The workers were forced to transcend the established boundaries and move into the hitherto undisputed domain of capitalist control: opening financial books, blockading products, controlling financial departments, taking owners or managers as hostages and occupying and running the factories.

In the first phase of the post-revolutionary labour movement, the phase of control from below, these were the basic forms of direct action. Resort to the forced re-opening of and occupying of plants, the taking of hostages and such actions would not occur in normal circumstances. In the third group of industries (those operating with their owners), the *shuras* emerged not, of course, because of the absence of an organ of management, but because of its very presence. Hence, the direct role of ideological mediation, the primary organizational form of which emerged as the Inquiry Committees of the factories.

Ideology

The very idea of the *shuras* came from the direct and immediate experience of the workers themselves. The working class is able, through its direct action and experience, to advance its struggle and question the fundamental principles of capitalist domination and legality. It is able to encroach in practice on areas of control which normally are considered to be the undisputed territory of capital. However, experience is one thing and conceptual understanding another. The role of the activists is to generalize from experience and demonstrate further possible steps.

In the Iranian case, we cannot deny the role, however limited, played by the left-wing organizations, in terms of agitation for, and direct involvement in, the formation of the *shuras*. However, we must assert that almost no political organization had any clear understanding of the *shuras'* significance, degree of control or functions. The chaotic democracy gained allowed revolutionaries and students to enter the factories, especially those located in Teheran. But we should not overestimate their role.

The working class lacked any historical traditional experience of such organizations as *shuras*. In Russia, before February 1917, the factory-workers had two distinct historical experiences of organization: the first was the experience of the Factory Committees and the Soviets of the 1905 revolution (Trotsky, 1973); and the second, as the historians would emphasize, was the *starosty*, the tradition of representation in the Russian villages from which most of the factory-workers in 1917 originated (Smith, 1980, pp. 141–2; Goodey, 1974).[3] Such experience was missing from the history of the Iranian workers. The experience of 'council societies' (*anjomanhay-e shuraii*), which emerged in some northern cities and among the urban people during the Constitutional Revolution in 1905–1907, were too far away to be remembered by the present generation of industrial labour.

After the insurrection of 1979, a sense of hatred for the past developed; the workers had defeated the past, so they tended to express their dislike for whatever belonged to it: they were feeling that now was the time to rebuild *their* society, *their* country, *their* factory according to their own ideas.

> Nowadays you don't need to tell a worker to go and work. He works himself; why? The reason why he didn't work [under the Shah] was because he was under the boss's thumb. He couldn't speak out. Now, he'll say, "the work is my own, I'll work" (Melli Shoe workers, in Ghotbi, 1980).

> After the revolution, the workers noticed that the country belonged to them, and so they should work harder (Metal Works worker, 1981).

The second important idea which developed rapidly was a sense of possession with regard to their own work. The landed peasantry would not and did not attain such a form of consciousness, for they already had control over their production process. For the workers in the morning of the Revolution, the country was owned by them. Hence the development of a strong sense of responsibility and care, commitment, sincerity and sacrifice. The following is an example of how such a sense was expressed in the words of an angry worker in the Pars Metal factory in Teheran.

> We have formed and appointed this *shura* with overall responsibility for the factory, for the investigation of work and problems. We formed this *shura* for the sake of our revolution . . . but we see that the Board of Directors which we have here by no means agrees with our *shura*. That is, they say we

111

can't go along with this *shura* . . . This factory is weak-willed. Since the revolution, we have done everything we can to keep the factory on its feet. But we have failed. Look, now what are the tasks of an engineer? An engineer must stay at the factory and work. Why has this engineer gone to stay at the boss's office? Who will pay for it? Isn't he going to ask for a salary? Isn't he going to get benefits? Our factory is a parent factory . . . This factory *can* stand on its feet. We produce so much! They [the management] say: "We have to take a loan from the government!" Where does our product go then? Where do the sales of this factory go, that they have to get credit from the government? What they get from the government belongs to this country's wealth. *I* am, here, under this burden, and then they go and get a loan from the government? This wealth belongs to the whole people, to everyone. Why should *I* benefit, although *I* am working. And then, where does the result of my labour go?[4]

Two examples will illustrate the process of *shura* formation. The workers' *shuras* of the Pars Metal factory emerged primarily not as *shuras* with a definite form, but as organs of discontent founded on the ambiguous ideology of possession and anti-authoritarianism. In the course of a struggle which passed through the stage of the formation of an Inquiry Committee to arbitrate on the misconduct of management and organs of the secret police, the workers conceptually articulated their activities in a *shura* constitution.

The struggle at the Eirfo factory was initially for the following demands:

1. wage payment without delay;
2. payment of year-end bonus of the profit-sharing scheme;
3. payment of child benefit;
4. permanent employment of the casual workers for a fair wage;
5. appointment of a manager independent from the shareholders;
6. supply of raw material; and
7. dissolution of the conciliationist *shura*, and the formation of a genuine one.

The workers pressed for the demands. In response the employer attempted to dismantle the *de facto shura*. In the course of confrontation, which led to hostage-taking by the workers of a few managers, and to the intervention of *Pasdaran* (the Islamic Revolutionary Guards), the demands were reformulated:

1. payment of the year-end bonus by the end of the month;
2. supply of raw material in ten days;
3. the director to work in the plant eight hours a day for at least one year;
4. the director to be accountable to the *shura* in financial and accountancy affairs;
5. the director to function under *nezarat* (supervision) of the *shura*;

6. the signature of the *shura* to be on documents of the sale of products.

The workers achieved their demands. In the five months following the Revolution, the workers in at least thirty factories followed a similar course.

The forms the *shuras* took varied according to the level of workers' consciousness, the ownership and management of the enterprise (absence or presence of the actual owner); and the degree of the opposition of the owner or director. The firms with an absent owner/director (who had fled the country or who was in hiding) formed the earliest and the most successful *shuras*. In the firms with owner/directors present, the *shuras* tended to be set up later, assuming a loose structure and rather legalist trade unionist attitudes.

The Legal Status of the *Shuras*

We shall consider two topics here: the law of the *shuras* prepared by the Revolutionary Council, and its relation to the real world of the revolution. We shall then go on to deal with the detailed practices of the *shuras*.

The Law of the *Shuras*

The most comprehensive document on the *shuras* appeared in August 1980 when the Supreme Council of Labour, of the Ministry of Labour, laid down the Resolutions of the Islamic *Shuras*. This followed the Regulations for the formation of Islamic *Shuras* in June 1980.

The Resolutions covered four major areas. The first was procedures for practical *shura* formation. This opened the way for control by the Ministry of Labour over the whole process of building the *shura*, the appointment of its constituent body (*Heyat-i Nezārat*), preparing (authorizing) the constitution and evaluating and recognizing (or otherwise) the qualifications of the candidates. The second section dealt with the units which were not entitled to *shura* operation. The third section authorized the mode of operation, tasks and responsibilities and the final section dealt with the way in which the members of the constituent body (*Heyat-i Nezārat*) were to be elected.

Compared with the Regulations released earlier by the Revolutionary Council, the Resolutions are more restrictive. The rights and responsibilities of the *shuras*, according to the Resolutions, can be divided into four categories.

a) Most of the Articles are concerned with co-operation with the management (Article 1, section 3); settlement of disputes with good faith; raising productivity; utilizing personal initiatives; decreasing costs (Articles h, d, j, b); co-operation with management in execution of plans in due periods; assistance in resolving problems; 'co-operation in order to decrease the economic and technical dependencies' (Article y).

b) Trade union rights exist to protect the material and the spiritual interests of all employees and collective bargaining; to supervise all welfare affairs (travelling costs, food, sport, co-operatives, loans, housing and hygiene); to raise the technical knowledge of the employees and to form educational classes in literacy, technology, Islamic ideology and military techniques (Articles l, t, h).

c) There should be consultation to evaluate and suggest useful proposals concerning planning; to consult with management over producing the internal (disciplinary) regulations of the units, including those on hiring and firing, leave of absence, absenteeism, illness and disciplinary procedures (Article 30).

d) Article 22 of the Regulations points out that, in units with less than two thousand employees, one member of the *shura*, and in those with over two thousand, two members of the *shura*, may be appointed in the management, provided that the members of the Board of Directors number five or more. The two *shura* members could act either as the members of the Board of Directors, or as the connecting members (*ozve-i rābit*). In the latter case, their roles would be limited to consultation. The whole Article obviously affected an extremely small number of the units bearing in mind a further constraint: the Law of the *Shuras* subjects *shura* formation in the large-scale state-controlled industries (oil, steel and copper, etc.) to the ratification of the Cabinet (Article 14).

These are the main tenets of the Regulations. The Regulations were not only a subject of struggle between the workers and the state, but within the state apparatus itself. Thus the hard-line Labour Minister, Tavakkoli, temporarily suspended the total project of *shura* formation in February 1981. In December 1982 the new Islamic Labour Law was introduced, which in practice made the whole notion of *shura* entirely redundant. The whole Law was based upon the Quranic notion of rent (*idjareh* = hiring) and individual bargaining (see Chapter 9). The Islamic Labour Law was opposed and rejected both by workers and the populist factions of the ruling clergy. Debate on preparing an alternative Labour Law continued through 1982–85; and owing to the factional conflicts within the government, the final draft of a new Labour Law is yet to be approved.

There are some formal similarities between the official Islamic *shura* and the strategy of co-determination. The Law intended to create the same relationship between capital and labour as co-determination: 'the spirit of co-operation and solidarity between the employees and the management', and the 'regulation of class relations' (Schaur, 1973, p. 224). Historically speaking, the official law of Islamic *shuras* reflected an intense class struggle, as did the strategy of co-determination in Germany, and Whitleyism in Britain during 1919–21 (Hyman in Goodrich, 1975) and all the strategies of control from above. The strategy is well expressed by Perry Anderson.

It is a rule in a capitalist society that any institution or reform created *for* or *by* the working class can by *that very token* be converted into a weapon *against* it — and it is a further rule that the dominant class exerts a constant pressure towards this end . . . The working class is only concretely free when it can fight against the system which exploits and oppresses it. It is only in its collective institutions that it can do so: its unity is its strength, and hence its freedom. But precisely this unity requires disciplined organization, it becomes the natural objective of capitalism to appropriate it for the stabilization of the system (Anderson in Nichols and Beynon, 1977, pp. 345–6).

The Iranian experience differs from this in at least two respects; in the historical limitations of Iranian capitalism and the absence of a strong trade union movement.

The Law of the *Shuras* and Balance of Forces
In reality the Law of the *Shuras* was recognized by neither management nor workers. The extent and degree of workers' *shuras* depended solely on the balance of forces between workers, management and the state. The laws the government laid down specifically about the *shuras* were not their only words on the matter. The Constitution of the Islamic Republic, prepared in 1979, mentioned the formation of *shuras* 'composed of representatives of workers, peasants, other employees, and the managers' in the productive, industrial and agricultural units (Article 104). 'Decisions taken by the *shuras* must not be against Islamic principles and the country's laws' (Article 105).

The Provisional Government rightly realized the danger of recognizing the *shuras* in any form. It did not hesitate to oppose them as disruptive, and advocated instead the formation of workers' and employers' syndicates.[5] It had already formed a special force (*Nirouy-e Vigheh*) to dismantle the genuine *shuras* by politico-military means. It was one-and-a-half years later, in June 1980, when the Revolutionary Council, after the collapse of the Provisional Government in the US Embassy seizure, recognized the formation of Islamic *shuras* composed of all the employees of an enterprise, in order to create 'a spirit of co-operation and solidarity between all of the employees and the management'. The law also encouraged *shuras* to raise the 'cultural, political, economic and occupational knowledge of the employees; to preside over the affairs of the enterprise and the better conduct of work; and to put forward constructive proposals, etc.

The source of legitimacy of the *shuras* was not, of course, the laws, but the dynamics of class struggle and the balance of forces in society which was reflected in the workplaces. Recognition of the law does not only imply the regulation of relations between two or more parties, but also regulation of the conditions of subordination of one party. A revolutionary situation is the negation of such regulation; it brings a fluidity and

115

anarchy and changes in the balance of forces; the law is no longer law. Neither the state nor the industrialists nor the workers recognized and practised the laws. The law became a point of issue in the ongoing class struggle; it could not manage to damp it down. When labour had the upper hand over management, it would go far beyond the legal and conventional constraints; and where management had the ability to suppress the workers' resistance, then it would do whatever was possible to prevent a representative *shura* forming, even if the *shura* wished to act within the legal procedures. The Law of *Shuras* failed to co-opt and integrate the working class into the system. The necessary social basis for such integration was lacking. The *ad hoc* government's recognition of the *shuras* only fuelled the offensive power of the labour side and led to a further escalation of class struggle.[6]

The *Shuras* and the Frontier of Control

The degree, extent and scope of workers' control cannot be revealed by a mere exposition of their forms. Any analysis must be located in the context of an investigation of the balance of forces between capital and labour. The balance of the latter is regulated by the position of a given industry in the competitive market; the nature of the labour process; and the stage of capitalist development in terms of development of organizations of the labour process; the organization of the workforce and the organization of employers (see Chapter 2).

We have some difficulties in our data. Table 7.4 indicates a spectrum of radical demands in the five months after the Revolution, the period of control from below. The table demonstrates only the forms of various issues that the workers were most concerned with — those which were still in the form of demands; and which might or might not be realized. In the rest of the units, the workers were either already practising such rights, or alternatively did not see them as serious matters at all. The latter was probably true of the small-scale workshops.

In this section, we shall explain the actual experience of control practices and the strong desire and ability of the workers to determine the production process for themselves. (Though we must point out that we are acquainted with a rather small number of workplaces which exercised a high degree of control). Whatever the numbers, the significance remains: if a single factory can be run by workers' control, why not all?

The functions performed by the *shuras* can be classified into five major areas: 1) trade union struggles; 2) struggle against authoritarian relations at workplaces; 3) control over conditions of employment; 4) control over financial affairs and contracts; and 5) management and administration of production.

Table 7.4
Areas of Workers' Struggle in the First Five Months

	March–April	April–May	May–June	June–July	July–August	Total	%
A. Radical Demands							
1 Dissolution of Hefazat, expulsion of counter-revolutionaries, trial of SAVAK agents & capitalists	3	4	4	1	6	18	8.3
2 Struggle for formation or recognition of *shuras*	11	9	4	4	2	30	13.4
3 Persecution of managers, foremen, bosses appointed before or after Revn.; appointment of new management	3	13	5	12	10	43	20.0
4 Control over production or distribution; management of the units; right to intervene in all units' affairs	2	6	4	4	6	22	10.2
5 Control over contracts; over distribution of Special Benefit	3	5	—	1	2	11	5.1
6 Control over hiring & firing	1	4				5	2.3
7 Nationalization or confiscation of capitals	1	3	3	3	2	12	5.6
8 Against censorship, mistreatment, discrimination; sacking of militant workers	3	3	2	11	10	29	13.4
9 Against conciliationist *shuras*		3	1		2	6	2.7
10 Right to assemble & strike	1	4	1			7	3.2
11 New Labour Law	2	3	2			7	3.2
12 Forty-hour week	5	6	2	4	9	26	12.0
						215	100.0
B. Economic Demands	87	91	66	85	102	433	
Number of units involved	63	58	47	52	67	287	

Some important points must be made about the significance of the precision of the sources of all Tables compiled on the basis of labour reports from Left papers.

a) Demands/actions in the Tables are only those *registered* and reported through the papers. Hence the number of industrial events is probably underestimated.

b) For a few weeks after the first extensive attacks on Left organizations (August 1979) Left papers stopped publishing. When illegal publication resumed, the scale of the labour reports in them declined.

c) Table 7.4 omits practices such as sabotage, or go-slows; these were the main forms of struggle in the second and third periods but no official registration of 'industrial disputes' took place at this time.

d) On the basis of the reports, any estimation of the numbers of workers involved/man-days lost is impossible.

e) The papers *Kar* and *Paykar* had a rather vague and imprecise conception of *shura* and syndicates. The possibility of confusing the two and some degree of exaggeration cannot be discounted.

Trade Union Struggle

The lack of any viable experience of independent trade union activities and an entirely negative view of the workers towards factory-based syndicates provided no reason for workers to organize themselves around the principles of trade unionism *per se*. The *shuras*, a number of which were formed as a channel for trade union-type demands, would inevitably act as direct, democratically-elected representatives of the workers at the workplace level, as opposed to the management. In this role the *shura* would negotiate over such issues as pay-rises, bonuses, profit-sharing benefit, job security, holidays, insurances, job classification and conditions of work.

Struggle Against Authoritarian Relations at Workplaces

> If Iran remains like this, it will fall. Because there haven't been any purges here. The manager is here still, still there are charlatans, knife fighters, thieves, bullies. In short, they are all still around. Only the Muhammad Reza [Shah] and a few people around him, like his brothers and sisters have gone. The rest are still here. Why otherwise should we work in a temperature of 80 degrees like this, and when the pay's due, we get fed up and tired out with all the shouting etc (Ghotbi, 1980, p. 7).

Authoritarian relations are a predominant characteristic of a factory system based on the capitalist division of labour. In Iran, the despotic attitudes of the traditional management was an additional dimension to industrial relations. Thus the Councils tended to struggle against these relations by attempting to change them. The workers' General Assemblies put on trial and sacked the elements responsible for maintaining such relations: directors, foremen, SAVAK agents, etc.

In the Arj factory,

> after the revolution, the management began to implement the same patterns of exploitation and oppression. But our lads had become conscious enough not to tolerate such a burden. As a result the lads threw the gentlemen out with a sudden rush. They threw them out, locked the warehouses and stopped delivering the products (my interview).

In the Yamaha Motor Cycle company in Ghazvin the *shura* initially dismissed two production and administrative managers and later seven others. The workers did not stop here. A number of them, with the *shura* members, travelled to Teheran:

> They went to central office, taking the director and major shareholder from their desks and threw them out of the office. The workers stayed there for three days to protect the available documents from access by the employers of the office.

At the same time they asked the Revolutionary Council, Revolutionary Tribunal and Ministry of Industry to investigate the cases and to recognize the dismissal of the eleven managers.

In some factories, the workers used the intelligence of the Department of National Documents (DND) to identify those connected in any way to the previous regime. In the Tehran Auto Company, 'we formed a Committee of Inquiry including a *shura* member, despatching them to the DND, to investigate the list of all employees. There was one SAVAK agent' (my interview). The same kind of inquiry in the Iran Cars company resulted in the identification of eleven agents. These forms of struggle did not only arise because the subjects were authoritarian and oppressive elements of the *ancien régime*, but because from the workers' viewpoint, their very function and position were seen to be unacceptable. Emphasis upon their pro-Shah character was conceived to be the best way of getting rid of them.

On many occasions the government would reinstate those elements. And in turn, the workers would continue their efforts to throw them out. In the Akrosaz factory in Ahwas, the workers, through strike action, forced the City of Ahwas' tribunal to sack two managers (in production and administration) who were accused of having links with SAVAK and of corruption. The tribunal had previously discharged them. Workers' pressure led to a change in the verdict.

Lacking any organization and, above all, credibility, the industrialists could not do much against such practices. The Provisional Government had to act on their behalf. Towards the end of May the government introduced the law of Special Force. This was to prevent the strike committees and *shuras* from intervening 'in the affairs of the management and of the appointments' (Appendix of *Labour Law*). The government's concern rose when the workers did not only sack old managers but also new ones whom the Revolutionary State had appointed. On the other hand, over a year later the state reluctantly had to introduce its own organization of Purifying Bodies (*Heyat-i Paksazi*). The law was introduced by the second cabinet with a social background and view different from those of Bazargan, that is, the Islamic government of M.A. Rajaii, committed to Khomeini's project of setting up an Islamic society. The law declared its objective to be 'the purification of production units from the conspiracies of the agents of the West, the East and the overthrown Pahlavi regime' (ibid.). The real aims, however, were twofold: a) in the first place it wanted to prevent the self-initiated actions of the rank and file workers and radical *shuras*, which were far more serious about purges than the government; b) secondly, the government aimed to purge, alongside the SAVAK agents, the militant workers, 'those responsible for retarding the plans, for go-slows, and for sabotages in production' (ibid.).

Control over Conditions of Production

When we speak of control by employees over conditions of employment, we are reminded of the practices of strong unions in Britain which make sure that none but their members are employed. Probably the most

119

extreme example is the present closed-shop system where the unions'
strict employment regulations prevail. Where such conditions are lacking, there cannot logically be such forms of control. In the Iranian
experience such unionization has been absent. However, there have been
a great many demands and direct action to control the conditions of
employment. In the *shura* constitution of the Philips factory-workers in
Teheran, a special Committee of Inspection was set up for Administrative
Affairs, to preside over and investigate administration and personnel
affairs, including hiring and firing (Article 2B). The Financial and Administrative Committee of the Arj factory considered its objective to be
'to preside over the financial situation and conditions of employment of
the company' (the *shura* constitution, Article 2). Such control was desirable for two reasons. The *shuras* wanted the re-appointing by employers
or the state of dismissed employees. The *shuras* were also keen to avoid
the employment of people on the basis of personal connections (favouritism). The more important motivation, though, was political; the *shura*
was an expression of the 'sovereignty of people over their own destiny' in
the workplaces (*shura* constitution of Leyland Factory Workers). This
explains much direct control action that goes beyond the immediate
utilitarian concerns of the workers.

Control over conditions of dismissal (firing) is undoubtedly of more
significance to workers than control over hiring. It is a general principle of
a trade union 'that no one should have more work than he needs until all
have as much as they need' (Goodrich, 1975, p. 73). This is an attempt to
reduce unemployment. The basis of such attempts is a tradition of strong
trade unionism, which in the Iranian experience was out of the question.

The right to sack had a twofold relevance for Iranian factory-workers:
the right to sack, and the right to prevent being sacked. The immediate
reason for the practice of the first right had been the desire to dismiss the
remnants of the previous regime or foreign experts in the factories. In the
Eadem Motor Company, in March 1979, the factory *shura* decided,
according to its constitution, to sack eleven managers, following an
investigation of their cases. They were dismissed as anti-worker. Twenty-
four hours after the *shura*'s verdict, the *shura* learnt that the director had
refused to carry out the order. As a result the *shura* ordered the factory
security to arrest the two highest-ranked managers and take them into the
factory where they were forced to pay back a Rls 70,000 loan. They were
then thrown out. The *shura* later put the investigation of the case of the
director himself on the agenda (*Kar*, No. 7). There are many other
examples of such direct action.

The right to sack is the foundation of the power of a *shura*, not only
against the authoritarian elements of the previous regime, but against any
authoritarian elements who do not come to terms with the workers'
shuras. The constitution of the workers' *shura* of Behshar Car Company
clearly saw it as its right 'to preside over the employment and dismissal of
workers'. The *shura* leader said,

Well, that is the way in our factory. We have changed any manager who does things wrong and the [organization of] Nationalized Industries accepted this. We had a director there (called Mr Bashirbord), who wasn't interested in working in the manner of the *shura*; he'd want to work individually; wouldn't take the *shura* into account. Despite the fact that the *shura* wasn't yet legal, we stood firm and said, "We don't want him"; we changed him (my interview).

In a quite different way, the workers' *shura* of the Philips factory in the spring of 1981 put a few managers, including a director, on trial and sacked them.

A further implication of the right to sack is more vital for the workers: it prevents the victimization of militant workers, including the *shura* leaders themselves. The necessity of this demand was felt more substantially as the trend of management from above began to develop and provided the basis for a confrontation and threats of dismissal on both sides. Bazargan fully backed both the new state managements and the private owners against the workers. His support was expressed in various circulars designed to curb direct action; the formation of the Special Force in the factories; formation of the Purifying Bodies and circulars to the public sector, warning the employees against the activities of the *shuras* (*Kar*, No. 32). The Prosecutor General of the Islamic Revolution in Arāk warned all the workers in the city:

> Memorandum to all Directors of the Arāk Factories:
> I hereby order you to ensure that your employees and workers clearly understand that they may not under any circumstances engage in propaganda in the factories. Should you observe any such case, it should be reported immediately, so that these elements can be prosecuted as counter-revolutionaries (*Kar*, No. 16).

The militant workers in some factories were indeed sacked.

The workers' *shuras* had to resist and secure the right to sack for themselves. Thus, the *shura* of Eir Persenan factory declared (in March 1978) that 'the employer has no right to sack any worker' (*Farhang-i Novin*, No. 4). The Nevasa Company workers and the *shura* went on strike, taking the employer hostage. They succeeded in getting their sacked fellow workers back to work (*Farhang-i Novin*, p. 7). When I visited Metal Works plant in Teheran, the managers had been on strike for 25 days. The reason was that the *shura* had opposed the firing of a worker by management, insisting on the case being closely investigated.

Securing the right to sack for the *shuras* would also be indispensable to secure the jobs of fellow workers in the event of lock-outs. The Chimco plant in Teheran, through its *shura*, refused to agree to a few workers being laid off; and in Arāk in March, workers and the *shura* of the Pars Car Plant stopped work, declaring 'the employer has no right to hire or fire anyone without consulting the *shuras*' (ibid., pp. 8–9). It is worth noting that all this was happening at a time when, according to Labour Law and Employment contracts, the employer still had the sole right to sack any worker without any explanation.

Control Over Financial Affairs

Although financial information is generally regarded as the sole concern of management, nonetheless, on some occasions demands for the control of these areas are advanced. Generally, such demands are the result of immediate concerns, as when an employer cuts wages on the grounds that the factory is making a loss, or when an employer intends to lock up the factory and put the workers on the dole. In such situations the workers may fight to have the financial books opened and they will be convinced of the correctness of management's decisions if they find the claims justified. The same demands can also be made in a rather different spirit, as part of a demand for workers' control. In the case of Iranian factory *shuras*, both aspects are of significance.

The example of the Fama Beton cement works in Teheran illustrates the first kind of case. Before the insurrection the employer began laying workers off; some 165 of them were dismissed and eventually the factory was entirely locked up two months before the insurrection. After the Revolution all the workers started a campaign for the re-opening of the factory and the payment of delayed wages. The demands were dismissed by the management. After forming a *shura*, the workers staged a campaign, putting forward new demands, forcing the employer to accept the following conditions.

> Return to work with the payment of delayed wages and benefits; forty-hour week; monitoring properly the decisions of the Board of Directors, contracts, new recruitments, the determination of wages and salaries; and an inquiry into the financial situation of the company (*Kar*, No. 13).

In the Iran Cars state-run plant, I was told that in March 1981 the *shura* was fighting against the management over the issue of profit-sharing benefit (Special Benefit), opposing the government's new scheme. When nothing satisfactory was gained by means of negotiations, the *shura*, through its access to the financial department, withdrew the required amount of cash to pay the workers.

The ideological dimension is more profound: it may be the product of either a preconceived ideological tendency, or the metamorphosis of an immediate defensive demand. Article 2 of the *shura* constitution of the Amazon factory workers is devoted to 'monitoring the financial and employment affairs of the company' which was to be conducted by the Finance and Administrative Committees of the *shura*. The same point was stipulated in the Constitutions of the *shuras* of Fanoos, Metal Works and Behshar Car Company. The real concern here was not necessarily immediate. In fact I put this to a *shura* member, asking what interests the *shura* and workers had in such practices. His answer was as follows.

Look, the reason why the Revolution was made at all, was because we wanted to become our own masters; to determine our own destiny . . . We did not want the situation where one or a few make decisions for two thousand. When we, 2,500 workers, are working around these walls, we want to know what is going on here; what we'll achieve in future, in what direction we are running the company, how much profit we get, how much we could take for ourselves, how much we could contribute to government for national investment. For this reason, we never let management employ somebody to make decisions. This would be a repetition of the same previous mistakes to the extent that it would violate the rights of the workers, which are in fact the rights of the Iranian nation (my interview).

This statement is made on egalitarian ideological grounds. This egalitarianism prevented the misuse of power, corruption and favouritism in the units. A *shura* leader in the Metal Works in Teheran here describes their activities:

During the second *shura*, of which I was a member in the Central Office, they [the management] had issued a cheque to withdraw a sum of six million, one hundred thousand toumans (about $762,500) from the company's account. We discovered that and stopped it. The cheque had been issued in the names of various branch representatives of the company. He [the employer] claimed he wanted to pay off a debt. Later we found out that only a very small part was debt in fact; the rest was to go to [the employer's] brothers (interview).

The *shura* constitution of the Philips factory workers regards the rights and tasks of the Committee for monitoring Finance, Administration and Management to be a) 'to list the entire property of the factory at the end of each year', and b) 'to prevent corruption; to cut superfluous costs, and to reduce high level salaries' [managers]. On the basis of these rights, the *shura*, in the winter of 1980 in the period of management from above, ordered the managers off the plant. It came across a case of scandal in the sales department. It then set up a committee of inquiry which after an investigation obtained sufficient evidence to hold a 'proletarian tribunal' in a factory mass meeting. The case was put forward and the accused persons (two officials of the Finance Office) were allowed to defend themselves. The verdict was announced by the mass of the workers: guilty. They were sacked. Within three weeks or so, the same procedures and processes were carried out to put the top director on trial: guilty. He also was sacked by the *shura*. In the second tribunal an official of the Ministry of Labour was present (my interview).

This egalitarianism leads to a variety of practices which necessitate control over finances. In the Caterpillar plant in Teheran, within the five months of the Revolution, the *shura* exerted control over finance, transferring all the cash from the employer's personal account into the factory account in order to pay off the wages when the employer had fled the country. The *shura* then gained the right of authority in financial matters, presiding over the 'monthly report prepared by the Financial Office about costs and incomes of the company, and direct control over the costs'. The *shura* authorized the cutting down of salaries and the increasing of low wages; it eliminated some existing privileges by issuing cards to check absenteeism at all ranks (including technical managers); it equalized the allocation of car parking spaces (formerly monopolized by particular managers), stopped highly ranked employees from misusing factory property and set up a single dining-hall for all employees. The *shura* also prevented all employees from taking a second job outside the company (Ghotbi, 1980, pp. 243–8). Such policies were common in all *shuras*. In the Melli Shoe Plant in Teheran 'previously the Special Profit used to be allocated on the basis of the level of wages . . . But this year we [*shura*] put a maximum limit of 12,000 toumans.' 'The amount of Special Profit paid to the workers and (white-collar) employees has been almost equal' (ibid., p. 25).

Management of Production and Distribution
'Here is the office of the boss, just here where you are sitting. Previously the boss was here; now *we* are here.' This is a remark of a *shura* leader in Caterpillar plant (ibid, p. 22). It shows a radical difference between the actual practice of control by the *shuras* and the formal degree and extent of workers' control in the advanced capitalist countries (practices such as control over special managerial functions such as discipline, allocation of tasks, safety control, the measurement of results (in piecework payments) or consultation over changes in techniques, insistence on improvements, joint actions in policy-making and worker-directors). Undoubtedly such strategies are gradual moves by the working class to gain control. Whether or not they can be successful and are compatible with the particular interests of the working class or merely serve capitalist control is another matter (see Chapter 10).

Let us now look at actual instances of control by the *shuras*. We have already discussed how the nature of struggle may transcend immediate demands. In this respect, the example of the Eirfo foundry works in Teheran is remarkable. The workers put forward demands for the payment of delayed wages, Special Profits and supply of raw materials; the dissolution of the conciliationist *shura* and the appointment of a manager independent of the shareholders. A long struggle proceeded in which Prime Minister Bazargan and the Revolutionary Council (the leadership of the country) were also involved, and in which workers took three managers hostage and imprisoned them, being confronted with the *Pasdaran*. Eventually they gained control and the following proposals were agreed by a leading director/shareholder: 1) the expulsion of a manager appointed by the owners; 2) Mr Gholizadeh [the leading director/shareholder] to report to the factory for one half-day a week and co-operate with the *shura*; and 3) the *shura*'s monitoring function over the factory to be supreme in the responsible management of the plant. Any company document without the signature of the *shura* would be invalid (*Kar*, No. 49).

In another example, in May 1979, the Mitusac Company workers were faced with redundancy. In response, they staged 'a 25-day sit-in and a 4-day hunger strike. Result? . . . Nothing!' 'There remained only one way out', they wrote in their leaflet, 'to take over the workshop, running it by our power' (*Kar*, No. 9).

A proportionately high number of brick-making workshops resorted to such forms of direct action and usually took over the factory. In Amol in the northern Caspian Sea area, the workers in a number of plants took control of the production and sale of products. A battle followed when, despite the warnings of the *shura*, the employers rejected some of their immediate demands. The *shuras* immediately formed special committees concerned with the order of the plant, inspection, sales and dispute settlements, etc. They started selling the products at a lower price (*Kar*, No. 6). In similar plants in the town of Gonbad in the north, the workers, after taking control of production, abolished the system of piece-rate with results and substituted a fixed daily wage (*Kar*, No. 12).

Some workers wanted control for the sake of control. This notion is expressed in the words of a Melli Shoe Plant worker.

> Nowadays [generally] you don't need to tell a worker to go and work. He works himself; why? The reason why he didn't work [under the Shah] was because he was under the boss's thumb. He couldn't speak out. Now, he'll say: "the work is my own. I'll work." But now [specifically] when you don't know where the products go, how much the prices are; for how much it is being sold; in whose pocket the profit goes, etc., well, he'll become demoralized. Now, it is the *shura* that must control all of them. It should know how much the company produces; how much is the price and the cost of production; how much the profit is; and where it goes. The *shura* must know all these, and let the workers know. Then, the workers wouldn't protest (Ghotbi, 1980, pp. 32–3).

This *shura* at its very inception expelled the existing boards of directors, most of whom were experts in various skills. It then succeeded in taking control of the plant and running it until state managers were appointed. 'Some people thought, if these managers and experts left here, the factory would be paralysed,' stated a *shura* leader. 'We even guaranteed and did succeed in running the firm' (ibid, p. 28).

Similarly, for a period of five months preceding the arrival of the state-appointed managers, the *shura* of the Caterpillar plant controlled 'all economic, social and political aspects of this company'. It controlled conditions of employment, finance, the purchasing of raw materials, sales and the co-ordination of work. The *shura* also dispatched a team of employees to Geneva to purchase raw materials. Meanwhile it established a committee of dispute settlement, sending the committee to various branches of industry at the same time, to encourage the spirit of *shuraism* among the workers (ibid., p. 28). In short, 'the *shura* made decisions on all aspects of the company until it became nationalized by the government. But, since its nationalization we have only had a consultative role with the state representatives' (ibid., p. 81).

The Fanoos Factory *shura* was initiated and encouraged by the management: it was a reformist strategy of a multinational company to contain the radical actions of the workers. But it did not work. When the workers were allowed to organize the factory committee, the extent of their expectations and actual practices went beyond the limits desired by the management. According to the workers' constitution, the fundamental right of *shura* is considered to be the overseeing of production, distribution and pricing. It reads, 'The task of this Committee is composed of complete oversight of the process of production, from the supply of raw material to its transformation into the saleable product.' In detail the rights and responsibilities of the *shura* were:

a) to raise the level of output in the interests of the public, including the employees of the factory;

b) to develop and organize the factory to cut dependency ties, in such a way as not to damage production or the supply of raw materials;

c) a just pricing of products in accordance with the internal market and income of the employees;

d) a just distribution of the products throughout the country, aiming to reduce the influence of intermediary dealers;

e) supervision of the sale of the waste products.

We have already mentioned the extent of control that this *shura* had over finance, administration and management in the plant. Another area of control which was of direct political significance was the task of the Committee of *Hefāzāt* and *Entezāmāt* (security), formerly conducted by SAVAK agents and the Army officials. Article 7 pointed to the *shura*'s authority over a) safety, hygiene and conditions of work; b) disciplinary measures in the workplace, inspection of absenteeism and guarding; c) dispute settlement; d) formation of security cadres, composed of the employees, against counter-revolutionary sabotages; e) military training; and most imortant, f) 'the purge of corrupt, anti-popular and idle elements, in any position'. In this connection, the constitution stated that

> following the presentation of evidence, the verdict will be binding with three-quarters of the votes of all employees or two-thirds of the votes of the Mass Meeting. The convicted elements will have the right to be present to defend themselves at the Mass Meeting.

There was a third group of *shuras* which did exert a considerable degree of control over production, distribution and employment. Yet the ideology of the *shura* protagonists was based neither on the class interests of their rank-and-file workers (because they did not view control as a means to meet immediate demands) nor primarily upon the class ideology of possession. They rather reflected the anti-capitalist ideology of the ruling clergy, and manifested a particular form of corporatism under the Islamic state. Such corporatism was almost totally absent in the private industries. The number of these *shuras* rose in the second period of management from above. A typical example were the *shuras* of the Behshar Car plant and Amazon factory. The Behshar Car factory *shura* was a form of co-determination. Two of the *shura* members were appointed to the Board of Directors. The *shura*, through its various sub-committees (of production, sales, administration and finance) actively participated in the organization of the plant. Rights and tasks were specified in a *shura* constitution. Here is the statement of a *shura* leader.

> The *shura* must be informed of the amount of raw material required, of the source of supply and the way it is purchased, so that the employer cannot paralyse the workplace by threatening a lock-out; and so that if he did, the *shura* itself would intervene directly. The *shura* should also obtain for themselves sufficient information about, or have advisers on, sales and marketing. The main issue here is that the worker is not to be separated from the product of his labour. He himself should have control over production, purchase and the sale of the product (my interview).

On the other hand, there seemed to be co-operation between the *shura* policies and those of the state-appointed managers. 'Fortunately, the director himself believes,' stated the *shura* leader, 'that all the affairs of the plant should be carried out with the consultation of the *shura*.' By way of reciprocation, the *shura* also made vital concessions:

> We are the followers of this government [pro-Khomeini Prime Minister Rajaii] which *is* revolutionary and believes in Islamic Revolution. We must obey the orders of the government, even if they are against us. We must appreciate the position of the government. We now have a war in our country with such high costs. I think it is wrong to press for benefits and such-like every minute.

Typology of the *Shuras*

When we speak of the workers' control movement, we tend to infer that it is homogeneous. Reality, however, is rather different. But it is crucial to make distinctions between organizations and to identify those motives which contribute to the class struggle.

The Iranian *shura* movement was no exception. Workplace organizations took a variety of forms. To portray the heterogeneity of the *shuras*, we have compiled a table of twelve factory *shuras*. The two extreme sides are opposite ends of the spectrum. We may identify one as the most successful and the other as the least successful; the area between them includes committees with varying degrees of control and contradictory tendencies.

127

Table 7.5
The Transformation of the Character of Factory Committees in the Three Periods

Products of the plants	Shuras	Form of ownership and management	Labour process	Market for products	Rank-and-file militancy	Nature of shura/degree of control			Relationship with 1A in 1st and 2nd periods	Political situation in factory
						1st period	2nd period	3rd period		
Shoes	Melli Shoe	Private + unknown + state control	Craft works and automation**	?	?	Militant, instrumental/ universal, full control	Independent, consultative; tense	?	?	Democratic (1st period)
Repair company	Caterpillar	Private + unknown + state control	Craft-based	Very good monopoly	High	"	"	Abolished	None	"
Radio & television	Fanoos	Jt. venture + unknown + state control	Assembly & craft work	"	Average	Independent, consultative	Independent, high degree of control; tense	Abolished, arrested	Not good	Very good 1 and 2
Foundry works	Metal Works	Private	Craft-based	Good	High	Militant, interventionist, ideological	Militant, interventionist	?	Not good	Quite good in 1st & 2nd periods; Tense
Car	Iran Cars	Private, joint + unknown +	Assembly and craft work	"	High	Militant, independent,	Militant, independent,	Abolished, arrested,	Not good	Good in 1st and 2nd periods

Domestic appliances	P.R. Plant	Private	Assembly and craft work	Very good	Divided – high militancy in some sections	Militant, interventionist	Trade unionist role	Trade unionist role	?	?
Car	Teheran Auto	Multinational + joint venture + unknown + state control	Assembly and craft work	Good	Ideological*	**	Interventionist/ corporatist	?	Good	Repressive
Car	Behshar	"	"	Good	Divided, low	Full control, Islamic ideology, corporatist	High control, corporatist	?	Very good	Repressive
Domestic appliances	Amazon	Private + unknown + state control	"	Good	Divided	Full control, instrumental/ ideological	"	?	Good	Repressive
Metal works	Teheran Steel	Private	Automation and craft-dominated	Very good	Low	Interventionist	Resigned	?	No 1A	Relaxed
Refrigerators	Alvand	Private	Assembly dominated and craft work	Good	Low	Trade unionist role	Limited trade unionist role	Limited trade unionist role	Good	Relaxed
Transformers	I.T.N.	State control & foreign capital	Craft work dominated	Good	Divided, with militant minority	Interventionist, ideological	Consultative	Consultative, low degree	No 1A	Tense

*Divided with a very militant minority.
**Full control, ideological, corporatist.

The most successful *shura* may be typified by the variables: full control, militant/independent and universal view. These successful *shuras* were those which exerted full control over and ran the workplace without (any effective control on the part of) the officially-appointed management. Their policies and activities were independent of the state and the official managers and were based upon the interests of the rank-and-file workers. The ideological motives for *shura* formation stemmed primarily not only from immediate working-class interests but from the ideology of possession (universal view). The Fanoos factory committee was an example of this type of *shura*.

In contrast, the least successful committees reflected the characteristics of the syndicate. From a defensive position, they in many respects co-operated with the owners/managers. The low level of rank-and-file militancy made the *shura* unable to take an offensive stand. The political conditions of such workplaces, therefore, were less tense. The Alvand factory *shura* seemed to be a typical instance of such *shuras*.

The militant interventionist tendency was found in popular *shuras* which were involved in a high level of class struggle (Metal Works and Iran Cars *shuras*). Despite the domination of state-managers, the *shuras* which relied on class interests and universal ideology were never subjected to the authority of management. At times they would encroach on the sphere of managerial prerogatives by taking out money and paying workers. Militant interventionism, though, unlike the control *shuras* did not exert a high degree of control. It rather reflected an ongoing struggle.

A less militant form was the consultative *shura*, such as the *shuras* of Bloom Helm and Melli Shoe in the second period. Here, the management saw the consultative function of these *shuras* as a channel to incorporate them, while the spirit of rank-and-file militancy still prevailed. On the other hand, these *shuras* rationally utilized their consultative role in the interests of their fellow workers. Such a form of *shura* management could not last long.

Lastly, corporatist *shuras* were another type. They would be composed of workers and *maktabi* (Islamic) management, working for the prosperity of the Islamic nation under the leadership of the clergy. In practice, these *shuras* exerted effective control over various aspects of management. They would not hesitate to launch a hard struggle to dismiss liberal, professional and non-conformist managers whose strategy negated the ideal of their work organization. Giving a contradictory impression, in the short run, to the workers, they played a significant part in the politics of industrial relations under the post-revolutionary state. Meanwhile the constitutions of these committees ensured that not a single non-Islamic and independent candidate could be accepted to *shura* membership.

We now turn to examine the major determinant factors which influence the success or failure of a *shura*. A successful committee was not an automatic outcome of pertinent objective conditions; the consciousness and ideological orientation of the *shura* members, expressing the consciousness of the total workforce, was equally crucial (Fanoos factory). It was also significant whether the ownership of the plant was state or private. Under state ownership, *shura* formation was less laborious in three respects: first, in that the ruling clergy put out remarkable anti-imperialist and anti-oppression rhetoric. This kind of rhetoric always has a double edge. While it might create the illusion of an anti-imperialist state, at the same time it mobilizes the workers, conferring upon them the power of manoeuvre, and hence a societal legitimacy to go onto the offensive. Workers utilized conflicts between the policies of the liberals and the clergy-dominated managers. And unlike the private sector, the state could financially, at least in the short run, tolerate the effects of workers' encroachments on the distribution of surplus.

The success of the *shura* further depended on the position of the enterprise in the market: in Iran, many of the worker-controlled industries were or later became state-owned and many of them enjoyed a semi-monopoly position. The character of the labour process and whether the workers were craft workers with a relatively high degree of skill or working within a division of labour with less room for manoeuvre was also crucial. Of the two successful *shuras*, the Caterpillar works may be said to represent craft-oriented work and Fanoos the latter kind. In the Philips case, the disadvantage of the detailed division of labour had been compensated for by co-operation between the intellectual labourers and the manual workers. Solidarity was a further important determinant for a successful workers' control movement.[7] In this sense, solidarity acted to 'subjectively' overcome the division of labour.

The Ideologies of the Shuras

Two main theories provided a rationale for the actions of workers of the *shuras*: firstly, the Marxism of left-wing organizations, which undoubtedly dominated debate, and secondly a considerable number of independent, militant and interventionist *shuras* adhered to the Mudjahedin Organization. The latter's conception of *shura*, as well as many of its political ideas, are influenced by the left conceptual framework, but are presented in the Islamic idioms and terminology.

The Marxian theoretical background of the workers' control movement has been widely discussed. At this point, we shall deal with the ideology of the corporatist *shuras*.

Corporatism of the Islamic Shuras

In the second and third periods of the labour movement, these *shuras* spread to the majority of industrial workplaces. Having termed them as *shura-i sazesh* (conciliationist) or yellow *shuras*, left-wing forces have identified them with the management, holding that 'their only role is to raise productivity, police the factory, serve capital and the capitalist state.' But there was a serious contradiction in the attitude of these *shuras* towards capital and labour.

Islamic Corporatism: Corporatism is generally a capitalist strategy which, unlike individual liberal capitalism, seeks to transcend class conflict by integrating the state, capital and labour by reliance upon economic motives or ideological appeal (such as nationalism). The strategy is adopted when capital is unable to prevent labour from organizing and is a classical pattern of control when market control is not possible. Corporatism may take different shapes. In democratic corporatism, state, capital and labour organizations are autonomous; this form is characteristic of a prosperous period or country (such as Sweden). Fascist corporatism, however, is non-plural and hierarchical; the relationship of state and capital is antagonistic. Corporatism may also represent a feature of a labour organization pursuing a policy of co-operation with state and capital. The peculiarity of the Islamic *shuras* was not their co-operation with state and capital, but their opposition to capitalist management – because as *shuras* they wanted to take control of management, and their alliance with the state led them to pursue a mystical and egalitarian Islamic doctrine.

The Islamic corporatist *shuras* were characterized by militancy in opposition to one-man management systems and to professional liberal managers. The *shuras* in such plants as Behshar Car Plant, Amazon, Gher Gehr-i Ziba and Darougar sacked the state-appointed managers after a bitter struggle. These were managers who had not co-operated with the *shuras*. There was a strong belief that the *shuras* had the right to supervise, exert control over management and the spheres of production, administration, hiring and firing, finance and discipline.

Kamali, a workers' representative in *Majlis* (Iranian parliament), a pro-IRP element, publicly announced, 'I believe that the *shuras* must be given the right to interfere in workplace affairs. But, we do not believe that any *shura* is a genuine one. Because we believe that a *shura* member before everything must be a true Muslim; otherwise it is not acceptable' (*Jelve-i Hagh Tāala*, No. 3).

Islamic *shuras* were religious, strongly anti-democratic and anti-communist. The Amazon factory *shura* leader stated:

> Just imagine that a member of the *Paykar* or *Mudjahedin* had advancement [becoming a *shura* member]: undoubtedly he wouldn't want the wheels of the country to turn, he'd always want to cause damage, to incite the workers to strike.
> — What if he were elected by the workers?
> — We'd continue to oppose him, even though he was elected . . . If two thousand workers elect a Paykari or Mudjahed, that is because 99% of them are ignorant. In fact they get elected because of their hypocrisy. They present themselves as Muslims and get votes. When they come up [as the *shura* members] they would be opposed by me, by the management or by the state, who would all see what they are up to.

On the other hand, the internal regulations of the Amazon *shura* stipulated that:

> should the aim and intention of a *shura* member be contrary to the interests of the Islamic Republic or violate laws, and disrupt the order of the company, it will be the Islamic and canonical duty of the other members to report him to the employees through the mass meetings.

There was a commitment to 'true' Islam and the *Imam*'s line, i.e. that fraction of the clergy in the state which followed the Khomeini doctrine of Islam and organized in the IRP.

This form of corporatism represents an aspiration towards a fraternal, egalitarian society without oppression and decadence, to be brought about by Islamic principles as an alternative to both capitalism and socialism.

> The revolution that we made was an Islamic Revolution. We didn't make a communist revolution. Therefore [the *shura* members] must act within the Islamic framework and ideology. The objective must be to implement an Islamic economy, which is neither a capitalist economy nor a socialist. It is an economy based on itself . . . and, that means "for each according to his labour". In a communist country people must work for the state. And in capitalist countries there is [a minority of] people in whose hands capital circulates. And in the communist system capital belongs to the state which exploits people and pays them something. But Islam says: "No! the worker who works should get the fruits of his labour" (the *shura* leader of the I.T.N. Company).

This corporatism shows an illusion of a mystical Islamic community in which class conflicts are concealed by the brotherhood of all *ommah* (Mass) and in which the Imam at the head of the state is the guardian of the community and the ultimate arbiter.

This ideological form stems from the ideology of 'possession' described earlier, and the unique contradictory nature of the Islamic state in Iran.

The Islamic State: The Islamic state is characterized by a dialectic between Khomeini's view of Islamic society and the objective reality of the Iranian society as a backward capitalist social formation. In theory, the project of the *valayat-i faghih* represents a view of a homogeneous, egalitarian, puritan and tribal form of community from the era of Muhammed — a vision of a society in which the main division is between the subordinate community and the dominant leader, or *imam*. As the arbiter and mediator between God and the community, he guides the community by the sacred rules of God of which he alone has a special knowledge.[8] This form of society, which may be an illusory ideal held by the most backward section of the traditional petty-bourgeoisie, is threatened by both bourgeois rule and by socialism.

A ruler's subjective perception of the state and government is one thing; the objective possibility for realizing this perception is another. The seizure of power by the ruling clergy was a reflection of a power vacuum in the post-revolutionary state. Neither the proletariat nor the bourgeoisie were able to exert their political hegemony. The reason for their inability must be sought in their historical development which is a testimony of the weakness of both.

The anti-capitalist and anti-Western rhetoric of the ruling clergy must be seen in the context of this contradictory state form. The initial impact of this rhetoric on the masses (and the traditional left) was undeniable. Such views of Khomeini represented him as anti-imperialist and pro-downtrodden:

> The deprived and oppressed [masses] should rise,
> They should not wait for the oppressors to save them (*Kayhan*, 19 June 1983).

> The basis of domination over countries, including our country, is those rich with big capital, who possess power to preserve themselves and their status.

> These dispossessed *(Pā berehneh ha)* are our masters. If they had not fought, we would have been either in jail or in isolation. It was those people who saved us, putting us in these positions (*Kar*, No. 149).

The anti-capitalist and anti-oppression slogans of Khomeini had practical/political implications. The pages of *Kar, Jelve-i Hagh Ta ālā* (Work, the Appearance of God) and *Salehan-i Sazandeh*, the magazine and the weekly paper of the *Khane-i Kargar*, carried reports of how Islamic *shuras*, or Islamic Associations fought the non-*maktabi* and non-conformist managements and slogans like 'The shining villas of the capitalists are the result of the exploitation of the oppressed (*peeneh dastan*)'.

Such slogans built up the corporatist ideologies of the Islamic *shuras*. They conceived the state not only as one which directed society to an egalitarian objective, but as a supporter of militant actions against managements. (No corporatist *shura* could be found in the private plants. The private appropriation of profit leaves no room for the corporatist ideology.)

In search of an Islamic tradition of the concept of *shura*, the Islamic activists and ideologues resorted to the *Quran*. This was an attempt to defeat the monopoly of the concept of *shura* (council) by the Marxists. Two major *ayāts* (extracts) were presented as the Quranic origin of the concept; they advocate, at a high level of generality, consultation in the performance of any work.[9]

The third period witnessed bitter conflicts between the Islamic *shuras* and both the liberal and *maktabi* managements. Ideological considerations apart, the corporatist *shuras* had by then gained a new social status. The dismissal of the corporatist *shura* members by the managements reached a point where the Ministry of Labour issued a Resolution against Article 33 of the Labour Law, excluding the Islamic *shura* members from arbitrary dismissals — 'preventing the conspiracies against the Muslim worker brothers by a few liberal managers and employers who disrupt the formation of Islamic *shuras*' (*Kayhan*, 10 August 1981). Following the announcement of the Resolution, the top authorities issued a series of instructions, warning the Islamic *shuras* and IAs not to overreach themselves (see Chapter 10).

The corporatist Islamic *shuras* resembled the fascist syndicates of Germany in their exclusiveness (anti-democratism), anti-communism, and anti-capitalism. But there were significant differences. The anti-capitalist and the radical slogans of 'towards factories' or 'workers' control under national ownership' chanted by the left fascism of the Strasser brothers were attributes of Fascism in rising, not in power. Fascism in power smashed even that kind of labour organization. In Iran, on the other hand, contradiction and chaos still remain. The ambiguous position of the Islamic state towards the limits of private property and the imperatives of the Islamic political system operate as a fundamental impediment to a peaceful compromise with the bourgeoisie. While the anti-capitalism of Fascism as a movement was a typical sign of the petty-bourgeoisie in revolt, the resentment of the ruling clergy was an apprehensive reaction of a puritan community against the invasion of alien forces.

Shuras and Democracy

One of the central themes of debate on the workers' council movement is the relationship between workers' councils and democracy. The notion of workers' democracy has been the focal point of both revolutionary and reformist strategies. On the left communism, the councilists have virtually identified socialism with the hegemony of workers' councils as grassroots organs of power from below (Bricianer, 1978), and for Gramsci the workers' councils were both the vehicle of the revolution, and the embodiment of socialist democracy (Clark, 1977).

The reformists seek industrial democracy under capitalist domination; this is practised in various forms of 'workers' control' policies in the advanced capitalist societies. The emphasis here is on the interconnection between the workers' council and democracy in the experience of the Iranian workers. Did the formation of the *shuras* in fact imply a strong desire for democracy?

For workers who had been under the scrutiny of the secret police for over two decades, freedom of expression, assembly and organization would have been extremely important. Speaking in the first period, a Caterpillar worker said: 'The greatest grace that the revolution has granted to us is freedom . . . Nowadays, a man can speak out and protest; he can criticize; he can read books, can breathe . . .' (Ghotbi, 1979, pp. 96–7). The indispensable role of freedom in unleashing the workers' power of creativity may not be appreciated by a Western reader who enjoys the fruits of liberal democracy. For a Third World working-class intellectual it is quite different.

While in their day-to-day debates and writings Iranian Marxists attribute special strength and ability to an abstract proletariat which it is assumed will take control of state power in the future, they are surprised when I describe aspects of my observations on workers' radicalism. Even for them, the working class has, in real terms, been identified with pauperism, misery, subordination and backwardness. This shows the extent to which repression has prevented the working class and its allies from appreciating its potential and actual radicalism.

In the backward capitalist countries democracy, albeit in its limited bourgeois sense, is indispensable for the working class to develop its potentiality in all political, social and cultural domains. Paradoxically, however, it is the working class itself that through its own organization can achieve democratic forms not only for its own benefit, but for the whole of society. The working class can assume this role for various reasons. In Third World countries, the working classes tend to grow comparatively faster than others. They have viable objective grounds for organization; and desire for freedom provides a bond for an immense majority of the population — peasants, déclassé masses and middle classes.

In advanced capitalist countries the state, generally identified with the bourgeois class, is able to provide values, norms and policies which are perceived by the nation as embodying universal values and interests: liberal democratic institutions and ideologies are the clearest examples. In Third World countries the bourgeois class is generally weak and is less able to fulfil this hegemonic role. This tendency generates a vacuum that either enables the working classes, in alliance with other masses, to play a major part in the total politics of these countries or, as in Latin America, provides the ground for the supra-class elites to take on state power, be they generals, emperors or Ayatollahs.

In Iran it was the working classes in general, not the liberal bourgeoisie, that brought about the universal conception of *shuraism*. The idea of *shuraism* transcended the domain of industry, permeating offices, schools, universities, farms and the army.

Throughout the first period, the Universities were run democratically by *shuras* composed of the elected representatives of students, teaching staff and administrative employees. In the rural areas where land had been taken over, the villages were administered by the village councils. In the armed forces, the Air Force technicians waged a sustained struggle to set up *shuras* and to have the right to elect and recall their officers. The bourgeoisie could never have invented the concept of a *shura*.

The workers' *shuras* were, however, limited to the workplaces. They were not extended to the whole community. They acted both as the organs of democracy (in terms of work organization and political considerations) and as instruments of repression — at the workplaces where the corporatist committees were dominant.[10]

The Political and Ideological Tendencies of the *Shuras*
Herein lies the basic politico-ideological distinction between the Islamic corporatist and the left-wing *shuras* (including those of pro-Mudjahedin). Factories were the first victims of the new state repression. Nonetheless, some progressive *shuras* worked hard to maintain a democratic atmosphere. From the first period, their policy was to maintain a coalition structure composed of anyone who was democratically elected by the rank and file. A left-winger in the Caterpillar plant *shura* argued for a coalition in the following way:

> The main issue that we discuss here is that of economic problems of the employees. Everybody, with any ideology [left or religious] holds the view that capitalism must be dismantled in our society. We all agree on this, that there shouldn't be capitalism in this country; and that classes in the forms of exploited and exploiter must be abolished. *We* are talking about a classless society; the Islamic ideology talks about *Tauhidi* [divine] society. When we compare the two, there is no difference . . . since there are various ideologies and religions, we have decided to abandon any [sectarian] political discussion here (Ghotbi, 1979, p. 125).

The religious member of the Factory Committee, however, provided a more realistic and immediate argument.

> The sole reason . . . is the election itself. We haven't elected each other. They (the employees) have *elected* us, getting us to get together. They have *elected* any views and any group they liked . . . We won't let anyone's views or ideologies, however respectable for their holder, affect our works and activities here (ibid., p. 127).

This was the main argument any left-wing worker could launch against the mounting waves of manipulation and exclusivism in the legal procedures to divest the *shura* elections of their substance.

Fanoos factory was probably one of the few plants which, in the second period, still enjoyed a high degree of democracy. That was because its left-wing *shura* exerted power over the management and Islamic Association (IA) as well as over other informal organizations. All leaflets, journals or any management announcements had to be confirmed and stamped by the *shura*. As a matter of fact, it was enough to curb the repressive activities of the IAs and the management, and workers' political-cultural activities would flourish. My own experience of conducting research provides a criterion for assessing democracy at the workplaces. As Table 7.5 indicates, there were only a few plants which were still resisting repression. In the factories with a democratic *shura* I was allowed to go anywhere, to talk to anyone (Fanoos, Metal Works, Bloom Helm). In the rest, I was under pressure to interview the fewest possible and preferably particular workers. Some corporatist *shura* members prohibited me from entering the workshops. Because I 'might cause trouble'. These *shuras* were all Islamic.

The corporatist *shuras* were ideologically repressive for they believed the *shuras* should comprise merely Muslim workers, the firm supporters of the Islamic Republic. The sympathizers of Mudjahedin, which is an Islamic organization, were also prohibited from standing for the election since they were seen as left-wing. The argument that the corporatist *shuras* (e.g. in Behshar Car Plant, Amazon, Teheran Auto) put forward is summed up in the following remarks.

> In an Islamic *shura*, all of the elected members must act according to Islamic principles: believers, supporters of the Islamic Republic etc. If a communist or one from these groups [left] is elected, he naturally would want to enforce his views or those of his organization. And this causes disruption . . . If they infiltrated into the *shuras*, they'd naturally oppose the Islamic Republic, and obviously would cause chaos . . . Our revolution is an *Islamic* Revolution. We haven't made a communist revolution. So the *shura* members must hold Islamic views (I.T.N. *shura* leader).

On this view, it is sufficient to condemn everyone who does not agree with the *shura* as anti-Islamic or communist. Radical Muslim workers, any worker who criticized the *shura*, the management or the government could be equally at fault (ibid., p. 127). While the corporatist *shuras* were naturally the major opponents of strike action, the left-democratic *shuras* advocated the right to strike even though it was illegal.

The Structure of the *Shuras*
The *shuras* in their essential forms do guarantee a certain degree of democracy in the workplace even when functioning under undemocratic rules of election. Theoretically *shuras* were the direct representatives of the whole workforce and would exercise power through the organ of the General Assembly (*Majma Omoumi*), and through recalling the Executive Committee of the *shura* at any time. Though the constitutions of the Iranian *shuras* varied in many respects, almost all of them conferred ultimate power on the General Assemblies. The latter had the duty a) to ratify the constitution prepared by the workers; b) to elect the *shura* members; c) to examine the report prepared by the EC: and d) to ratify the formation of the Union of the *Shuras* (US), and to consider whether or not to join the US.

In many factories, in practice, major unexpected and/or unspecified issues were brought to the General Assemblies. In no constitution was anything said about strike action, for officially it was strictly forbidden. But in practice, strike or other forms of industrial action did take place during the first and second periods, and most of them were debated and decided in the General Assemblies.

The Committees possessed the power of both decision-making and implementation of their decisions. In this spirit they would distribute their executive power among various sub-committees, depending on the extent of workers' control. The EC of the Fanoos factory *shura*, for example, set up seven sub-committees, each with particular rights and responsibilities specified in the constitution: a committee to oversee supply, production, distribution and pricing; a committee for finance and administration, for welfare, for cultural activities, for communications, for technical affairs and security and order. More or less the same sorts of committees operated in other factories, such as Behshar Car Plant, Amazon, Teheran Auto and Saypa. All of these committees were accountable to the ECs of the *shura* which itself was accountable to the General Assemblies.

That, however, is by no means the whole matter. Not all the *shuras*, in any period, acted in accordance with the interests and in response to the actual demands of the rank and file. And that explains why in most of the factories frequent *shura* elections were held. *Shura* elections were strongly influenced by political considerations and the factories were the most sensitive sector of society. The state, directly or through formal and informal mediations, would do anything to dismantle the *shuras* which were thought to be infiltrated by militant workers. As an angry worker in the Metal Works explained,

> the capitalists don't allow our *shura* to work . . . We have had seven *shuras* so far. But they don't let them work. [These managers] now have gone off in a huff, and have gone up there, to delay our advances. They want us to stop working. They want to make us go on strike. That's it. They've gone up there because they want to dismantle the *shura*. They've already dismantled two, claiming them [*shura* members] to be agents of SAVAK; and [then] they paid them 55 thousand toumans (£5,500) [for their dismissal]; paying money to SAVAK agents? And then they've said they [the *shura*] spoke to Farah during the *Taughout* [time of the Shah].

There was a tendency towards bureaucratization of the *shuras*; the mass of the membership became dependent on the intitiative and strategic experience of a relatively small cadre of leadership. Explaining the bureaucratic trend in British shop-floor organizations, Richard Hyman proposed three objective influences restricting the official activity of even a militant shop steward: 1) external pressure which acts against the security of the organization and leads it to become cautious; 2) an ongoing relationship with external parties, usually committing the official to respect the rules of the game; and finally, 3) the rationale of officialdom (Hyman, 1979, p. 61). These considerations are most influential in politically normal conditions. They are subject to modification in critical and revolutionary situations. Indeed, the element of external pressure was fatal for the *shuras*, and they had to respond against it, not only with cautious conservatism, but at times with resolute militancy, depending on the balance of forces at the workplace. Though the second tendency was dominant in the first period, the strategy of conservative caution prevailed in the second, when the rank and file would appear to be more militant than the *shura* leadership.

The second consideration, i.e. respect for the rules of the game, went with the first one. The balance of forces, however, would at times diminish such respect on the part of the militant *shuras*. The rationale of officialdom explains a great deal. To elect a worker as the *shura* member, the rank and file not only considered a candidate's militancy but his competence and ability to represent them. The wide range of activities and committees required that the *shura* members become full-time officials, dealing with the complex matters of totally intellectual labour. The result was a new division of labour. (In almost all factories, officials had offices with full facilities.) In these circumstances, the accountability of the *shura* depended on how and to what extent the rank and file monitored the elected representatives.

The democratic *shuras* would have no fear of holding a General Assembly to supply reports. Indeed, the dependence of *shuras* on the General Assembly, not vice versa, proved to be the major source of any *shura*'s bargaining power. The *shuras* of the Fanoos and Iran Cars factories were of this type. In the former there was continuous contact between the *shura* and the rank and file. The result of any activity or negotiations with any authority would be reported to the workers. This form of rank-and-file intervention reduced the bureaucratic tendency.

On the other hand, a corporatist *shura* could not be democratic, either internally or externally. It had to be bureaucratic, for fear of disclosing its activities and policies to the rank and file. In principle, the *shura*'s activities would become exclusively a matter of *shura* concern and not the business of the mass of the workers. In practice, the committee members evaded General Assemblies, or frequently postponed them.

Composition of the Shuras and their Unifying Role
Unlike the shop-floor trade unionism which protects the legally specified interests of particular sections of employees, the *shura* represented the whole workforce including white-collar workers and technicians. Such representation was carried out at two levels: legally and socially.

In legal terms any individual employee was entitled to stand, with qualifications, for the *shura* membership and be represented by it. Objectively, any *shura* requires a kind of managerial competence and technical expertise, in order to be able to supervise management. A *shura* therefore encompassed not only manual skilled workers, but also white-collar, administrative employees and even, at times, engineers.

This characteristic composition of the *shura* membership was one of its contradictions: on the one hand there was a need for the competence of certain personnel, and on the other, the most competent members were objectively authoritarian and anti-*shura*. The collapse of the second *shura* in the Pars Metal Works plant resulted from such a contradiction (see Chapter 9).

Yet an important feature of a *shura* was its unifying role. A *shura* would essentially be a socially unifying organ against capital. It acted as a medium between the social position of the manual and intellectual workers. This function was crucial, bearing in mind that the objective division between the two has historically been very wide. In general, the institution of the *shura* is a moment in the transcendence of the division of labour between manual and intellectual, precisely because it encompasses practical and intellectual activities simultaneously.

The socio-political predicament of a society enmeshed in the practices of a new repressive state (from wage-cuts to the violation of democratic rights and harassments) would generate general discontent; and thus general solidarity among the different ranks of the workforce. In these conditions, the potentiality and flexibility of the *shuras* to deal with all-embracing economic and socio-political matters would render them the institutional manifestation of these discontents and opposition to the state.

Notes

1. This consolidation of power at state level and the following events do not mean a solution of the labour problems. For an analysis of the contradictions of this repressive strategy, and a more detailed examination of Islamic Management, and Islamic Associations, see Chapter 10.

2. Even a prominent industrialist like Haji Barkhordār declared his support for Khomeini when he donated Rls 200 million (£1.33 million).

3. Another writer puts emphasis on the War Industries Committees initiated by the *Kadets* and the Octobrists in 1915 as a measure to free factories from the Tsarist bureaucracy (Siriani, 1982, pp. 19–20).

4. By the term 'people' the worker means only *working people*. This is their response, as I asked them to explain it.

5. *Labour Law and Social Security Regulations*, Institute of Labour & Social Security, Appendix of publication no. 9, 1359, Teheran, p. 63.

6. Ibid.

7. Hence the argument of Beynon and Nichols that 'skill is not essential to control. It is possible for unskilled workers, subdivided into routine repetitive jobs, to use their collective strength to oppose capital' (1977, p. 108).

8. For an historical examination of *Shia't* and Islamic rule, see Ja'afar and Tabari, 1981; and Tabari, 1981.

9. The literal translation of the extracts is 'To conduct a work, the Muslims should consult among each other.' See Shoār, 1981.

10. For this discussion see my 'Labour and Democracy in Post-Revolutionary Iran', in M. Parvin and H. Amirahmadi (eds), *Post-Revolutionary Iran* (Westview Press, 1986).

Chronology of Post-Revolutionary Events

11 February 1979	The radio declares the victory of the Revolution.
February–March	Mass demonstrations of military personnel, Kurdish people, Turkoman people, and women for democratic rights.
April 1979	Iran becomes an Islamic Republic after a referendum.
August 1979	Attack against the left, Kurdish and other ethnic minorities. (The second phase of industrial relations begins.)
4 November 1979	US Embassy is seized; the hostage crisis brings down the Bazargan government. Meanwhile, following the embassy seizure, a new wave of labour struggle escalates.
2–3 December 1979	The Islamic Constitution is ratified after a referendum.
25 January 1980	Bani'Sadr is elected as Iran's first president.
April 1980	The start of cultural revolution, Islamization of educational, cultural institutions and industrial workplaces. Meanwhile, a new crackdown on labour militancy is waged.
25 April 1980	An American rescue mission to free the hostages fails.
25 July 1980	The deposed Shah dies in exile in Egypt.
11 August 1980	M.A. Rajaii, a *maktabi* Prime Minister, forms a cabinet. From this period, the Islamic Associations begin to dominate the workplaces.
22 September 1980	Iran-Iraq war begins.
20 January 1981	American hostages are freed.
February 1981	The working-class struggles escalate as the state abolishes Special Benefit (year-end bonus).
March 1981	The conflict between Bani'Sadr and the Islamic Republic Party surfaces violently when a rally organised by Bani'Sadr is attacked. Meanwhile, in the factories, the confrontations between the IAs and the liberal managements accelerate.
June 1981	Bani'Sadr is dismissed as Commander-in-Chief and goes underground.
20 June 1981	Massive demonstrations against Khomeini in Teheran turn into a bloody confrontation with *Pasdaran*. Widespread guerrilla warfare against the Islamic regime starts. (The third phase of industrial relations begins).
July 1981	Bani'Sadr and Masoud Rajavi (the leader of the Mudjahedin) escape to France, setting up the

National Council of Resistance.

September 1981   Liquidation of opposition elements in the industrial workplaces. The beginning of new inter-state factional conflict between the '*Imam's* line' and the *Hojjatieh*.* The confrontation between the IAs and the *Maktabi* management escalates (the fourth phase).

---

*Fundamentalist (*vs* pragmatist) faction within ruling clergy.

8. The Leaders and the Led

The workers' understanding of their situation was based on their own experience; on the other hand, the left, the leaders, either lacked the ability to analyse these experiences correctly, or relied on abstract concepts which ignored reality. This chapter is therefore devoted to considering how the left-wing organizations conceived of the *shuras* and locating the *shura* experience in the context of the broader historical experiences of the working classes in developing similar movements.

The Shuras and the Left

Each socialist group claims that it alone is the theoretical mentor of the working class; the misunderstanding of political events by leaders affects the conditions of the led.

The Confusion of the Central Concepts
In analysing the workings of the *shuras* we find that four main concepts are used: *control-i kargari* (workers' control), *edareh* or *modiriyat* (management), *nezārat* (supervision) and *dekhālat* (intervention). These concepts have remained undefined and have been loosely used. The terms used have different connotations in the different workers' movements.

Control-i Kargari (Workers' Control): In general, workers' control in the European Trade Union movements is taken to mean control by workers of the labour process and the organization of work. The term is equivalent to job control and various forms of restrictive practices, that is, the demands and practices conducted under capitalist relations of production.[1] Historically, the notion of workers' control derives from the revolutionary situations in European capitalism at the end of the First World War (in Russia, Germany, Italy and Britain) and the critical periods of capitalist social instability especially in Europe in 1968 (see Chapter 1).

There has almost always been a tendency among shop-floor workers — both unskilled and skilled — to resist domination and alienation in the workplace and to demand a restriction on management's powers of control and genuine participation for workers. This tendency, along with, but distinct from, capital's requirements for the co-operation and involvement of the workforce in the production system, encouraged the re-emergence of the debate on workers' control among the Western labour movement. One definition of workers' control (which is widespread among social democrats) involves the securing for labour of some rights to determine the organization of the labour process in capitalist production. In both definitions, control is limited to the point of production itself.

Edareh/Modiriyat (Management): While the management by the *shura* of the affairs of the unit is not exactly the same as workers' self-management, it is distinct from workers' control. The essential attribute of self-management is the 'exclusive control and management of productive organization by [the] full membership on a basis of equality of vote' (Vanek, 1975, Introduction). In Yugoslavia, for instance, the organs of self-management are to a very large extent autonomous of the state, operating in the context of the law of the free market (Baumgartner, 1979). In (Yugoslavian) self-management, the income of capital is assigned not to the active participants (as is probably the case in producers' co-operatives) but to the owners of capital (society) (Vanek, ibid.).

Nezārat (Supervision): This is widely used and is a vaguer term. Observation of the actual practices referred to by the term would lead us to conclude that *nezārat* (like the term *control* in the Russian language in the early development of the factory committee movement) signifies a system of checks and veto by the *shura* on the activities of a capitalist system of management. The term *dekhālat* (intervention), which is again widely employed, points to direct action as a means of enforcing the right of *nezārat* in specified areas where it has not been respected by the management.

The Shuras in a Wider Context

It seems appropriate at this point to consider the characteristics of the three major radical forms of workers' movements — syndicalism, guild socialism and the factory committee movement — which bear some resemblance to the *shuras*. An analysis of these movements may also help to define what was specific to the *shura* ideology of the Iranian workers.

The origins of syndicalism go back to two historical experiences. The first was the strategy of the Industrial Workers of the World in the US, under the influence of the ideas of the Marxist Daniel de Leon. Their idea was to re-organize the American unions on an industry by industry basis, rather than trade by trade. The second source was the philosophy of the Frenchman Georges Sorel, who argued for winning control of the state through a general strike (Pelling, 1983, p. 125). This idea later spread throughout most European countries, including the Welsh mines in the 1910s and Spanish industries after the First World War. The labour radicalism that became identified with the syndicalist movement was before then unprecedented. In Britain it took the form of 'challenging the existing industrial order in a more fundamental manner' by a struggle 'to oust the capitalists from the control of industry'. This involved 'a revolutionary struggle for power' (Gallacher and Campbell, in Clark and Clements, 1977, pp. 125–7). Also the National Council of Scottish Workers' Committees called for a strategy to attain the 'industrial republic of labour' (ibid., p. 130).

The syndicalist movement, however, confined its activities to the industrial workplace, assuming in principle that 'social relations at the point of production [were] the determining factor in the social structure' (Hinton, 1973, Chapter 11). The syndicalists ignored the need for wider political struggle by not acknowledging the dialectical relationship between economic struggle, and the revolutionary political party. By the same token, the syndicalists put more emphasis on the tactics of class struggle and less on long-term strategies; more on action and less on theory. In addition, like the theory of industrial unionism, it argued against state socialism (Hinton, ibid.).

Guild socialism is a mixture of syndicalism and collectivism; it assumes that the means of production should be owned by the state but that control of production should be conducted by the guilds. Within a pluralistic framework, guilds would be democratically organized and bargain on equal terms with the state. When the different guilds merged to form a single union, capitalism would then, in practice, be transformed by industrial unionism itself (Cole in Vanek, 1975).

The *shuras*, as perceived by the workers, bear some affinity to the above movements insofar as their activities were confined to the point of production. But, unlike these other movements, the *shuras* were based in single factories; they did not last long enough to generate a theoretical perspective for the future; and they never had the opportunity to act as a united political force in society. This was undoubtedly one of the major defects of the movement. The *shura* organization, as conceptualized by the industrial workers, was reminiscent of the characteristic features of the Russian Factory Committees that emerged following the February Revolution of 1917.

Misconceptions About What Happened
Almost all of the left was surprised by the sudden emergence of *shuras*. Almost all left-wing organizations, as well as the *shuras* themselves, were confused about what to do and about what kind of possible role the *shuras* could play politically. The left's theoretical knowledge about workers' councils did not extend beyond a few articles by Gramsci. That the *shuras*, as conceived by the leftist forces, were reminiscent of the Russian experience, was based overwhelmingly on a version of that history which is crude and mechanical methodologically, and uncritical politically. No

other experiences are viewed or evaluated, nor have they learnt from them — for example, those experiences of Germany, Italy, Portugal, Spain, Chile, Eastern Europe — nor those particular forms of workers' organization that emerged in advanced capitalist countries like Britain in the Revolutionary conjuncture or those theories and practices developed during stable periods.

Most of the literature on the workers' councils confuses two distinct forms of workers' organization, through a misconception of the terms factory committee and council/soviets, when applying them to the Iranian experience. These terms are generally employed to describe the experiences of the Russian masses in 1905 and in the February–October 1917 Revolutions. In 1917 in Russia three types of workers' organization sprang up in the early days of the February Revolution: factory committees (*fabzavkomy*), councils (*soviets*) and trade unions (*profsoyozy*).[2] In Farsi, the term *shura* is used by commentators in all three meanings. In the experience of Russian workers, the factory committees were the product of specific revolutionary circumstances and of particular political, economic and ideological transformations (the vacuum of power in the workplaces and the emergence of a new ideology amongst the workers). The factory committees were shop-floor workers' organizations which were attempting to exert control over the process of production and distribution. They were rarely involved in high level planning. They were threatening the domination of capital at the point of production. In terms of the formal extent of workers' control, the British shop-steward organizations of the inter-war period were more successful than the Russian factory committees (Smith, 1983). But the socio-economic conditions and the balance of forces within which those two forms of workers' organizations sprang up were radically different. While the shop-steward movement was basically a defence by skilled craft workers against deskilling, the Russian factory committee movement was part of a struggle to weaken the position of capital in the workplace.

On the other hand, the term soviet (or council) referred to two forms of organization: first, to the actual Soviet of Factory Committees (the Executive Committee of the Conference of Factory Committees held in late May 1917) and secondly, to the Soviet of Deputies of Petrograd (Ferro, 1977, p. 150). In this Soviet, the workers could be elected from the members of the factory committees, or elected from all the workers representing a given factory on it. It was this last organization, the Soviet of Deputies, which eventually questioned bourgeois state power, becoming a state within a state.

A number of commentators compare the functions of the *shuras* with the *shuras*(?) of the Russian Revolution — the soviets. They conclude that the Iranian workers' *shuras* were not in fact shuras, but a distorted type of the Workers' Councils/Soviets; and that workers' *shuras* were a kind of syndicate (*Paykar*, 25 and 58), at best a radical syndicate, because they did not question the bourgeois state power and because, unlike the Russian soviets, they did not constitute an alternative rudimentary form of proletarian state.

On the other hand, there was a tendency among most of the left-wing groups to dismiss the *shuras* as a spontaneous activity of the working class. Yet their emergence delighted the left, because they created a justifiable ground for the left's relevance and rhetoric.[3] Theoretically, for these groups the concept of *shura* hardly went beyond ahistorical quotations from Lenin, for whom the *political* role of such organizations, to stand against the bourgeois state, was the most important one.

The traditional left viewed the *shuras* in terms of their oppositional role against the employers, or the government, a role that any radical workers' organizations, including trade unions, could in certain circumstances play. Little attention has been paid to the most significant and distinctive character of the *shura* as an organization of workers' control which seeks to defy the division of labour at the point of production (the division between management and executive).

Defining the success or failure of the *shuras* by their militancy, left-wing groups divided them into three types: yellow *shuras* run by pro-Khomeini and fanatical Islamic workers; 'real' *shuras* elected directly by workers who might or might not serve the interests of rank-and-file workers (if they did not, they were simply viewed as ignorant); and lastly, the revolutionary *shuras* whose members were sympathizers with left-wing organizations. The political tendency of the *shura* members therefore became the criterion for the success or failure of a *shura*; to what extent and degree, over what areas and in what condition a *shura* exerted control became irrelevant. Such an approach was furthermore unable to explain the antagonism between the yellow *shuras* and liberal managements.

The Workers' Conceptions of the Shura

We will now consider what conception the rank-and-file workers had of the *shuras*. It is naturally difficult to draw up a clear-cut categorization of their views. Some workers had already translated their perceptions into the common terminologies such as *nezārat* or intervention; but these were too vague to be useful.

We limit ourselves, here, to the data collected through in-depth interviews in three factories in Teheran: Metal Works, I.T.N. Company (producer of electricity transformers) and Arasteh (producer of domestic appliances). I limit my quotations to a few statements by workers, each representing a distinct conception.

The statements suggest that three conceptions might be identified.

The Trade Unionist Conception

Q: What do you think the *shura* should do?

A: *Shuras* must represent the real wishes of the workers; must get the rights of the workers from the boss; mustn't let them be violated.

Q: Could the syndicate do this job?

A: The syndicates have been infiltrated by the boss's guards; if they had not been, they would have been OK.

Very few workers expressed such an opinion. The *shura*, for them, was only a means of representation of the workers in their economic demand-making process.

The Universal Conception

Syndicates take only the workers' [economic] interests into consideration, not the social [total] interests, or the interests of the whole country. But the *shura* concerns itself with the whole social interests, the country's interests . . . the syndicate would defend only workers' money [wages], getting some money to the workers and forgetting about the rest! Where the products will be going, into whose pocket, etc. — these things are not the concern of the syndicate (an I.T.N. Company worker).

Workers holding this view maintain that the *shuras* must have responsibility not only to the workers, but also the society as a whole. This ideology expands the social role of the *shuras*, as opposed to its being limited inside the factory fences. On the other hand, however, it wishes to act not simply beyond the factory walls, but beyond their *class* boundaries. This populist aspect of this conception could not last long unless its material basis is provided.

Control and Nezārat

We do want the *shuras*. It is not possible for seven hundred workers to go up [to the management office] and negotiate with the factory directors. We want a *shura* to be appointed, going up, solving *our* problems.

A: What kind of problems?

Q: *Any;* about wages, about the function of the factory, about sales, orders, etc., those which are recognized by Law . . . The *shura* must intervene in all these cases which are legal.

The first part of the statement seems to suggest a rather trade unionist conception: the *shura* is conceived as the workers' representative in negotiation with management. However, from the viewpoint of this worker, its function goes beyond demanding the legal rights of the usual shop-steward committee. For this worker, the problems of the factory *as a whole* — its functioning, sales, purchases and so on — are considered to be *his* problems. He feels his right to have a say, to interfere in factory affairs. This is an expression of the ideology of possession.

It is striking that a large proportion of workers conceived of the *shura* as the sole responsible body in the factory — the organ through which the workers could exert their power, could question those who until recently were ruling them in the factory.

> We have formed and appointed this *shura* to be in charge of the factory, to sort out the affairs and problems. We have built the *shura* for the sake of our Revolution . . . But now we see that the directing body by no means agrees with our *shura*.

And describing the anti-*shura* character of the directing body, he goes on to say with outrage,

> We produce so much! They [the management] say, "We have to take a loan from the government!" Where does our product go then? Where do the sales of this factory go? . . . What they get from the government belongs to this country's wealth; it belongs to the whole people.

Worker B

> The *shura* must be Islamic; must be recognized by law.
> Q: What are its duties?
> A: Its tasks should be that it must be resolute in the face of the directing body and the like; must intervene in *everything*; must run this factory. But this directing body destroys any *shura* we build.

Worker D

> At the moment we are not talking about the economic interests. First of all the factory should have an income, so that we can get some. But it hasn't had any output; that is, it hasn't been found out whether it has or not. Because we don't have a real *shura* to control the input-output issues, keeping them under its own control . . . The *shura* must have the right [to control]. In order to be able to do that it must be recognized.

And lastly, Worker E of I.T.N. factory:

> We have built the *shura* to defend our rights, to be able to speak out.
> Q: The syndicate could do the same job, couldn't it?
> A: Well, the syndicate was economistic: it expected us to work eight hours for some pennies; that was it. It didn't involve questioning who the management was, what it was doing, what it bought, where the money came from and so on. We were not involved in [these things] in the past. But the *shura* tells the workers where the money (capital) comes from, where it goes. The *shura* checks (*nezārat*) and intervenes in all things; for instance, financial affairs; employment, purchase, sales and the rest.

There is, however, no mention of the management. So far everything evolves around the *shura*. The workers proved to be extraordinarily committed and responsible for the affairs of the enterprise. They considered it their right to intervene in its running. It was their right to

150

question the managers. 'Where does our product go?' 'Where do the sales of this factory go?' 'Where does the result of my labour go?' For these workers, the concept of *shura* implied the material expression of their strong desire for control over the organization and administration of production. And this is indeed the definition of a *shura*.

Some Reflections on the Workers' Subjectivity

During the interview, the workers were keen for the legalization of *shuras*. A positive attitude towards law, legitimacy and the like was not limited to the sphere of workers' struggle. This could be recognized in the social behaviour of most people. Any positive attitudes towards undesirable laws do not necessarily imply obedience to them. Four areas can be identified where the workers expressed such views.

'*Shuras* must intervene in all those areas that are recognized by law.' Such statements were mostly made by the workers who appeared to support the Islamic regime. The politics of the workers depended less on economic and sociological stratification (skill, sex, age, occupation) and more on ideological considerations. Working-class support for the regime has been contradictory. Initially, the working class expressed large but confused support; while it participated in official rallies, it rejected government labour policies in the workplace. (This confused support has now been replaced with clear opposition by the large majority of the workers.)

Pro-regime workers were a tiny stratum which was sub-divided into three groups. The first group were those who had been granted some social or ideological role as functionaries of the formal or informal labour organizations such as *Khane-i Kargar* (Labour House) or the Islamic Associations. This group benefited materially from its privileged position.

The second group might be said to feel and articulate an identity of ideological interest with the regime because of kinship relations; workers whose close relatives held significant positions in the regime either as an influential clergyman or as state agents fell into this category. Such adherence reflected a tribal form of solidarity (probably an ideal form of social relations from the point of view of the ruling clergy).[4]

The third group were influenced by the contradictory nature of the Islamic state. They regarded the state as anti-capitalist and anti-oppression. The mechanism of this influence has already been described in the discussion on the ideological sources of the corporatist *shuras* in the previous chapter. Any support, on this count, could be expected to be highly vulnerable. Let us consider the statement of worker B.

The *shura* must be Islamic, must be recognized by law.
Q: What are its tasks?
A: Its tasks should be that, it must be resolute against the Board of Directors

and the like; it must intervene in *everything*; must run the factory . . .

While Worker B believes in an Islamic *shura* and its recognition by law, in practice he opposes the government's conception of the *shura*. This contradiction in support is the reflection of a contradiction in the state and between the workers' class interests and their views on the state.

Recognition by Law as a Guarantee

Our major problem is that the authorities do not recognize the *shuras* as such . . . If they don't then they will be exactly like the syndicates, without any difference . . . Now these days, the employees, how shall I put it, in fact threaten the management. In such situations, then, the *shura* has to accept the responsibility, meeting the demands of the workers. If it doesn't, then how does it differ from the syndicate? What is it, then, that constrains the *shura*? It is its non-recognition. If the *shuras* are recognized, then any other problems will simply be tackled.

A struggle for reform is not necessarily reformism. The reform can be a basis for a further advance. Demanding a guarantee from the state is a common practice, from the Western trades unions to the Polish Solidarity. The workers who had similar views to Worker B upon legality might mean to get a *recognized* concession from the state. If they were legalist, i.e. accepted the government's Resolutions on the *shuras*, they wouldn't say 'the *shura* must intervene in *everything*.'

Caution before Repression

A cautious mentality is the product of a society dominated by repression and a secret-police order. This atmosphere produces fear of colleagues, lack of trust and a culture of insecurity. Such a social order was reproduced by the Islamic state; formal and informal state organizations carried out the task of social and ideological control in almost all public places.[5] (To the causes of insecurity we must add the notorious Article 33 of the Labour Law according to which workers could be dismissed without explanations, and the high level of unemployment.) In the course of conducting an interview on the subject in the *shura* office in the Metal Works factory, a *shura* member made the point clear.

Excuse me, I think you will get better results if you talk to people one by one, without anybody else being present, rather than talking to them altogether in a group. You went into the shops — but perhaps the workers can't speak the truth: *there, here* or *anywhere*. For this reason, I told you that I wouldn't be interviewed.

Legalism as a Tactic

Having been produced by despotic socio-political conditions, tactical legalism is a distinct form of popular culture. The logic is to defeat the enemy with its own weapons. There are countless examples of this tactic.

In the infamous event of Carvan Sara Sangi, the workers were reported to have held the Shah's pictures in their hands.[6] In a strike action, under the Shah, in the Plasco factory in Teheran, the workers, by covering the machines with the Shah's pictures, made them virtually idle. In the Iran National Car Factory (Talbot), in a strike incident under the old regime, a meeting at which one of the managers was giving a speech was disrupted by workers who were chanting, 'Long live the Shah'. This tradition is still alive, but of course in different forms. Chants such as 'In the name of *Imam* Khomeini', 'in the name of God', are utilized for protection, neutralization and for further offensive purposes.

In the state-run Iran Cars factory, a severe confrontation occurred after the *shura* withdrew funds from the financial department to pay the workers their year-end bonus in March 1981. Some of the *shura* members were jailed as the state reacted against the action. The workers withdrew their claims in order to get their *shura* members released. The day I visited the plant, the representatives of the *Iman* (Khomeini) and of the Prosecutor-General turned up at the factory to settle the continuing dispute. After a bitter argument between the workers and the representatives, one Azerbaijani worker stood up and declared, 'Just as we brought down the Shah's regime, we are able to bring down any other regimes.' At this moment the workers started clapping. The worker stopped them by saying, '*Takbir*,[7] please, my brothers' (Bayat, 1983).

In a society where self-expression and protest are banned, the workers will take any possible channel to advance their struggle which might not assume a conventional form. Perhaps that is why it appears to be so hard to grasp, let alone foresee, the abrupt extraordinary mass eruptions, unless we comprehend the complex social psychology and the forms of expression of mass militancy in such societies. Those kinds of mass eruption were well demonstrated historically in Russia in 1905 and February 1917 (Smith, 1980; Liebman, 1975), in Iran in 1978 and Poland in 1980 (Singer, 1982).

Notes

1. This position is criticized by Coates, 'Democracy and Workers' Control' in Vanek, 1975, pp. 90–91. I have examined confusions surrounding the concept 'workers' control' in European literature, in Chapter 2.

2. For an analysis of factory committees in Russia, see Smith, 1983; Avrich, 1963; Ferro, 1980; Kaplan, 1969 and Siriani, 1982.

3. See for example *Kar*, no. 62. The traditional left includes organizations and tendencies both of the Stalinist line, such as *Tudeh, Fedaeen* (both factions) and Maoist groups.

4. See the remarks on the character of the Islamic state (Chapters 7 and 10); also notice the paternalistic ideologies prevalent in the countryside, being carried by the migrant peasants into the factories, in Chapter 4.

5. After 20 June 1981, Khomeini ordered people to spy on their neighbours. Children were interrogated in the schools about family conversations.

6. Carvan Sara Sangi is on the road between Teheran and the town of Karadj, where the striking workers of *Chit-i Jahan* textile factory, who were demonstrating along the road, encountered the gunfire of the Shah's paramilitary forces in 1976. In this event at least three workers were said to have been killed.

7. As regards the term *takbir*, it should be noted that conventional kinds of applause are considered to be an unIslamic form of praise, and have been replaced by *takbir* — a call for the slogan *Allah Akbar*. Applause has thus become a form of collective expression of opposition to, and independence from, the regime.

9. Historical and Structural Limitations of the *Shuras*

In this chapter the two major causes of the *shura*'s disintegration are discussed. Political pressure is analysed in terms of the policies of the state and capital on the *shuras*, and historical/structural limitations which were most clearly manifested in the contradiction between two aspects of the work of management, that is co-ordination and control.

Political Pressure

The political factor is related to the attitudes of both the state and capital towards the *shuras*. Although, for the reasons previously mentioned, the relationship between the Islamic state and capital has long remained contradictory, it was primarily the anti-authoritarian orientation of the workers' councils to which they both expressed their opposition.

The State and the Shuras
At different times different fractions in the Islamic state adopted different attitudes towards the councils. The Provisional Government of Mehdi Bazargan, composed of liberal-religious elements, categorically opposed the *shuras* and the notion of workers' participation. The provisional government set up a Special Force composed of appointed inspectors inside the plants to report on councils' activities. The P.G., instead, advocated the establishment of syndicates.

The populist fraction of the Islamic Republic Party (IRP) known as the 'Imam's Line' aimed at creating a form of Islamic corporatism in order to integrate labour into the Islamic state. In general, corporatism is a form of populist strategy which attempts to integrate the tripartite forces of labour, capital and the state in order to make them work co-operatively for the good of a 'beloved nation'. Corporatism in Iran had a further ingredient of Islamic ideology: a corporatism of Islamic workers, *mashru*, legitimate capital (or *maktabi,* literally Islamic, management) and the Islamic state, all co-operating for the common cause of the Islamic nation. By attempting to adopt such a policy, the IRP in practice strengthened the notion of *shuraism*, albeit with an Islamic character, employing it both in workplaces and in society at large in order to discredit the values and the elements it considered 'liberal'. The policy also aimed to pre-empt the socialist ideas and organizations with which the idea of *shuraism* had been intertwined. The policy in practice also weakened the position of workers by dividing the councils into 'Islamic' and 'non-Islamic'. The non-conformist councils were later dismantled.

The 'fundamentalist' faction of the IRP, the *Hojjatieh* sect, believed that the very concept of *shuras* was irrelevant to Islam. It was argued that power in Islam emanates from God, through the mediation of *Imam* and, in his absence, through *naib Imam* (the *Imam*'s substitute on earth). As institutions of power from below, *shuras* were considered to be unIslamic. In 1981, Ahmad Tavakoli, the then Labour Minister and a follower of *Hojjatieh* sect, prohibited the formation of the new *Islamic shuras* for a year. But the workers' resistance and the power struggle within the state led to his dismissal. The power struggle over the nature of a new Law of *Shuras* continued. Khomeini himself largely shared the view of *Hojjatieh* on the issue of the *shuras*, and observers consider this to be the main reason for the conflict between Khomeini and Ayatollah Taleghani — a popular clergyman who died in 1979 and who advocated *shuras*.[1]

The State and Management Sabotage

The management and the Ministry of Industry were aware of the workers' technical failings, and knew that they would be unable to pose a proletarian solution to end the crisis in industry by running the workplaces properly by themselves. A worker in the Metal Works clearly explained this to me.

> Mr T [the owner] is a capitalist. He is now in the National Organization of Industry, with Mr Neemat Zadeh who was the Minister of Labour. At the moment our engineers are also there, all conspiring against the workers.

The strategy of the liberal managers and the Ministry of Industry, under the Bazargan cabinet, was to defeat the workers through the paralysis of production by, for instance, going on strike or passive acts of sabotage in production and administration. After the revolution when the ideology of possession and control developed, the workers would no longer tolerate authoritarian relations within the workplaces. The strategy of managers was to re-establish, as far as possible, the previously existing authoritarian relations. Having failed to provide an institutional medium between themselves and the workers, the liberal managers attempted to undermine the workers' confidence. They were trying to shatter the authority of the workers through their role in the technical division of labour. This effective and rather common strategy was supported by the liberal faction within the government, as a worker at Metal Works reflected:

> These [state] managers are plotting with the boss against the workers. They want to destroy the factory and then pretend it was our doing. We have been

to the Ministry of Industry on several occasions. The answer was, "You go and take to the streets, start striking and demonstrating!"

Management's competence in its functioning was a factor of production which managers and the state refused to allow the *shuras* to use. The state also used economic blockade as another strategy to make the independent *shuras* yield by denying them access to other components of the productive forces. Through its control over economic life via the credit system, market and international transactions, the state could easily manage to halt production. The impact of such intervention will be clear when we remember that over 70%, and in some sectors (like chemicals) almost 100% of industrial raw materials, were imported from abroad. According to one report, transactions with the SAKA plant *shura* were banned by the state and the bazaar merchants, on the ground that the *shura* members were communists (*Rah-i Kargar*). In the Orkideh Chinese factory the state cut off the import of raw materials from West Germany after the workers had taken control of the plant. Credit to two factories of the Naz-Nakh and Isfahan Wool Industry were cut back by the state, in order to dismantle the *shuras*. This was one reason why the *shura* workers interviewed were sensitive about their competence to conduct transactions with foreign countries.

Physical Liquidation
The use of force is always the last resort in exerting illegitimate domination. It may take arbitrary, legal-systematic and institutionalized forms. The state used all of these means to liquidate the independent *shuras*.

The wave of struggle based around workers' control in the first period forced Bazargan to use legal forms or force to put down popular agitation. The law of formation of Special Force in industry was passed and implemented only three months after the Insurrection. The Special Force was conceived to prevent the intervention of the *shuras* or strike committees within managerial selection and management operations and to control and report on the elements who were waging acts of sabotage and disruption. The policy of use of force, in the first period, culminated in August 1979 when the first wave of suppression was launched. Many independent *shura* activists were arrested and a number of them executed.

The second wave of liquidation followed the closure of the universities, when a substantial number of independent-interventionist *shuras* were dismantled. The factory *shuras* in Tabriz, an industrial zone in Azerbaijan, were the primary victims. In Machin Sazi plant, the office of the *shura* was sealed up following a demonstration by the loyalist workers who had been organized by the Islamic Associations. The 40-member *shura* was dissolved, and the members were sacked. A similar process occurred in other plants (Tractor Sazi, Lift-Truck, Pompiran and Compidro). The strong union of factory *shuras* of Gilan province was the next victim. Later followed the liquidation of factory *shuras* in the armament industry Union of Factory Committees of West Teheran, the oil industry, the railways and a number of others. Another strong union was the Union of Factory *Shuras* of the Organization of Industrial Development (UFSOID). This organization owned and controlled several state industrial plants throughout the country. The UFSOID's intention of holding a country-wide congress was opposed by the Ministry of Industry. The UFSOID, however, went ahead with organizing the congress, after which the Minister of Industry ordered its dissolution. The order was implemented after the holding of a counter-seminar by loyalist workers and the members of the Islamic Associations. (Islamic Associations, the organs of pro-regime workers, played an important role in harassing the interventionist *shuras* by spying on and watching the movements of the *shura* members and through organizing anti-*shura* activities.)

The role of the military forces, *Pasdaran*, in terrorizing and liquidating the *shuras* was also crucial. *Pasdaran*'s involvement in industrial disputes started right from the insurrection when the new state authority still had not been institutionalized. Their role increased, particularly after the events of July 1981 when the clergy seized the state apparatus by deposing President Bani'Sadr and instituting a crack-down of opposition forces. I managed to observe the operations of the *Pasdaran* who, in the Fanoos factory, rushed into the factory searching for the *shura* members. In this event a number of the *shura* members were arrested and the *shura* itself was dismantled. In the Iran Cars factory, I was told, following the June Days of 1981, the armed *Pasdaran* had rushed into the factory and begun arresting *shura* members and other activists according to a blacklist prepared by the Islamic Association. In one day 73 workers were taken away. The *shura* leader, a pro-Mudjahedin worker, had already been kidnapped at the factory gate, and a few days later I found his name in the daily paper in the list of executed people of the day.

It may seem confusing when I limit the workers' control activities to only a few months after the insurrection, the first period, and yet still speak of the liquidation of the *shura* members in the third period. This only shows that although the period of actual workers' control practice did not last long, the desire for *shuras* continued.

The political crack-down was indeed a devastating blow to the structure and the activities of the independent councils. It is, however, a mistake to attribute the disintegration of the councils wholly to the political factors. I would argue that the internal contradictions of the *shuras* should be considered as the major factor responsible for their failure. In other words, for the reasons provided below, the real (*vs* the formal) power of the *shuras* would have been undermined, even in the absence of political pressure.

The Internal Contradictions of the *Shuras*

In the previous chapter we concluded that for the workers the *shuras* were the organizational manifestation of a desire for control over the processes of production and administration of production. We have characterized the first period of five to six months as the phase of control from below. The *shuras* then began to be replaced by a one-man-management system.

Did the workers give in to the return of professional managers? Did they launch any resistance against the professional managers and the system they represented? While on several occasions the workers had put the managers on trial and dismissed them, later — and months after running the companies themselves — they requested the state to send back these same professional managers. In our own research sample, the workers in three factories — Amazon, Teheran Auto and Behshar — themselves requested the Ministry of Industry to dispatch state-managers. And in other factories the workers and the *shura* felt the need for professional managers. That approach, however, by no means reduced their commitment to the *shura* and their desire and demand for control. In order to investigate this contradiction, it is necessary to understand the workers' conceptions of management.

The workers wanted professional managers becuse they needed their technical competence without which the very existence of the *shuras* as effective organs of control over production and distribution would be in jeopardy. A militant employee and the leader of the first *shura* in the Iran Cars factory, explained that fact with regret.

> As soon as the regime toppled, the *shura* was formed. The workers believed it to be their right to interfere in any job. Management no longer made any sense for them. They replaced the managers. They halted any "anti-worker" plans. They launched efforts to provide raw material. Foreign managers were all sacked. The management had actually been paralysed . . . However, the level of output was pretty low. The *shura* would have to pay salaries and wages. They still would have to get raw materials to the plant. But it was a hard job. The *shura* then had to appeal to the government for help. You know, the *shura* wasn't able to pay the wages for even one month. Therefore, it had to come to terms with the state-appointed managers. As a result, the *shura* in fact lost its genuineness!

A *shura* member in the Amazon factory was also convinced of the necessity of managerial competence.

> A question which one should not really deny is that, if a *shura* does not possess the expertise of supplying things and of management, then it can by no means replace the management. It has to have that expertise. There is no question about it . . . If we had carried on in the same manner, i.e. running the plant without the management, it would certainly have been a failure; a one hundred per cent defeat. Because, where I [as a *shura* member] do not

159

know anything about supplies, any foreign language and about how to import materials, or when I do not have a legal authority, I wouldn't be able to run things.

Workers' requirement for the technical competence of management was not in accord with the whole management rationale. (The character of the workers' struggle around the *shura* in the second phase has to be seen in relation to this.) This implies that the workers had to accept only one aspect of management: the technical side. The case of the Metal Works in Teheran is instructive here. Unlike in the other factories, the Metal Works workers (with the *shura*) and the management were in the midst of a bitter struggle on this very issue when I conducted my research. Following the dispute the management had gone on strike for 25 days when I visited the factory. I shall, therefore, concentrate on this particular factory.

Pointing to the management's strike, a *shura* member complained bitterly.

When that gentleman [engineer-manager] says "I won't come under these conditions", it was *we* who appointed them as provisional managers. Now, they must come back and do their proper work. If they've resigned from management, then they must turn up to their usual work. We will appoint some other managers. At the moment a number of furnaces are out of order — the two 12-ton ones, which are the heart of the factory.

Asgar, a skilled worker, reacted angrily.

Since the revolution we have tried to keep this factory on its feet; but we have failed. [Why?] Because *they* don't allow it . . . These people [managers] have gone and sat in the Central Office! What are the tasks of an engineer [now one of the elected managers]? The engineer must stay at the factory and work. Why has this engineer gone and sat in the boss's office? Who's paying for it?

Other statements reiterate the message: 'The factory will be paralysed while the management sits on its arse up there. The management must work, to find out what the [technical] problems are' and 'My friend, this factory needs only *one* manager, and *one* good engineer.'

A technicist conception of management might be defined as a tendency among the workers not to accept the basic division of labour between the functions of conception and execution; and yet, due to technical inability, they have to come to terms with the necessity of using the technical competence of the management. A 'natural conception' is the tendency of workers who regard a division between the two functions of conception and execution as essential and natural.[2]

The workers, in practice, both wanted and did not want the management. This is not a contradiction in workers' behaviour, but rather the reflection of a contradiction within capitalist management.

The Functions of Control and Co-ordination
The work of management or supervision is itself a specific performance of productive labour.

> Flows of input materials and instruments of labour must find their way to workers at well-timed intervals for each activity. Finances must be available for sales and borrowing to pay for labour power, materials and tools. The final output must be marketed. (Friedman, 1977b, p. 77)

When a manager, a functional capitalist, performs the work of management, he in fact creates surplus-value. 'He creates surplus-value not because he works as a capitalist, but because he *also* works, regardless of his capacity as a capitalist' (Marx, 1977, p. 382). This work, the function of co-ordination of production, is necessary in any complex economy. For 'all directly social or communal labour on a large scale' requires a 'directing authority' in order to co-ordinate individual and social behaviour (Marx, 1979, p. 449).

The second function of management is the exercise of authority and power, the 'function of control' which is specific to 'all modes of production based upon the antithesis between the labourer as the direct producer, and the owner of the means of production' (Marx, 1977, p. 384). In capitalist production relations, it is the major aspect of the work of management. For the capitalist production process is never just a technical process; it rests upon social relations of production — the relation between labour and capital which is by nature antagonistic (Marx, 1977, pp. 449-50; de Vroey in Nichols, 1980). Historically, the function of control became dominant, especially with the advent of manufacturing, and hierarchical management systems, and with the domination of real subsumption of labour to capital. In the course of transformation from craft production and co-operation to the manufacturing system, as with the development of the division of labour with the manufacturing process, the labourers who had control over the production process became subordinated to the requirements of capital (Braverman, 1974; Littler, 1982). The individual labourers became deprived of their 'knowledge, judgement and will'; what they previously possessed was now in the hands of 'the capital which [confronted] them' (Marx, 1979, p. 482). These two functions of management under capitalism are separated only at the level of abstraction. Under capitalist relations, they in practice reproduce each other.

The function of co-ordination, in capitalist production processes, developed after the transformation of craft production, the detailed division of tasks, the deskilling process and the advent of the collective worker: these fragmentations created by capital had to be co-ordinated in turn by capital itself. Historically and theoretically, then, the work of co-ordination corresponds with the diminishing autonomy of the labourer. The diminution of autonomy necessarily infers the domination of authority and power[3] over the labourer (see also, Palloix, 1976).

Any form of organization of production and of labour, influenced by the requirements of the accumulation process tends to require a strict division of labour and an ever widening gap between the functions of conception and execution. Such a technical division of labour corresponds to the social division of labour and the relations of power and authority. An agent who performs the function of planning or supervising carries a certain degree of authority over his/her subordinates. The larger and the more complex the structure of industry, the less visible the actual power of the agents, since power tends to become depersonalized.[4]

Let us now return to the workers in the factories of Teheran. On the one hand they were determined to exert control over the processes of production, distribution and exchange in their enterprises. They demonstrated a strong desire to make decisions and take part in future planning and they struggled to direct factory affairs. Practically, however, they felt that they were unable to do so, because of the persistence of the existing capitalist division of labour.[5] For the Metal Works workers the most viable method was to appoint managers accountable to the workers. As a result, three members of the Board of Directors (two of them engineers) were appointed. The result was that no substantial change occurred to realize workers' desire to control. Contradictions, conflicts and confrontations continued to prevail. Simply speaking, what the workers aimed to do was to assign the function of control to themselves, and that of co-ordination to the managers. But as soon as the workers appointed the managers as the co-ordinators, they inevitably had to accept their authority and control. Neither the goodwill of the managers, nor their accountability to the workers, were capable of creating workers' control and allowing the workers to exert power over their own work relations. For power is no longer personal but functional.

If the workers did not appreciate that reality, then it was most likely to bring the *persons*, the agents and the personified power under their mounting attacks. They, however, had started thinking beyond the immediate personalities involved. The basic contradiction is expressed by an angry worker in the Metal Works.

> The capitalists don't allow our *shura* to work. They [the *shura* members] do want to work [for us workers]. We have had seven *shuras* so far. [But] they don't let them work. [The managers] now have gone off in a huff, and have gone up there, to delay our advances. They want us to stop working. They want to make us go on strike. That's it. They've gone up there, because they want to dismantle the *shura*.
> They've already dismantled two, claiming [the *shura*] to be agents of SAVAK, and [then] they've paid them 55 thousand toumans [about £5,500] [for their dismissal]! Paying money to SAVAK agents? Then they have said they [*shura* people] had spoken to Farah [the Shah's wife] during the *Taughout* [Shah's rule]. Using this excuse, they've sacked them. And now

also, if this *shura* is dissolved and if we build another *shura*, they will certainly dismantle that too. *Because the power is in their hands*.

The traditional sectors of industry are characterized by quite simple labour processes and division of labour, and with more team work (for instance, in the brick-making industry). Simple organization of co-ordination and a much higher degree of autonomy for the workforce combined with an easy supply of raw material made it possible for workers to exert a great deal of control over the process of production and distribution. In the brick-making industry an insignificant dispute would lead workers to take control of the industry; this happened in the cities of Tabriz, Amol and Maragheh in the northern provinces. The main factor preventing workers' control in these industries was political-military.

The Role of Skill
A brief review of the majority of workers' control movements attests that skill and expertise have been determinant factors in the success or failure of the movements; and that the skilled workers have been in the forefront of them. In the German council movement of 1918-1919, the highly skilled tool-makers, in particular the turners, were the leaders (Bologna, 1976, p. 68; Geary, 1976). In the defensive control movement in Britain in the 1910s, the skilled craftsmen were the fundamental agitators (Walker, 1981; Hinton, 1973; Zeitlin, 1980); in the Russian factory committee movement after the February Revolution in Petrograd, the strong skilled workers (of Putilov) were the most active (Smith, 1980, 1981). Skill and expertise were spontaneously used as a demonstration of workers' ability to go beyond the predetermined bourgeois relations of domination at the point of production; as a factor to break down the fetish of managerial imperative; and as an ideological mediation to reveal the historicity of the capitalist form of work organization.

Skill is necessarily an element of a (skilled) workers' ability; but it will not necessarily develop class consciousness and class solidarity. Instead, it has tended to be a source of craft consciousness, shopism and occupational sectarianism (Rosenburg, 1980), narrow-minded ideas and sectarian interest-seeking mentality (Hinton, 1973; Stein, 1978). The labour aristocracy of the late 19th Century in Britain was of this kind (Hobsbawm, 1979, chapter 16): viewing their skill as their property. The defeat of the shop-steward and German council movements are the result of the sectarian mentality of those privileged skilled workers who possessed a strong bargaining power (Walker, 1981; Hinton, ibid., chapter 10; and Bologna, 1976).

The conflation of skill and sectarianism is not inevitable. It is subject to two qualifications: firstly, the sectarianism of the skilled and privileged strata of a working class can be, to a very large extent, modified by the political conditions of an undemocratic system. The metal-workers of pre-revolutionary Russia were radically different in political terms from the British labour aristocracy. Secondly, it is wrong to speak of skill in an abstract sense. Skills are also class-divided and ideological: there are managerial skills and workers' skills. In this respect, the political orientation of each is conditioned by the positions of their holders in the process of production, that is, whether they perform work in the labour process or surplus-value extracting process. In taking skill as an abstract notion I am here reflecting the spontaneous conception of the workers.

The Iranian Case
While the engineers in the Metal Works could have been the source of a movement for offensive control, they turned out to be moving in exactly the opposite direction. In Iran, an engineer is privileged both in terms of his position in the social division of labour and in the technical division of labour. On the other hand, in a relatively backward labour process, as at Metal Works, the 'proletarianization of the new middle class, through the social and technical dequalification of their positions' (Carchedi, 1975) develops rarely, if at all. Furthermore, in the small, individual factories we can hardly trace a bureaucratic managerial hierarchy and hierarchical authority relations. Thus, the engineers in such plants as Metal Works were themselves in authority, and thus within the surplus-value extracting process.

The workers appointed the engineers as skilled agents, in order to enable the workers themselves to exert technical (and, along with it, social) power. But in practice this appointment defeated its purpose. Though necessary, the move ultimately resulted in the defeat of the *shura*. The political/ideological solidarity of engineers could not effectively help a *shura* to sustain itself and to exert power; so long as the predetermined division of labour remained, the objective and real division would transcend the subjective intentions of solidarity.

In a dual power situation at the point of production, the mass of unskilled or semi-skilled workers (contrary to what Nichols and Beynon assert) could only exert what I would call a negative economic power;[6] they could oppose capital and halt production. In order to exert a positive economic power, replace capital and reproduce and sustain their power at the workplace, they had to transform the capitalist division of labour. To achieve this necessitated the seizure of political power. For many Marxists the question ends here. That is because for them power is conceived as an abstract notion, to be exerted in the same way by any group or individuals or to be transferred as soon as the agents change positions (this is formal power). Real power can be exerted by each class only in the ways appropriate and viable for that class. For example, the working class cannot exert power by the same methods as those appropriate and feasible for the bourgeoisie. Power is not a subject, but 'a system of relationships, a structure' (Gorz, 1982, p. 52). And power is meaningful only as long as it is exerted.

It seems reasonable to conclude that while the seizure of political power, i.e. the defeat of the old rulers, is necessary for workers' control and for the exertion of workers' power, it is not sufficient. A systematic attempt to change the dominant subordinating division of labour is the only viable strategy.

Notes

1. I am indebted to Professor Envard Abrahamian for bringing this to my attention.

2. The natural conception is expressed in the statement of a typical trade unionist worker, now a *shura* member in the Arj factory.

Q: What is the necessity of a management while you have a *shura*?

A: Well, I think there must be a management. I think (well, this is what I personally think, others may think in some other way) we cannot manage [without them]. Because in terms of literacy or intellectuality, we are not in the position, say, to contact abroad. You know 95% of our materials come from abroad; we must send telegrams, telex and such like. Therefore, we need a management to supply raw materials, and somehow run the factory.

Q: Is the problem just the fact that you can't speak English or you need some people to contact other countries?

A: Well, it *is* the problem. *But apart from speaking English and the rest, the fact is that, that is not our task; that is, everybody must do his own job. Suppose I am a worker, I must do my own work.*

3. Alan Fox distinguishes the two concepts of authority and power. The former is taken to refer to a relation in which 'subordinates legitimize the order-giving role of the superior, and although sanctions are deemed necessary to deter or punish transgression, these too are legitimized.' Power relations exist 'where sanctions are used to enforce conformity to norms which the subordinate perceives as illegitimate' (Fox, 1971, pp. 36-7). In our discussion, both of the concepts are applicable.

4. For an analysis of the notion of power in capitalist enterprise, see the highly controversial book by André Gorz, 1982, chapter 5.

5. Some writers underestimate the question of technical competence of the managers, technicians or other experts, arguing that it is possible for the workers to exert workers' control merely through a change in production relations. They ignore the technical division of labour itself as the source of differential power relations. André Gorz, for instance, in previous works (1978) advocates that view. While he rightly stresses the ideological role of technology under capitalism, he separates the two functions of management. This leads to his erroneous conclusion that it is possible to use the expertise and skills of engineers and experts without accepting their authority.

6. Nichols and Beynon argue that 'Skill is not essential to control. It is possible for unskilled workers, subdivided into routine repetitive jobs, to use their collective strength to oppose capital' (1977, p.108). As a matter of fact, opposition to capital is one matter; exertion of control over the production process another. Every day we are witnessing opposition by the workers against capital throughout

the world. But the opposition has *not* yet led to their actual control over the production process. The question of whether or not, and how, the division of labour can be abolished constitutes one of the most crucial issues of Marxist theory. For some remarks on this, see the concluding chapter.

10. The Politics of Industrial Relations in Post-Revolutionary Iran

Introduction

Industrial relations is a term widely used by industrial sociologists as well as by state officials; it is disliked by most Marxists. It has been defined as 'the study of processes of control over work relations' (Hyman, 1975a, p. 12) and deals with the attempts to exert control over work relations made by labour on the one hand and capital on the other. Work relations covers all relations to do with work and the workplace. 'Industrial relations' is, therefore, the study of aspects of class struggle in a particular sphere — the workplace — manifested in and mediated by various institutions and regulations.

In the case of Iran we have so far examined only one side of the struggle for control, that is, the exercise of control by labour, reflected in the *shura* movement. This chapter will analyse the other side: the strategies of state-capital to control work relations and the workforce. We shall deal with the objective and historical possibilities, limitations and contradictions of these strategies in the period 1979-83.

We have counterposed against labour the term state-capital instead of capital. This is because, as we have pointed out, the Islamic state in the form of *valayat-i faghih* took a somewhat autonomous position to capital. This implies that there was both correspondence and conflict between the interests of capital and state.

The reflection of this tense relationship may be most readily seen in the sphere of industrial relations. Below we start by examining the types of managerial strategies devised to control work relations and to overcome labour resistance and industrial crisis in the three periods following the Revolution.

The Strategies of Control

Ever since the emergence of capitalist industry various strategies to control work relations have been practised. Determined on the one hand by the law of value (i.e. the accumulation requirements in particular

Table 10.1
Types of Managerial Strategies

Forms of Strategies	*Technical Character*	*Social Character of Control* *Labour-Management Relationship*	
Structural strategies:			
Craft control	Control by labour over the means of production, unity of execution and conception	Formal subordination Simple control Master-apprentice relationship	Craft control
Taylorism	Detailed division of labour (DL); separation of conception from execution	Real subordination (RS) Bureaucratic control	Direct control
Fordism	Detailed DL based on automation	Bureaucratic, structural control (RS)	
Neo-Fordism	Job-enrichment	Bureaucratic control with autonomous work-group (RS)	
Relational strategies:			
Human relations school	Same techniques, but appeal to the sentiments of the labourer	Bureaucratic control with autonomous self-regulating work-groups (RS)	Responsible autonomy
Industrial psychology	Appeal to the instincts of the labourer		(RS)
Short-term profit maximization	'Irrational'	Ideological, political, military control (RS and FS)	Non-structural functional strategy

circumstances of capitalist development), and on the other, by the workers' resistance, managerial strategies were faced with inner contradictions and were thus transformed (see Friedman, 1977a). Table 10.1 summarizes the main strategies.

The strategies should be considered as falling into two broad categories: long-term steady profit maximization and simple short-run maximization. Any strategies are constrained and conditioned by the level of accumulation of capital and the character of the class struggle. A long-term strategy requires a systematic, thoughtful and detailed plan. This is distinct from the strategy of short-term maximization.

Let us first briefly clarify each of the concepts introduced in the table. Craft control has already been described in Chapter 5. This is not really a strategy of capital. Historically, subsequent strategies were initiated as alternatives to this form of labour process which is characterized by the high level of control, both technical and social, exerted by labour over the labour process. Craft control was dominant in the pre-monopoly stage of capitalism, and relied upon the detailed knowledge of all aspects of commodity production. The contradictions within this form of work relation were first revealed when the control exercised by labour over the production process ceased to be compatible with the requirements for capital accumulation. The second bottleneck is quite distinct from, though interrelated to, the first. In response to resistance and opposition, capital needed to adopt a strategy of real subordination of labour, not immediately for maximization purposes, but in order to subordinate labour ideologically, by dividing up the labour process, separating individual labourers and divesting them of judgement and will, so making them dependent upon the direction and control of non-labourers (Marx, 1979, pp. 449-50; Burawoy, 1982 and Gorz, 1978).[1] The development is not just a technical transformation, but also an ideological and social one. Hence the emergence of Taylorism.

Taylorism did not simply replace the craft control system, which continues, in a limited degree, even now. But capital required a new strategy compatible with its project of long-term profitability. Taylorism assumed that workers were motivated by rational calculations of their individual self-interests. Therefore it could be desirable to divide, as far as possible, the various motions of a single performance, assigning each to a single worker to perform. Payment of a higher wage to the first-class workers was assumed to compensate for the monotony and meaninglessness of work. At the same time, as well as the technical subordination resulting from the detailed division of labour and the strategic separation of conception from execution, hierarchical and structural control replaced the simple control of the craft system (Edwards, 1979 and Littler, 1982a; Rose, 1975). It was the accumulation process and progress of early twentieth-century monopoly capitalism that set up the material basis for this strategy (structural control). This is what Friedman calls direct control (1977b). The contradictions of Taylorism or direct control are demonstrated in the first instance by the fact that widespread division of labour extended the Taylorian labour process to most parts of an enterprise or industry, thus categorizing almost all workers as first-class workers with supposedly higher wages. In the second place, with the universal practice of this strategy in the competitive market, the law of value forced wages lower. Thirdly, contrary to Taylor's assumption, the will of the worker is not simply guided by economic motives (Friedman, 1977a, pp. 49-50). The ideology of possession among the Iranian workers offers relevant evidence to counter this.

Fordism, employed in America after the First World War, could not be an alternative to Taylorism. Fordism was the mechanized version of Taylorism. If, in the case of Taylorism, workers as fragmented organs were controlled immediately by piece-rate or time-rate mechanisms and supervisors, under the Fordist system they were controlled by automation, getting direction and guidance from the machines. Alain Lipietz, together with Aglietta, has conceptualized Fordism as a particular stage of global capitalism, and in so doing has added another important dimension to the concept. Lipietz refers to '*the continual adjustment of mass consumption* to the historically unprecedented rise in productivity generated by intensive accumulation' (my emphasis) (Lipietz, 1982 and Aglietta, 1979). This tendency for increase in the workers' real wages — due to the cheapening of goods necessary for the reproduction of his/her labour power because of higher productivity and despite a probable decline in the value of wages — has a decisive ideological impact upon the working class in their opposition to capitalism (Seabrook, 1978) and capitalist work organization. It is therefore not unlikely to alleviate the tensions resulting from the contradictions of Taylorism discussed above (in particular the wage cuts due to market competition).

The limitations and contradictions of Taylorism and Fordism produced resistance from the workforce in the forms of a 'high rate of absenteeism and of turnover, a large amount of wastage and of rejects, and an increase in stoppages and sabotage' (Palloix, 1976, p. 62). This led capital to seek alternative measures. As a result, a range of theories of industrial behaviour developed and were used experimentally with the aim of making work more interesting. Human factor industrial psychology (HFIP) emerged in Britain; the Human Relations school in both America (the Harvard Group and Chicago School) and in Britain (Tavistock Institute) (Rose, 1975). These schools, as Friedman (1977a, p. 52) summarized, with their emphasis on human instincts and sentiments,

> have suggested a combination of making the work itself more interesting (appealing to individual desires for sociability, security, challenge and variety), choosing workers who best fit in with the tasks required, and the sensitive and subtle exercising of managerial authority through the manipulation of sentiment — encouraging venom against competitors (particularly foreign), "counselling" non-cooperative workers, and encouraging a

feeling of team struggle through participatory and rewarded suggestion schemes, and the judicious payment of loyalty-inducing perks, such as company recreational facilities.

Industrial psychology and human relations theories were not the only alternatives. The main alternative strategy was the actual reorganization of the labour process in a way that was responsive to the resistance of the workforce such as neo-Fordism (Palloix)[2] or responsible autonomy (Friedman) or restrictive practices (Hyman and Elger) or job enrichment.

The new strategy, responsible autonomy, involves

allowing individual workers or groups of workers a wide measure of discretion over the direction of their work tasks, and the maintenance of managerial authority by getting workers to identify with the competitive aims of the enterprise, so that they will act "responsibly" with a minimum of supervision (Friedman, 1977a, p. 48).

The strategy of responsible autonomy or neo-Fordism is also prone to contradictions as long as it is operated in the context of a market economy. In contrast to the situation that predominates in Third World countries, in the advanced capitalist societies the rate of capital resiliency — the rate of response of capital to opportunity costs and the effects of market rationale — is high and enterprise management has become an active process. Management has to prepare to respond through continual reorgnization of tactics to ongoing changes and requirements which are independent of it. The need for higher rates of productivity brings a change in the pace of work and the introduction of new machinery, which require the consent of the workers, and thus an elaborate ideological apparatus for co-opting the leaders, and in particular the rank and file.[3] It is therefore likely that, as Friedman argues, the management will resort to the older strategies of direct control, in which case this would lead to the emergence of new fundamental tensions and contradictions (1977b, pp. 106-8).

Limitations and Historicity of Managerial Strategy

What followed were structural strategies of managerial control for a long-term profit maximization. The strategy of structural transformation of the labour process has to be compatible with the long-term functional policies of dominating the market, safeguarding opportunities for innovation, promoting brand familiarity and so on. The alternative to this strategy may be called short-term profit maximization, which is a set of functional policies.

According to this perspective, the manager/owner aims to achieve a rapid turnover of capital, lower costs and higher profit, even though these short-term objectives be in contrast to long-term stable profit maximization. He prefers raw and unskilled but cheap labour to expensive but skilled and stable labour; he prefers to produce goods of poor quality and lesser costs to better but more expensive ones. In short, the policy is a non-strategy which the manager inherits or has imposed upon him involuntarily through the logic of accumulation and political insecurity. This is the situation in most Third World countries.

Structural strategies have emerged in particular stages and conditions of capitalist development. Some require an ability for a drastic change in the organic composition of capital in favour of fixed capital share, like Fordism; for some — a change to a system of co-operation or Taylorism — this is not indispensable. Some strategies have as a prerequisite an ideologically paternalized workforce; such is the strategy of participation and any form of responsible autonomy. While craft control was the product of the strong bargaining power (of the skilled workers) in the late 19th Century, responsible autonomy is the product of monopoly capitalism, a strategy offered by capital in response to the resistance of a workforce.

An analysis of the limitations and possibilities of managerial strategy in post- (or pre-) revolutionary Iran has to be located in the context of the global distribution of technology and expertise which to a large extent, though by no means entirely, determines structural strategies both in the centre and the periphery. At this stage, therefore, the managerial strategy of the periphery has to be characterized.

Managerial Strategy and the Labour Process in the Third World

Frances Stewart, in her book *Technology and Underdevelopment* (1977), wrote,

> two or three hundred years ago, organisation [of production] in the now-advanced countries was probably not all that dissimilar to conditions in large parts of the underdeveloped countries today: traditional employment ties of a feudal or semi-feudal nature operated side-by-side with self-employed units (p. 61).

Despite the qualifying phrases this statement deserves criticism. Our whole argument is against such approaches. One of the major features of Third World development is its unevenness. As far as the organization of the production and labour process in these countries is concerned, this unevenness applies not only to a single country, but to the whole of the Third World. The Third World is not an homogeneous entity, but is characterized by, as Lipietz said, 'explosive fragmentation'.

Alain Lipietz divides the Third World into three categories. First, there are those countries mainly dominated by Taylorism in labour-intensive industries. This is the case in countries like Taiwan, Hong Kong, Singapore and South Korea which pursue the policy of export substitution. In such sectors 'the transferred jobs are typically fragmented and repetitive, not linked by any automated system of machinery' (1982, p. 41) e.g. they are jobs linked to sewing machines or electronic products such as calculators. Alongside the repressive Taylorist administration (structural strategy), political strategies are also required: the strategies of regulation (social legislation), repression and regimentation (p. 43).

The second category consists of those countries generally described as periphery Fordism. This is the strategy, adopted in countries in Eastern and Southern Europe, Brazil, South Korea, Mexico and Iran, of import substitution. The 'sub-Fordism' or the 'caricature of Fordist industrialization' in the Third World, according to Lipietz, is characterized by: (a) a combination of import- and export-substitution economies (as with Brazilian car assembly); (b) both a skilled and industrially-familiar unskilled labour force (cheap, close to major markets and endowed with a skilled component); and (c) commodities (e.g. cars which, unlike T-shirts or pocket calculators) have to find a large market nearby. The main thrust of Lipietz's argument is that this strategy of Fordism has failed in practice because of the industrial inexperience of the working class.

The third group consists of those countries whose economies are not dominated by Taylorism or Fordism.

I shall now return to the particular case of Iran, which is characterized by periphery-Fordism.

Firstly, there is an indigenous labour process (craft, Taylorism) which, even if overtaken by the modern technology introduced by foreign capital, continues to be reproduced. In this situation the two (modern and indigenous) labour processes either co-exist uneasily or co-operate alongside each other — albeit with tension.

The second characteristic, which is common in most Third World economies, is that alongside the backward indigenous sector there exists a relatively modern sector. As far as the choice and importing of technology is concerned, technological developments in the advanced industrialized countries impose their dictates upon the host economy by introducing highly modern techniques (Stewart, 1977, p. 59). Thus modern organization of production and management techniques (or the way in which the modern fixed capital is to be operated) is also imported.

Thirdly, despite the above point, the Fordism of the periphery is, technically speaking, still labour-intensive. This is because most modern industries tend to acquire a monopoly position because of the small size of the Third World market (see also Stewart, ibid., p. 64). The non-competitive conditions lead them not to bother to search for the most up-to-date technologies which would increase the fixed-capital cost.[4] As a result, the tendency towards deskilling does not occur at the same rate as in the centre. The organized workers therefore possess a strong bargaining power. Skill is still in great demand by capital in these countries (Bartsch, ILO, 1973).

The counter-tendency is for the modern technology in these countries to employ workers who come directly from the countryside and who are devoid of any industrial experience of wage labour. For them, therefore, real subordination takes place without resistance, unless they acquire sufficient work experience and industrial familiarity and the values which go with them.

Fourthly, Fordism is not simply a change in technology, but also a total change in the whole economy: introducing capital-intensive techniques, dramatic rise in labour productivity, mass production, production of cheaper commodities and higher real wages. Thus, mass consumption and change in the content of labour struggle going beyond wages and conditions. The periphery Fordism, however, is unable to adjust mass consumption to the rise in productivity generated by the modern technology. Higher wage demands are still more important than the demand for re-organization of the labour process; at best, protest over the latter issue expresses itself in the demand for higher wages. In this situation, the workplace becomes the centre of everyday tensions, and (if the opportunity arises) coherent industrial action. This means that, in Iran (and similar countries) the available structural strategies are unable to provide an appropriate strategy for control. In the absence of an ideological medium, the alternative strategy of responsible autonomy is likely to create a chaotic workplace, the alternative to which would be a return to direct control.

Managerial Strategies Under the Islamic State

We have analysed the patterns and limitations of the management system in the Iranian industry in Chapter 5. The same underlying trend still exists after the Revolution. The three forms of management, semi-craft, traditional and modern rational, which characterize the management system should be regarded as the consequence of the form of industrialization in Iran (as a part of the Third World). We also concluded in Chapter 5 that the failure of structural strategies to control labour made the alternative strategy of political oppression inside the factories indispensable.

We are now in a position to analyse the possibilities and contradictions of the alternative set of strategies, functional strategies, which the Islamic state has attempted to pursue in the face of industrial crisis. By controlling the labour force and raising labour productivity, the regime hopes to recover from the crisis, the political consequences of which are of great concern to the regime. All these measures have to be analysed bearing in mind the unique and contradictory nature of the Islamic state.

Two Forms of Management: Liberal and *Maktabi*
Industrial relations in Iran have strong political connotations. This trend was reinforced after the Revolution when inter-state factional conflicts

were directly reflected in industrial relations. The dual forms of management are one outcome.

Liberal Management: This policy was in line with that of Prime Minister Bazargan in the second period. It obeyed the logic of capital (as a social relation), and involved respect and support for technocracy and the implementation of rational, scientific management, dispensing with Islamic idiom. Liberal management advocates one-man management from above; maximization of profit through structural and functional strategies; work ideology in its utilitarian concept; secularism in production (people can hold what opinions they like so long as they do not disrupt profitability) and the policy of containment in the sense of less use of naked force and more peaceful settlement of disputes.

By the end of the second phase, and with the clergy possessed of the entire state power in June 1981, liberal managers were losing the battle to the *maktabi* management. Three trends played a part in this transformation. Firstly, the limitations and contradictions of liberal management in relation to the *shuras*, that is, one-man management vs. control by the *shura*. The logic of liberal management was totally unacceptable to the *shuras* (both independent and corporatist) who resisted, fought and expelled the former. Secondly, as a direct reflection of the anti-liberal campaign of the IRP, liberal managements were under attack from Islamic Associations. And thirdly, these managers did not show much resistance against such opposition; they were either tried and/or sacked by the workers (in Fanoos Company), or simply resigned (Pars Metal). They did not see any attraction in staying in positions which did not fulfil their socio-political interests.

Maktabi Management: This was a form of managerial control and industrial rationale which manifested itself in the policies and attitudes of particular managers and was introduced late in the second and throughout the third periods. *Maktabi* management arose because of the inability of liberal management to bring about industrial peace. It was mediated, in post-Revolutionary power politics, by the ideology, rationale and policies of the ruling clergy.

It is management by those whose position derives not from certain relevant skills (education or experience) but is based mainly on character and personal, or more importantly, ideological connections with the ruling clergy, especially the IRP. (This does not imply that all managers lacked managerial skills.) They were in authority to preserve the presence of the ruling party in the factories, these being the most vulnerable parts of Iranian society. For them the policy of worker participation was limited to the corporatist *shuras* and Islamic Associations. In essence, their major policy was repressive one-man management; if they did not achieve this, they demanded workers' cooperation in a participatory management structure. Their strategy was hierarchical Islamic corporatism. Whilst profit maximization was their main objective, it was not the only one. By nature, *maktabi* management is committed to certain ideological and political measures, the implementation of which disrupts production or wastes working time. This is only one of the contradictions of Islamic management: in order to exert ideological control over the workplace, i.e. in order to identify the non-Islamic workers and to cleanse the factories of them, the management has to Islamicize the factory by holding compulsory daily prayer ceremonies, delivering speeches and so on. These practices create disruptions and wastage in production.[5] This type of manager views the secularism of liberal managers as anti-Islamic. They use force and tight control instead of peaceful dispute settlement and reformist mediums — a policy of repulsion rather than incorporation.

The implication of this approach is that, in practice, there is a tendency to create and support ideological gangs — informal workers' organizations which are the functionaries of different external organizations of factional powers, such as Islamic Associations of IRP, *Pasdaran* (Revolutionary Guards) and *Basij* (mobilization organization) etc. Such alliances are based on ideological/political and tactical considerations. This tactical aspect is crucial for a management which seeks to spy on militant and politically independent workers, to crush the militant *shuras* — in a word to use force.

This strategy has its own contradiction. The use of pressure gangs (such as IAs) as executive agents for implementing unpopular policies in essence grants them (IAs) a degree of power which, because of the strong support of the state, is likely to assume a relative autonomy against the (Islamic) management itself. This is indeed what happened in the third period. In some cases it involved armed confrontation between the two old allies.[6]

Maktabi management, when confronted with the workers' militancy, employs repressive methods; and unlike liberal management they struggle to stay in their positions, since they do have an interest in the system. *Maktabi* management reflects the character, contradictions and the crisis of the ruling clergy, mediated by the realities of industrial life.

The limitations and internal contradictions of these two types of management have been examined. But, as Friedman rightly states, contradiction does not mean impossibility, but rather, the persistence of fundamental tensions deriving from within (1977a, p. 53). Whatever the contradictions of the *maktabi* management, it is not tolerant of diversity and the autonomy of labour. So if managers remain in their positions they do not tolerate the development of independent unions. This will be a crucial hardship for the working class in future.

Let us now turn to see what strategies the state had to adopt to deal with the fundamental questions of control of labour power on the one hand, and of the workforce on the other.

Industrial Crisis and the Management Strategy

The metamorphosis of managerial types and managerial strategies should be conceived as the product of the dialectic of capital and the state: the requirement of capital to reproduce itself (in terms of economic and social relations) and the restrictive imperatives of the Islamic state.

Thus the assumption is that the economic, and in particular the industrial crisis, following the Revolution (in the second period) is of a more political than economic character. Economic crisis applies to a situation where capital with a power of free movement falls into a contradiction created from within. During this process, it may call external determinants (state, religion, family) into the service of solving its contradictions. However, the crisis becomes political when those external forces affect the 'natural' movement of capital and its ultimate goal of accumulation.

In post-Revolutionary Iran the profitability of capital came under two pressures: direct and indirect pressure from the state and workers' class struggle.

Direct and Indirect Effects of State Pressure: The state was unable to define its position toward capital, especially industrial capital. The clearest indication of this was the fact that by this date (late 1985) and after years of debates and seminars the state has been unable to set limits to private capital accumulation, i.e. the limits of *mashrou* or acceptable or Islamic private property holding.[7] As a result of that matter and political insecurity private capital is therefore reluctant to invest in the productive sector. After a sharp decline during the revolutionary upheaval, industrial investment in 1982-83 was still only one-third of its 1977-78 value.[8] Small-scale workshops, however, are likely to have grown as a result of the crisis in large-scale industry, protectionist measures such as exemption from unpaid insurance rates, and, more importantly, reviving the master-client relations of production as the only structural managerial policy toward self-sufficiency (*Jomhour-i Islami*, 23 May 1962).[9] These policies are underlaid by a populist ideology of 'small is beautiful' dominant among the ruling clergy.

The lack of appropriate conditions for industrial capital has inevitably led to a boom in mercantile capital which is characteristically functional almost in any circumstances, be it in war or famine, or pre-capitalist social formations.[10] The inevitable concentration of (70% of value of ouptut) large-scale industry, after the nationalization of ownerless plants, under the direction of the state has created a chaotic bureaucracy. This chaos has had a direct impact in particular upon planning strategy, purchases and credit systems.

The state-run industry is supervised by 15 state organizations, including banks, *Bonyad-i Mostazafin* (the Downtrodden Foundation), the Organization of National Industry (ONI) (with about 600 plants) and the Organization of Development and Reconstruction of Industries. In this situation, as the Minister himself stated, 'the management of one single factory may be shared by five or six organizations!' The mismanagement of plants is the consequence.

A rational systematic management (capitalist or whatever) requires a highly skilled labour force and technocrats whose particular cultural and political interests (let alone economic) have to be provided for. If those cultural or political relations are not reproduced in the new environment, the intelligentsia is unlikely to co-operate under the present conditions. The socio-political relations (social 'Islamicization') that the state requires is by nature in contradiction to the socio-political aspirations of the intelligentsia.[11]

Table 10.2
Selected Indices for the Large Manufacturing Establishments (1974=100)

	1976/7	*1977/8*	*1978/9*	*1979/80*	*1980/81*	*1981/2*	*1982/3*
Production	134.6	150.0	129.1	129.7	121.7	137.5	157.6
Employment	117.3	119.6	126.3	132.8	136.8	141.9	149.4
Compensation paid to workers	167.8	209.8	325.7	526.7	630.3	683.4	762.6
Per capita production	113.9	125.5	100.7	92.7	83.0	89.7	98.8

*Excludes the sugar industry and slaughter houses

Source: Bank Markazi Iran, *Annual Reports*, various issues.

Workers' Class Struggle: This is another major determinant of the industrial crisis of productivity. The state/capital attacks against the *shuras'* imposition of authoritarian measures, and decline in real wages, have led the workers to resort to various forms of struggle. Workers' initial ideas of 'work as ideology' and commitment to work 'for our Revolution' have declined drastically. 'Both at the time of *Taughour* [Shah] and now, there are only words — all talk and no action. Both then and now; nothing happened. It's just bloody show.' (Arasteh factory worker, February 1981)

> If they outlaw the *shura*, from then on the workers will never let them [the managers] inside here. If they dissolve the *shura*, they *themselves* must go. (A worker in Metal Works)

Workers, thus, have resorted to a variety of protests and illegal industrial actions: petitioning, sit-ins, the detention of managers, strikes, sabotage, go-slows and poor quality production. In the post-revolutionary era, the year 1979-80 marked the climax of the working-class industrial actions. In this year some 366 industrial incidents (see table 10.3) were reported. The number declined to 180 in 1980-81, and to 82 in 1981-82 as a result of the mounting repression which forced the workers to resort to covert industrial action. 1984-85, however, marked the start of a wide-spread working-class struggle when 200 industrial incidents were reported. Of these 90 were illegal strikes, the most important of which being the strike of Isfahan Steel mill workers against the redundancy programme (see Chapter 7).

Figure 10.1
Trend of Wage Increases, 1977-83

Source: *Quarterly Economic Review*: Iran, 1985

The working-class struggle together with disruption in management and administration contributed substantially to the negative growth rate of industrial productivity in the post-revolutionary years. According to the official figures, production per worker declined with an annual rate of 10.6% since 1978 (table 10.2). In 1981, the Minister of Labour admitted that the 'disturbances within the factories' resulted in a production decline of 30% (*Jomhouri Islami*, 20 May 1981). There is no accurate figure for 1981-82, except that the state industries made a loss of Rls 60b (£04.b), and that the industries overall were running at just over half their capacity (51.2%) (Ministry of Planning and Budget). It was not until 1982-83 that the adequate supply of raw materials resulted in positive growth in the rate of production-per-worker in relation to the loss of the previous years. Yet, after five years the net value was still 27% below its pre-revolutionary peak value (table 10.2).

Table 10.3
The Forms of Workers' Struggles in 12 Months after Revolution

Forms of struggle	Feb-March 1979	March-April	April-May	May-June	June-July	Total 5 months	July-August	Aug-Sept	Sept-Oct	Oct-Nov	Nov-Dec	Dec '79-Jan '80	Jan-Feb '80
1. Verbal protest, petitioning, leafletting	4	20	10	11	16	61	2	1		1	5	2	1
2. Formation of assembly (stopping work temporarily)	12	9	5	5	5	36	1	1		1	2	1	1
3. Strikes	19	2	14	11	30	76	2	3	5	4	3	2	1
4. Sit-ins	18	15	8	13	17	75	1	1		1	2	1	1
5. Street demonstrations	4	3	2	1	1	12	1	1	1	1			1
6. Ban on the sale of product	2	2	2	7	5	18							
7. Detaining employers, managers; preventing them attending the plant, or sacking them	5	2		9	3	19					1	1	2
8. Occupation of plants, controlling and running, or managing it by workers, or formation of shura	7	6	4	5	6	30	2		2	1	2		2
9. Other forms	2	3	5	6	4	20				1	1		
Total reported confrontations with the Pasdaran	8	3	8	11	11	41	3	3	2	4	2		3
Total no. of the reported affected units	54	51	44	45	61	255	6	6	9	7	11	4	10

Source: Compiled from various Registered Labour Reports in the left-wing papers Kar and Paykar.

The Crisis of Productivity

The concept of a crisis of productivity is intimately related to the structural limitations of state-capital to exploit and control the labour power at the point of production. It seems obvious that the most appropriate method of countering such a crisis would be to set up a structural strategy to exert structural control (as opposed to simple control); to set up the labour process in such a way that the objective process and structure extract surplus-value. This would require a transformation in the labour process and high expenditure on fixed capital, machinery, managerial education and so on. The present state in Iran is unable financially and private capital is reluctant to carry out this modernization.

The alternative policies have been a return to the past and a resort to a) absolute extraction of surplus-value (in conditions of real subordination), b) Taylorism (in the large-scale industries), and c) master-apprentice systems (in small-scale ones). The two first strategies have acted as alternatives to, and are being replaced by, one another.

Absolute Surplus-Value Extraction

Hours of work have been extended and wages have been cut. A shorter working week (40 hours a week) was one of the major demands of the industrial workforce after the Revolution when, in many places, the workers themselves put the demand into practice (notably in the oil industry and in car manufacturing). Despite the resistance and non-recognition by the state of the 40-hour week, and despite the formal ratification of a 44-hour week by the Revolutionary Council, the practice continued unevenly in various workplaces (in the oil industry for over two years until after the June Days of 1981). This achievement was attacked as the independent *shuras* were disintegrated.

The policy of wage cuts was implemented through a series of cuts in benefits and perks. The most important of all has been the abolition of profit-sharing schemes which operated in 1,200 large industrial units under the Shah. A major year-end bonus had become customary. Abolished in February 1981, it was replaced by a formula of 20 days' wages times the number of years worked (with a maximum of Rls 85,000), which was by and large below the customary year-end bonus. This led to widespread wild-cat strikes and protests in February-March 1981. Although independent from the state, the private sector wholeheartedly obeyed the pay policy. In May 1981 the Job Classification scheme was virtually dismantled. The scheme would have financially benefited those qualified by skill and long periods of service. The new policy of annual wage increases (which did not increase the minimum wage), treated all strata of workers as equal (an increase of Rls 40 = 25p per day) and inflicted a wage cut upon the well-paid workers. The rest of the wage increase (up to Rls 50) depended on harder work.[12] In summer 1982, Tavakkoli, the Minister of Labour, cut back the every-other-year bonus (a car) plus some other bonuses which had been won by the car industry workers.

Shift work (quantitatively more utilization of the existing fixed capital) has been put into operation. The problem with this programme is that the machines are all too old for over-utilization. As the industrial officials admit, one of the major technical problems is the amortization of the machines, which, if shift work continues, might lead to their total collapse (*Kayhan*, 17 January 1983). The alternative strategy is to exploit labour without necessarily increasing the cost of fixed capital — that is, a version of Taylorism.

Taylorism?

The strategy of raising productivity, through bonus systems, above the standard level, and based upon work study, was first proposed in the Arj factory in May 1981. The objective of the plan reflected the prevalent crisis at the time: 'with the implementation of the Plan the worker will be given a better impetus for higher productivity' and, more crucially, 'because of the interdependent nature of production line and existence of motivation, *the workers will prevent some of their colleagues from engaging in go-slows*' (*Jomhouri Eslami*, 30 May 1981).

Two months later, the Ministry of Labour announced a plan of a similar nature (the Plan of Bonus Payments to the workers in *Ettelāāt*, 3 August 1981). According to this plan, which was to replace the abolished profit-sharing and year-end customary bonuses, each worker would get a 1% wage increase for a 1% increase in total standard output. The standard level of output was to be calculated on the basis of the point of balance (a level of output in a situation where the income and the cost of a workplace were equal), the average output of the previous four years, timing and customary practices. The ultimate criterion would be the one which indicated the highest figure (Articles 1-3). The more interesting point is the very short period of calculation of standard output — monthly, though with mutual agreement up to a maximum three months (Article 5). This meant that if the workers wanted to get a (1%) wage increase they themselves would have to raise the level of standard output on a monthly basis, while their wage basis would remain the same. This would result in output rising higher than actual pay. Even in capitalist logic, over-production of output means *over*-work (such as overtime) the monetary equivalent of which is higher than the normal wage. In addition, in terms of labour relations, as an act of collective bargaining, this plan required an independent workers' organization to exert control over its implementation. This right is continually violated in Iran.

Introduced under Mir Sadeghi, a Labour Minister who supported the corporatist *shuras*, the plan was virtually repudiated by Tavakkoli (the new Labour Minister not sympathetic to even corporatist *shuras*) who proposed a Labour Law which was founded upon the free agreement of the individual employer on the one hand and the individual labourer on the other.

Master-Apprentice System

In May 1981 an official seminar on labour relations proposed a bill to the Supreme Council of Labour, that

> for the purpose of support for the master-apprentice system as a means to cut dependency ties, and to give technical training to the raw labour force, the trades and craft works may be allowed to operate outside the considerations of the Labour Law (*Jomhouri Eslāmi*, 23 May 1981).

The proposal, which was later ratified, implied that in order to raise the level of output with lower cost the employers were allowed to disregard basic workers' rights, such as limited hours of work, a minimum wage level, restriction on child labour, conditions of work, internal work relations and so on which had operated under the Shah. It could cover the areas characterized by the semi-craft system of control analysed in Chapter 5, encompassing some 300,000 workshops and 500,000 workers. This strategy was another example of how the productivity crisis encouraged paradoxically pre-industrial production relations. Despite its considerable impact upon employment creation, the workshops, because of their very low productivity of labour, were unable to contribute substantially to the demands of the market.

Crisis of Hegemony

The productivity crisis was a crisis of the control of abstract labour. However, the working class under capitalism is not merely a commodity (labour power) to be exchanged; it is above all a number of human beings who are historically located in particular economic and socio-political circumstances, and who react, resist, oppose and think. In other words, the labour force (as distinct from abstract labour) also has to be controlled itself in and outside the point of production, for short- and long-term purposes. If a state-capital is by nature unable to exert that control over its labour force, we may characterize this as a crisis of hegemony. We shall discuss below the various strategies adopted by the Islamic state to secure that hegemony, categorized into three main areas of control: institutional, ideological and political.

Institutional Control

The Islamic state is characteristically afraid of any form of autonomous organization. For the latter, as an earthly entity, is very likely to develop and become a rival to the government of God mediated by the present mundane state. However, organization as such is a major aspect of this state apparatus. Thus, any existing institution has to serve the Islamic state.[13] In reality, however, the state organizations serve not as a structure for integrating the populace — i.e. as a means of creating a feeling of unity and identity — but as an organization of control. In short, the attempts by the state to institutionalize discontent among the working class have by and large failed.

Ideological Control

Ideology plays an underpinning role in the regime of the *valāyat-i faghih*. For the latter, Islamic society means, in one sense, bringing all aspects of individual and social life under the observation and interpretation of the Islamic ideology as interpreted by the ruling clergy. Intervention in and interpretation by the latter of work relations result in distinct forms of ideological control over the working class. Ideological control may manifest itself in the particular interpretation of work ideology, corporatist ideology and Islamization of workplaces.

Work ideology is concerned, on the one hand, with the question of how people perceive the very act of working, and of why they work; and on the other, with the idea of work which the dominant classes or elements advocate. Work ideology both specifies and is the product of a particular historical conjuncture, depending on a complex of determinants.

For the ancient Greeks, work was simply a curse. So was it for the Romans. Up to the time of Luther and the early development of capitalism, which was seen as being without intrinsic value, 'simply an instrument of purification, charity and expiation' (Fox, 1971, p. 3). In the Protestant ethic, however, all distinctions between religious piety and worldly activity were swept aside (ibid). The Calvinist ideology of work was the foundation of modern factory discipline. Meanwhile, as Hill argues, work was praised and idleness was regarded with contempt, since 'property was justified by work and was not justified without it, so that idleness should be followed by expropriation' (in Anthony, 1977, p. 45). This was a utilitarian conception of work. A work ideology may be one which values 'work as a social and moral duty (implying stigma and shame for those who did not fulfil it)'. This was part of the pre-Fascist Italian working-class culture (Passerini, 1979, p. 93).

The crisis of productivity and a strategy of ideological control combined with the religious character of the Iranian state to advocate work, first and foremost, as a religious duty.

> The hours of work are the moments of *(ebādat)* worshipping God, paying debt to martyrs, the deprived people and the downtrodden of society. Wasting even one moment is equivalent to violating the rights of the deprived, and to disrespecting the blood of the martyrs.[14]

Based upon a *hadis* (quotation) from Prophet Mohammed that 'to work is like *Jihad* in the service of God', the instrumentalist religious conception of work is widely employed by the *valayat-i faghih* to raise the productivity of labour. It advocates that the performance of work brings rewards which are not material, but spiritual, granted not in this world but in the next, in heaven. However, the penalty for misconduct is a matter for both worldly punishment as well as God's revenge, in the world to come. This view is widely propagated by the special factory clergies.

Quite distinct from an instrumentalist (tactical) application, the ruling clergy still propounds the principal (ideological) conceptions. One version is the same as the work ideology of early primitive Christianity: a means of promoting the health of the body and soul, guarding against evil, idleness and decadence. It is in this context that Khomeini addresses the workers: 'One day of your life is worth all the lives of the capitalists and the feudals put together' (Khomeini's speech on May Day 1981).

As for the individual labourer, there is a wide gap between the fundamental and pragmatic view of the ruling clergy. Pragmatically, primarily as a reaction to the socialist and radical views on labour, the regime grants great dignity and religious piety to labour and to the labourer. The case is exemplified in the widely expressed *hadis* that 'Prophet Muhammad kisses the hands of a worker', and that 'labour is the manifestation of God'. And,

> the value of work and the worker in Islam is higher than that in any other materialist ideology (*maktab*). Following the Islamic world view, we view work and the worker to hold divine value, not merely material value. A worker is one who, obeying the command of God, endeavours to develop the earth and its materials . . . Thus, the workers are of divine value; and obeying that command is a divine and Islamic duty; it is not merely of a material value (President Khamanei, May Day 1981).

On the other hand, the worker is essentially assumed to be a mere commodity or an object so that the procedures for its exchange, according to Labour Minister Tavakkoli, are to be found in the section on *hiring* (not employment) in the Islamic *Feghh*. While under German Fascism, 'the labour relationship is a community relationship based on honour, faith and care' (Neumann, 1979, p. 342), the proposed Iranian Labour law is based on individual agreement according to which labour is hired for a certain period to conduct certain kinds of work.[15]

The other contradiction confronting the regime is the fact that by dignifying the work and worker the social and political significance of workers becomes manifest; interestingly, the alternative strategy, that of terrorizing the workers, would have the same result. There are countless examples suggesting that the state equates any limited trade union demand and action with the 'extended operations of imperialism', and so places it next only in abhorrence to Iraq's invasion or the abortive US operation in the Iranian desert (see *Jomhouri Eslāmi*, 5 December 1981).

In the *valayat-i faghih*'s ideology, atomization of workers in the workplace goes side by side with the integration of the whole working class into one single ideological mass: *Ummat-i Eslāmi* (Islamic mass). In Fascism, the denial of individuality took the form of a massive labour front with 25 million members. The Islamic state, however, strives to deny the 'classness' of the working class.

The workers must approach the labour questions through the Islamic view. The differences in expectations and trade demands must not divide the various layers of population, must not damage the Islamic brotherhood. The *(elhadi)* atheist ideologies attempt to use these means to define the workers as a class, so separating them from the Islamic *ummat* (people) crushing the unity of Muslim *ummat* (President Khamenei, ibid).

The denial of the working class has been accompanied by a denial of those manifestations and symbols which express it; by changing the word *kārgar* (worker) to *karpazir* (one who agrees to do work). This is an attempt to destroy the main identity of a worker — his name. By such a strategy, the Labour Ministry attempted to end the idea of *kārgar* which is so widely associated with the words socialism, left and *enghelab-i kargari* (workers' revolution). This shows how certain historical-cultural symbols become a subject of (class) struggle.

Referring to the massive propaganda campaign carried out by the Nazis, Franz Neumann reflected, 'Propaganda is violence committed against the soul. Propaganda is not a substitute for violence, but one of its aspects. The two have the identical purposes of making men amenable to control from above' (1969, p. 356). *Valayat-i faghih*'s means of commanding people's will is the use of massive propaganda machines based on modern and traditional mediations. As for the workers, Islamization of workplaces goes hand in hand with the Islamization (better to say regimentation) of leisure. The factory is assumed to be a barricade against *koffar* (infidels), where the *agirs* (labourers) have to listen to official religious sermons as well as perform 'the divine duty of production'. Hence, massive dispatches of factory *mullas*, a religious transformation of the atmosphere in factories, the putting up of special pictures, posters, huge slogans on the walls and the loud broadcasting of official speeches during break and lunchtimes etc.[16] At every moment the state is announcing its presence to each and every individual.

Political Control

When ideological control fails, political control becomes inevitable. The state strategy of ideological control has, to a large extent, failed among the working class. They have rejected work ideology based upon religious duty, even though the workers themselves had initially developed a strong populist work ideology and work commitment immediately after the revolution.[17]

The strategy of political control of the workforce functions through the mediation of some workers' organizations (Islamic Associations) and direct political-military liquidation by the repressive Islamic state apparatuses: *Pasdaran* and the committee guards.

Islamic Associations: Islamic Associations (IAs) are the most important labour organizations the *valayat-i faghih* can utilize to exert political control over the workforce. They therefore merit a more detailed consideration. According to the constitution of the Islamic Republic, the IAs were set up for Islamic educational, cultural and social purposes. In practice, however, they acted, with the encouragement of leading founders of the IRP, as an alternative labour organization for the independent *shuras*. The internal dynamism and socio-political role of the IAs are determined by the dialectic of, on the one hand, the inter-factional conflicts within the state, which we have referred to frequently, and on the other, by the internal (ideological) attributes of the IAs.

The IAs were gradually set up in the first period of control from below. The second period of management from above saw their rapid growth as the conflict between the ruling clergy and the liberals erupted during the US embassy seizure. The Labour House (*Khane-i Kargar*), once the central headquarters of the independent and radical *shuras*, was ransacked and became the headquarters of the IAs, and later, of the corporatist *shuras*. The IRP now utilized the IAs as its direct arm inside the workplaces to oppose resisting *shuras*, on the one hand, and liberal managements on the other, advocating instead Islamic *shuras* and Islamic *(maktabi)* managements. When the inter-factional confrontations surfaced after the war (with Iraq) and culminated in the July Days, the IAs enjoyed great support. Prime Minister Rajaii, a man of the ruling clergy — whose strategy of merging IAs and *shuras* had been defeated — addressed the workers in March 1981 and said, 'I am standing by my word; and I am proud to say again, that "we shall support the IAs as long as there is blood in our veins",' and continued, 'You! Member of IA! You would have reached the point of purity when you recognize only the *Imam* as political leader' [as opposed to President Bani'Sadr]. The third period, following the July Days of 1981, was characterized by the consolidation of the positions of Islamic management and IAs, followed by a period of confrontations between the two. The historical mission of the IAs seemed to be over. The growing authority of the IAs, which would in practice threaten the authority of management, was opposed by the new Labour Minister Tavakkoli. Khomeini and other officials called on the IAs to concentrate their activities only on social and cultural matters. This official rebuff to the IAs resulted in managements (both *maktabi* and liberal) gaining the upper hand, and a wave of dismissals of the activists of both the IAs and Islamic *shuras*.[18] While such moves were backed by the Labour Minister associated with the hard-line *Hojjatieh* faction, the populist and pragmatic faction, followers of the *Imam*'s line, still did not (and do not) wish to alienate such instrumental organizations; though at the same time they attempted to limit their power to the sphere of consultation instead of decision-making. Musavi Ardabili, the head of the judiciary, formulated their function in the statement, '[in a factory] the management is the brain, the IA the eyes, the rest the hands' (*Kayhan*, 11 March 1983). Following this shift in policy, the settlement of disputes between the IA and Islamic *shura* members was assigned to a revolutionary tribunal situated in the Labour Ministry.

The IAs, it is clear, were the product of a particular set of contradictions. They themselves, by their very nature, also continue to be contradictory entities. The role of IAs is one thing for each faction of the ruling caste in their power struggle and quite another for workers. It is to the latter that we now turn. The actual functions of the IAs may be summarized as follows:

1) Indoctrination of labour with the ruling ideology. The official title given to this function is cultural activities.[19] It is concerned with the Islamization of the whole atmosphere of the factories through organizing meetings, exhibitions, mass prayers, publishing and distributing Islamic papers, organizing ideological classes and eliminating Western culture (ibid., pp. 23-36). In this sphere, the translation of the concepts of labour relations into Islamic idioms assumes a particular significance: a sit-in or strike becomes an anti-Islamic action *(heram)* and the price to be paid is defined. It is the IA which decides what actions are Islamic and what anti-Islamic.

2) Policing the workplace. The official version of this function is political activity. The *Guideline* is absolutely clear on this crucial task: 'To reject the elements opposed to the Islamic revolution' (p. 37), 'to fight against [political] groups and counter the deviationist lines; to stop and search those non-workers intending to enter the factory' (p. 38), 'to give resolute support to Islamic [political] currents, and to condemn and liquidate entirely the anti-Islamic currents'. This official task gives total authority to its members to check and spy on the workers who complain or put forward simple economic demands. The Commission for Identifying the Labour Force, organized by the IAs of ONI, provided the criteria for identifying counter-revolutionaries inside the factories (in *Internal Bulletin*, March 1981); that is those involved in 'discouraging workers to the future of the revolution; unreasonable demand-making; provocation of workers and rumour spreading; unjustifiable criticisms; lack of honesty; dependence on East and West and affiliation with counter-revolutionary groups' (i.e. socialists and Mudjahedin or any other pro-working class organizations). These criteria speak for themselves.

The effect of such policies, in particular in the July Days and after, was devastating for the workers' movement. In this period, long blacklists of opposition workers were submitted to the internal and external armed *Pasdaran*, who, with the close co-operation of the IAs, carried out mass arrests.

Prior to the July Days, the *Khane-i Kargar* (Labour House), the centre of IAs, became so powerful that it could independently organize resistance cells inside the factories. Their tasks were intelligence, military and ideological-political. A document explains the tasks of the intelligence unit as, among others, 'to identify reliable individuals and those committed to the Revolution'; 'to identify non-Islamic, deviant elements'; 'to infiltrate the members of *shura*, IA and the management, checking their move-ments'; 'to report the available information to the leadership of the cell'; and lastly 'to obey conscientiously the leadership of the cell' (*Enghelab-i Islami*, 17 March 1981). Pursuing a political objective, the IAs were committed to give military training to their members, forming military *Basij* (mobilization) groups.

3) Mobilizing role. This was what the *Guideline* termed 'social activities' (pp. 41-51) and concerned not only the workplace, but also, more importantly, society at large. At the workplace they mobilized their members or other amenable workers to break strikes; to collect contribu-tions for war refugees, to encourage workers to be dispatched to the war fronts; to secure constant contact with the workers' families of war victims. In this sphere, IAs attempt to mobilize the workers on moral and ideological bases.

The external role was more significant, as the IAs attempted to mobilize workers in pro-regime demonstrations and rallies, or — in official terminology — 'to be present actively on the political scene of the country' (*Guideline*, pp. 40, 45). The July Days of 1981 saw the IAs adopt an active mission of mobilization to organize counter-demonstrations against opposition rallies.

Who are the activists of the IAs? No research has ever been carried out to identify who these workers are, and why they are so destructive. Our observation at a car factory in Teheran suggests that four groups of workers were members of the IA. a) The ex-foremen or ex-supervisors whose interests, in terms of both financial and authority relations, were jeopardized by the revolutionary movement. They joined IAs by adopting an appearance of Islamic behaviour because they saw the IA as a vehicle for disruption; b) a few workers who, apart from work in industry, had land and agricultural activities near Teheran, who were probably in search of a position through the IA and who had no fear of risk of indirect wage cuts or of the management strategies which the IAs would defend; c) the workers whose close relatives were influential in the government or in clerical circles; and lastly d) those workers who believed that the state was pro-*mastazaf* (downtrodden). The agents in higher echelons of the IA enjoy the material rewards of their social position and political status and role.

The nature of their tasks (and my observations) suggest that, quite apart from even corporatist *shuras*, their power rests not on workers' support, but rather on careful support by the state which gives them significant power of manoeuvre. By the mass of workers, they are viewed as new SAVAK agents who grow beards instead of wearing ties.

Militarization of the Factories: Policing the factories was completed by a militarization process. Its major function is the creation of an atmosphere of terror and insecurity for the militant. In their turn, various formal and informal organizations have set up their own labour military units which are designed to organize their own loyal workers and give them military training: among these are the Organization of *Mudjahedin* of the Islamic Revolution (not the opposition *Mudjahedin-e Khalgh*), *Khane-i Kargar*, *Sepah-i Pasdaran* (revolutionary guards), committee guards, *Basij-i Mustazafin* (mobilization units). In the troubled factories armed and uniformed military units patrol, and in some plants, notably car plants, full units of committee guards are stationed to be in control of the day-to-day movements of the workers.

Conclusion

We have seen so far that industrial relations in post-revolutionary Iran (and probably any country with similar circumstances) have been extensively intermingled with politics. This implies that the present industrial crisis is not merely economic but is also political and has, in practice, been caused by and resulted in a perpetual covert resistance and non-co-operation of the labour force. The co-operation of labour (by any means) is indispensable for industrial prosperity in a situation where the implementation of the structural strategies of managerial control (advanced Taylorism, Fordism, neo-Fordism and so on) suffer from severe limitations — the characteristic of most of the Third World countries.

This has two important implications. In the specific case of Iran, the present political form is unlikely, by its very nature, to be able to secure the co-operation of the labour force. The crisis is therefore likely to remain. On the other hand, it is possible for an alternative democratic political form to transcend the existing crisis, despite the persistence of structural limitations; but this can only happen by the strategy of extensive democratic participation and free involvement of the producers in their actual process of labour.

Notes

1. See in particular the historical study by Marglin in Gorz, 1976, p. 20. Palloix is right to criticize the one-sidedness of such a position; but he underestimates capital's need for profit maximization (Palloix, 1976, p. 62).

2. Neo-Fordism is not an appropriate term, since it implies a continuity with Fordism, whereas the actual practices and ideological effects of the two strategies are different.

3. The resistance of the workers in the printing (newspaper) industry in Britain is noticeable; in particular the long strike of SOGAT members in 1983 against the *Financial Times* management plan to introduce new machinery.

4. There is a big difference between the techniques used in Talbot in Iran and that in Britain for production of the same car.

5. This contradiction is obvious in the two statements made by the Minister of

Industry in one interview. On the one hand he stated,

> A maktabi manager, the one who runs a factory in an Islamic system, is not merely a manager, but also the leader of that small society. He has a duty to direct the society towards ideological, cultural and economic dimensions; his task should not be just to achieve a high productivity (*Ettelāāt*, 1 August 1982).

On the other hand, in reference to the existing conflicts:

> I view the problems as social [in fact political]. If our chaotic social problems were solved, that problem will also be tackled . . . We haven't still been able to find a specific social relation (mechanism) to explain whom these difficulties originate from, and how they happen (ibid.).

6. The political confrontation and power struggle between the two organs culminated in Telecommunications in Teheran, in 1982. Wondering about the sources and the logic of such conflicts, the Minister of Industry commented,

> We have still not beeen able to find a specific social relation to explain whom these difficulties originate from, and how they happen. We have factories whose IA and Islamic *shura* are in conflict with the *Sepah-i* (*Pasdaran*) of the region. Sometimes there are two-two or three-three ambiguous composition; it is not known who is with whom. This differential pattern leads to the situation where you do not have a specific, unified system. I have documents indicating that in some factories, for instance, management, *shura* and IA are all in good relations, but have conflicts with the *sepah*; or on the contrary, management and IA are in good relations, but are against the *shura* (*Ettelāāt*, 1 August 1982, Appendix).

7. There are factions in the state which advocate free enterprise. The so-called *Hojjatieh* faction is the main one. However, they are not the determinant tendency. Various elements committed to what is called 'Imam's line', the Minister of Industry, the Prime Minister and the Director of the Organization of National Industries (ONI) — opposed the privatization of state-run plants (see *Ettelāāt*, 1 August 1983; *Kayhan*, 12 and 13 April 1983).

8. The Director of the ONI states:

> One of our major problems is the interference of irresponsible organs; the problem derives from the fact that these organs lack procedure and the knowledge of management. It even entails interference from outside the factory, which naturally inflict undesirable impacts, obscuring the responsibilities. (*Kayhan*, 13 January 1983).

9. According to official figures, industrial investment increased with an annual average rate of growth of 11% in value terms over the period 1977-78 to 1982-83. However, the very high growth of the *numbers* of the industrial establishments (average annual rate of growth of 166%) indicates that mainly small capital tended to invest (Bank Markazi Iran, 1980-81).

10. Merchant capital is believed to have made a considerable profit. However, there is no evidence to suggest that the big bazaar merchants give support to the regime. My own conversations with a few leading political figures in the bazaar gave quite the reverse impression in late 1980-81. In an attempt to offset the bazaar discontents and to rationalize the economy, Khomeini eventually ruled out the nationalization of foreign trade in 1984.

11. See A Bayat (1986), 'The Politics of Economic Disorder in Post-Revolutionary Iran'. Paper presented at the 4th Annual Conference of the Center for Iranian Research and Analysis, Washington DC, 5-6 April 1986.

12. This was to be evaluated by a committee composed of representatives of the Islamic *shura*, supervisor and the employer (*Jomhouri-i Eslāmi*, 25 July 1981).

13. Islamic attitudes toward [institution of] consultation is different from those attitudes on council systems in socialist and Marxist societies . . . we do not consider it to be correct that administration system of a country to be based on election from below to the top. That's not the case in our system. We believe in *valayat-i faghih*, and in the fact that *valayat* (government) is authorised from above to bottom (Labour Minister Tavakkoli, *Ettelāāt*, May 1983).

14. President Khomeini's message for May Day 1981.

15. Article 10 of proposed Labour Law defines the labour contract as the *ta-ahhod* (obligation) on the part of the *karpazir* (worker) to perform work for payment of *ojrat* (wage); and acceptance (*paziresh*) by the employer (*sahebkar*) to pay *ojrat* for the ownership of the work (*amal*). The word *ojrat* is not equivalent to wage (*dastmozd*) but a payment for the hiring of objects or animals. The proposed Labour Law was rejected by workers and by the populist faction in the state. The Labour Minister, Tavakkoli, was later pressurized to resign.

16. The official ideology could not tolerate even the historical origin of May Day to be secular. 'This is,' says an official of Labour House, 'a distortion that the Marxists of Second International in Paris have committed . . . On the basis of our researches, we have found out the fact that the attitudes of the protagonists and the main participant force of the May Day were in fact religious' (*Jomhouri-e Eslāmi*, 22 April 1982).

17. In a metal factory in Teheran, I attended a mass prayer at the factory's mosque. Out of a workforce of 700, less than 20 workers, most of them old, were in attendance. The rest of the workers were playing football in the factory yard or chatting. From then on (spring 1981), participation in mass prayer became compulsory in the factories and offices. In another plant, a junior manager explained that the workers themselves demanded prayer sermons, but did not participate. Instead, as I observed, they would sit in the sunshine talking.

18. A review of the internal debates of the regional IA's weekly meetings indicates that a considerable part of the meetings are devoted to the tensions and confrontations between them and the managers. In one meeting it was said, 'The ONI with unIslamic managers has a new plot against the IAs. It wants to dissolve the IAs and put its own men in (*Jomhouri Eslāmi*, 26 December 1982).

19. The details of the functions of the IAs have been spelled out in Pamphlet No. 3 of the Bureau for Mobilization and the Development of Islamic Culture of Workers, *A Guideline for the Functions of Islamic Associations*, Ministry of Labour.

11. Workers' Control and Political Democracy

Introduction

If the councils (*shuras*) in Iran failed to sustain themselves partly owing to their own internal contradictions (leaving aside the state's political pressure) why was it correct for socialists to support *them* instead of the syndicates which fight for limited and immediate demands for better wages and working conditions?

Such a question could be applied to most of the failed experiments of the world working class. In the history of the international labour movement, there have been numerous examples of working-class struggles that have failed due, in part, to their own shortcomings; and yet they have been enthusiastically advocated by socialists. Indeed, the basic problems with which the Russian factory committees and the Italian factory councils were confronted were the same as those of the Iranian *shuras*. In the revolutionary situation and as a part of revolutionary process, a dis-equilibrium arose in the workplaces between personal and structural power relations; that is, while the *personal* authority of the functionaries of capital (managers, technicians and supervisors) was seriously questioned by the working class, the division of labour inherited from the past tended to persist because of the practical impossibility of altering it overnight while maintaining production levels (Bettelheim, 1978; Smith, 1980, 1983 and Siriani, 1982). As the inherited capitalist division of labour persisted, the corresponding authoritarian power relations were in the long run reproduced. And this, as far as the workers' councils were concerned, meant defeat.

The formation of the *shuras* should be viewed as part of the anti-monarchic revolutionary process. The idea of the *shura* was not invented by the theoreticians; it emerged out of a new working-class consciousness, the ideology of possession, and the inability of capitalism to respond to working-class demands. Many demands made by the workers in the revolutionary situation were of trade-unionist character, that is for limited and immediate ends. Yet the failure of capital to meet these demands provided a condition for the working class, through direct action, to take control of industrial enterprises. The combination of these practices and

193

the ideology of possession provided them with the concept of the *shura* and workers' control as a solution to the post-revolutionary economic crisis. The *shuras* served as an organizational means and way of transforming existing power relations at workplaces. In my view, a call for trade unionist action and organization would have been wrong. It would have been subjective, because as stated above, the councils emerged through the working class in response to an objective economic-political situation in which capital was unable to meet the labour demands. Conversely, a trade unionist approach — preventing labour intervening in managerial prerogatives — would have lagged one step behind the militant approach of the working class itself. My interviews clearly indicated that almost all of the respondents resented the syndicates. Thirdly, it would have denied the working class a unique historical experiment — an experiment in which the class could test its capacities and experience new areas of control both at the workplace and in society at large which had previously been the undisputed domain of capital.

This chapter is devoted to discussing and speculating about the impact of council organizations upon institutionalization of democracy in society at micro and macro levels, envisaging a socio-economic order within which such democratic practices might exist, and finally making some general points as to how workers' control itself can be reproduced.

The General Implications of Workers' Control

Much has been written about the general significance of workers' control. Numerous versions have been put forward from syndicalism to guild socialism, the co-operative movement, workplace unionism, socialism and above all councilism (Hinton, 1973; Gallacher and Campbell, 1977; Cole, 1975; Pannekoek, 1950; Rene, 1978; Coates and Topham, 1968). In the present section I shall restrict myself to the workplace and social implications of workers' participation.

Workplace Level
Alienation is the chief characteristic of capitalist social-economic organization and the capitalist workplace, which is regulated by the traditional division of labour. In discussing the alienation of labour, Marx identified three aspects: alienation of the labourer from a) his/her labour, the products of his/her labour and thus from him/herself; b) the conditions of his/her labour, meaning that the social and technical conditions within which the worker performed his/her tasks were controlled by others; c) other people who controlled his/her labour (Marx, 1964, pp. 112-13). Since Marx's time the degree of alienation has deepened dramatically. The development of new technology and methods of production has increased productivity and the rate of exploitation, transformed the labour process by intensifying the detailed

194

division of labour, and deepened the subordination of labour to the modern structure of management.

This intensification has not proceeded without resistance. The workers have responded to it by strikes, absenteeism, sabotage and growing demand for participation (Palloix, 1976; Friedman, 1977b). Reacting to such disruptions, management has tended to propose from above various strategies of participation and work humanization.

An important dimension of workers' control is the reducing of alienation in the workplace. By our definition, workers' control means exertion of control by the workers over the processes of production and administration. This points to the workers' ability to determine how, how much and what to produce, and in what ways things should be organized. As Bahro wrote, this restructuring of the division of labour is 'far more than a remedy against monotony, as it is often envisaged today' (1978). Genuine participation means, above all, restructuring the organization of production and administration in such a way that the workers can re-assert their humanity as free producers.

The Problem of Efficiency and Workers' Control

It is not uncommon to find opposition to workers' control on the grounds that it is inefficient and chaotic. To begin with, inefficiency may be a problem of not merely workers' control but also of an authoritarian one-man-management system. Under workers' control a possible ineffi-ciency should be attributed not to the alternative organization of produc-tion *as such*, but to the fact that, in most cases, workers' control is expected to function in an unfertile ground, that is, in the context of inherited capitalist technology and hierarchical management regimes. It is this contradictory combination that may cause disorganization and dis-ruption. What is required is a way of transforming the existing technology, making it compatible with a new organization of labour.

The very concept of inefficiency is problematic; it is an ideological concept and an area of class struggle. For a capitalist management, it may mean reducing costs (including that of labour), higher output per worker and competitiveness in the market. In contrast, for workers it may imply job security, higher living standards (higher wages) and the usefulness of their products to society as a whole (even if they are not competitive). Thus we may use the concept of socialist efficiency as an alternative to 'efficiency'. This concept transcends the narrow one of industrial efficien-cy and includes also the social development of labour, initiatives, emancipatory work organization and socially useful products.

Workers' participation can cause higher output on both ideological and structural grounds. 'It is almost a matter of common sense' as Paul Blumberg wrote two decades ago, 'that men will take great pride and pleasure in their work if they are allowed to participate in shaping the policies and decisions which affect that work' (1968, p. 123). My own observation on the Iranian experience suggests that as long as the workers feel that they really participate, that they really exert power, productivity rises (e.g. in brick-making plants in Azerbaijan, Chite-Jahan textile plant in Karadj). But an awareness of the merely formal nature of participation leads to passivity and opposition. A similar pattern was reported in Chile under Allende (Zimbalist and Espinosa, 1978, p. 185; Levenson, 1979) in the USSR in the 1920s (Rakovsky, 1980) and Cuba (in Carciofi, 1983, p. 202).

In real participation, output may rise not simply because workers work harder or longer, but because they find a situation where they can express their initiatives and their latent abilities and develop themselves. Capitalist production relations and work organization suppresses initiative and uses only a limited range of workers' abilities.

It becomes clear, as many have suggested (see Marglin, 1978), that in general management's concern about the organization of production is not merely to promote efficiency for higher profit, but to restrict the influence of labour over the conditions of production and administration. In 1973 some experiments in work humanization and job-enlargement were put into practice in the American Polaroid Company. Despite a rise in the productivity, management stopped the experiment. In an interview with *Nation*, the manager explained why.

> It was successful. What were we going to do with the supervisors — the managers? We didn't need them any more. Management decided that it just didn't want operatives that qualified . . . The employees barely revealed ability to carry more responsibility was too great a threat to the established way of doing things and to established power relations (in Jenkins, 1973, pp. 314-15).

Social and Ideological Implications

The establishment of workers' control from below, however embryonic it may initially be, is not simply a technical change, nor just a modification in the organization of production at enterprise level. It has important social and ideological implications.

By striving to restructure the production process and alter the traditional relations and hierarchies the workers experience a new area of control, achieving a new power status which was previously an exclusively managerial prerogative. As they experience this process, workers' perception of work, power and society tend to change. Such an experience confers on the workers a new perception of their role in society; they cease to be subordinate and exploited and discover their right and ability to determine the direction of production. This change in ideology, if sustained, is in social terms immensely significant. For it not only involves the workers in thinking differently about themselves and about other classes, but also involves the rest of civil society, notably the dominant classes, in acquiring different attitudes towards these workers and their relations with them. 'Working people should no longer be identified as subordinate, miserable, crippled and regrettable creatures, but as human beings with initiatives and ability of offering alternative ways of organizing the economy and society.' This change in mentality means that the workers acquire a confidence in their ability to offer an alternative mode of work and make other classes *believe* in their (workers') ability to carry out such an historic task.

Political Implications

In the preceding section we envisaged a learning process within which workers' control might be accomplished and workers achieve an ability to maintain that process. This learning process, however, does not occur in a vacuum. A free political climate must exist to allow labour to demonstrate its initiative and develop itself. A genuine industrial democracy can be implemented only in the conditions of political democracy and free and collective decision-making. But how can such conditions be brought about?

In the actually existing socialist states, where state power is exerted in the name of the working classes, the scope of industrial democracy does not not much exceed that of the market economies (Harastzi, 1977; Holubenko, 1975; Tiktin, 1973). The partial control enjoyed by workers in the USSR is only negative. Negative control is the ability by the workers to disrupt production, administration or planning without the state being able to do anything about it, precisely because the state is officially ruling in the name of the working people (Tiktin, 1973). In the Yugoslavian self-management system, on the other hand, a more democratic form of state goes hand in hand with democratic control at enterprise level.

The situation in the Third World is still very different. Lack of political democracy, let alone workers' control, is almost universal in the capitalist peripheral countries. Given our argument that workers' participation can be meaningful only in democratic conditions, it might seem that industrial democracy in the Third World is impossible. But in the first chapter, I provided evidence to show that Third World workers have in practice fought for workers' control and in some countries, have achieved it. Here, I want to argue that workers' participation in a wider sense can be a means of achieving political democracy in Third World societies.

Capitalism and Democracy

The concept of political democracy is relevant to both capitalist and socialist social formations. In socialism it refers to a system of self-administration and popular control over the political and economic organization of society. In a capitalist social formation, political democracy is manifested in bourgeois democracy. This is the rule of capital in the context of a democratic government under which citizens are legally

197

entitled to participate in the determination of the policies 'to be executed by the state in its capacity as sovereign legal subject' (Jessop, 1982, p. 274). In order that such participation can be realized, some other pre-conditions are necessary, including the institutionalization of certain political freedoms (freedom of association, freedom of speech, free elections) and parliamentary control over the executive and administration (ibid., pp. 274-5). Yet within this political framework, the reproduction of capitalist relations is guaranteed by the capitalist state.

Bourgeois democracy can vary in terms of the actual formal legal procedures and extent of political rights. There exists an enormous variety, in terms of the degree of democratic practices, in today's capitalist societies.[1] Only a few Third World countries are administered in a bourgeois democratic manner.

What then determines the degree of democracy in a capitalist society? A relationship can be established between the nature of capitalist development and the form of the state at the level of a social formation. Milton Friedman argues that democracy can be realized only in a free market economy which he regards as non-exploitative and crisis-free. This theory is hardly tenable, as the free market exists in many Third World countries which are ruled despotically. It might be argued that in the latter countries the free market is disturbed by state interventions. Against this argument, Sweden illustrates that state intervention in the economy is not necessarily an obstacle to democracy.

As against the Friedmanite theory, the capital logic school of the British left maintains, following Lenin, that 'a democratic republic is the best possible political shell for capitalism' which is both exploitative and crisis-stricken. Some sympathetic critics of this view go on to suggest that the bourgeois-democratic state is the best possible political shell for capital to the extent that 'the bourgeoisie is politically and ideologically dominant' (Jessop, 1982). These critics, however, do not explore the reason for the weakness and strength of the bourgeoisie; and further their analyses one-sidedly concentrate on the logic of capital, giving little or no attention to the role of labour.

I sympathize with the view that the establishment of democracy, like the enactment of laws, is the result of the conflict between social forces (classes) in a given society. More specifically, in a given capitalist social formation and at a given historical moment, the scope and depth of democratic practices depend upon two factors. Firstly, the degree of capital expansion; secondly, the intensity of class and popular struggle.[2] By capital expansion I mean the scale of capital accumulation, productivity, the extent of the development of productive forces and social relations. By class struggle here I mean the degree of the historical development, the organization and militancy of the social classes and other social groups (e.g. women) in a given country — the classes and groups where the self-realization of democratic freedoms are an objective necessity. (The working class and the new middle class are in this category.

Whereas the mode of reproduction of existence of the self-sufficient peasantry or the traditional petty-bourgeoisie does not necessarily require democratic conditions.) A high degree of class struggle may arise in the independent and militant activities of class and popular organizations, such as working-class organizations like trade unions, social and cultural societies, political parties, professional societies, cultural and ethnic establishments and so on. Thus the degree of democracy, in a given historical situation, depends primarily on the dialectic between these two determinants.

How is political democracy related to capitalism? This relationship may be characterized by the following features.

1. Hegemonic rule. The establishment of hegemony is the ideal type of capitalist and indeed any other rule. An hegemonic capitalist state is one which rules with the consent of its subjects. This arises out of the integration of the whole civil society into the state through some kind of representative (democratic) political system in which the principal objective, capitalist socio-economic organization, is guaranteed. As far as capital is concerned it is only under such conditions that democracy can be tolerated or even be desirable. Whereas advanced capitalism may be able to set up the conditions for a hegemonic state, backward capitalism cannot guarantee such opportunities.

2. Bourgeois class rule. Advanced capitalism implies the development of a bourgeois class in terms of economic and political organizations. Such a class may be capable of establishing a socio-economic and political order (modern state) controlling the state apparatus. However, where a weak bourgeoisie exists the state tends to dominate and be independent of civil society, including the bourgeoisie itself.

3. Economic satisfaction. Advanced productive forces and high productivity offer a higher standard of living by raising real wages much higher than the value of production. Economic betterment and a higher living standard for the working classes can be an important ground for political integration. Weak capital and a low level of accumulation cannot offer such rewards.

4. Impersonal relations. Advanced capitalist social relations tend to objectify and depersonalize the existing dominant class and power relations. This characteristic of advanced capitalism presents the state as a neutral agent acting for the well-being of the whole community. This is the ideological basis of integration. In backward capitalism, on the other hand, the residues of traditional (ethnic, kinship and patriarchal) relations lead to the retention of *personal* relations between the individuals, and between the latter and the state.

The interaction of the two determinants — the degree of capitalist development and of class struggle — can result in at least four possible political conditions. At the risk of a gross simplification, these may be presented as follows:

1. Strong C + low degree of CS → Democracy
2. Strong C + high degree of CS → Instability (Democracy —
   non-democracy)
3. Weak C + low degree of CS → Non-democracy
4. Weak C + high degree of CS → Instability (Non-democracy —
   democracy)

C = Capital
CS = Class struggle
+ combination
→ consequence

It is possible to argue that the reason why liberal democracy is practicable, at the present time, in the advanced capitalist societies is because capital has developed sufficiently to enable the (capitalist) state to co-exist with the struggle against it, with the democratic institutions which 'historically have come to exist in opposition to capitalism' (Therborn, 1977). Capital in these countries can contain the fluctuations of the class struggle. The periods of capitalist boom are not only periods of capital's economic hegemony, but also of strength in the labour movement. In periods of crisis, however, a weakened capital is obliged to encroach on the existing democratic rights in order to save itself (as in the UK now). If the labour movement is divided and weak at such times, anti-democratic legislation is inevitable. However, if popular organizations are united and militant, the outcome can be different: either a chronic crisis and instability, or a dual-power situation which, depending on numerous mediations, may lead to the defeat of either the labour movement or capitalist state.

It should now be clear why democracy in the backward capitalist societies is scarce or highly fragile. In these countries, in general, a weak capital is operating — that is, the scale of capital accumulation and productivity are low, the propertied classes are politically weak and social relations are to a considerable extent personalized. In such circumstances, if popular forces are unorganized, the weakness of capital opens the way for the domination of undemocratic state power (Situation 3). These authoritarian state-forms are objectively required to control the potential forces of the populace and its spontaneous movements which result from the contradictions of the socio-economic system that these states strive to construct, i.e. backward capitalism (as in Pakistan, the Shah's Iran, the military regimes of Latin America).

Are undemocratic political systems a permanent feature of the Third World? No doubt, weak capital in the Third World is forced to retreat where a rich political culture — in the form of traditions of organization, solidarity and democratic institutions — exists. In these circumstances the resultant balance of forces does give rise to an exercise of democracy. Yet these democracies tend to be restricted, tense and fragile and thus cannot last long (Situation 4). The history of capitalism in

Latin America has been a history of weak capital integrated with international capital, combined with a tradition of organization and struggle, giving a history of precarious and intermittent democracies.[3]

Popular Democracy and Transition

For reasons outlined in the first chapter — the crisis of hegemony of the state or ruling classes and failure of reformist policies — revolutions and radical changes do occur frequently in the Third World. Between 1974 and 1978 alone 15 countries in the Third World went through major revolutionary upheavals (Halliday, 1983). A revolution may sweep aside an old socio-political order, but it will not necessarily lead to a new democratic system. In a revolutionary situation, the fact that no one group *effectively* exerts power offers the possibility of change and a free political climate. Yet, in the process of the consolidation of the new regime, this freedom may be curtailed and eventually the revolution may be defeated. What conditions are required to institutionalize and reproduce a stable democracy?

Some tend to see the solution in strengthening the position of capital. It is argued that in these societies, owing to the historical weakness of the ruling classes and, for that matter, the strength of the state (in particular the rentier states which control the major economic resources), the strategy must involve making the civil society, especially the bourgeoisie, independent of the state. This strategy envisages a liberal market economy like those of Western Europe.

This argument is like Friedman's: it involves the freedom of the capitalist class (among other classes) from state control and the freedom of the market from state domination. This view has already been dismissed. The very concept of periphery capitalism implies that Third World countries are not experiencing the same pattern of development and class formation as the advanced capitalist countries did.

To envisage the feasibility of a democratic order in a backward capitalist social formation, we have to take into account the specific situation of each country. Yet, situations are related to and influenced by a general rule which is the conclusion of our discussion so far. Since weak capital (as a totality of socio-economic relations) cannot provide the conditions for a democratic state in backward capitalist social formations, then class struggle should be the point of attention. Let me elaborate this with reference to Iran.

Theoretically, in a capitalist social formation such as Iran, the consolidation of political democracy cannot simply be brought about by the goodwill of the political leaders, however sincere they may be in wishing to establish democracy. A strategy of mass democratization is necessary to establish and strengthen popular organizations and develop a culture of free participation. The balance of forces between class struggle and the accumulation rationale can be altered to the benefit of the former only by creating and extending the economic, political and social organizations of the working class, political parties, professional societies, women's organizations, peasant organizations, neighbourhood and regional councils and above all the organization of workers' participation in production, services and state administration.

But the extension of such mass organizations will come into conflict with the requirements of capital, eventually creating a political impasse in which violation of democratic gains and frequent coups would seem to be inevitable. Hence, to achieve a democratic rule in these societies a revolutionary change is vital. First and foremost it must transform the existing power structure through subverting the social, military, administrative and economic bases upon which the old regime rests. Though necessary, this is still not sufficient to guarantee democratic practices and processes. It is not hard to imagine that the new state can easily be bureaucratized, the new army transformed into a repressive organ, and the state become a capitalist enterprise running an inefficient nationalized economy.

To avoid such a tendency a new set of power relations must be established with the following features:

a) Political order

1. The old power structure must be transformed so that it rests upon the democratic mobilization of people at the grass-roots in the economic sector, state administration, neighbourhoods and nationalities. Here, civil society can express its opinions and influence the political processes through its immediate organizations which would send elected representatives to form a national legislature.

2. This state form would derive its legitimacy from the representation of popular mobilization and mass organizations. In this it differs from the liberal democratic state.

3. Under such a state, the freedom of intellectual activities and expression of political ideas of any kind is conceivable. (It must be stressed that we cannot afford to regard one particular ideological orientation as the truth and suppress the rest.) Such a political order will be able to provide conditions for the realization of pluralism — a pluralism of the transitional period.

b) Economic order

A mixed economy should be established. The state would own the large and strategic sectors, and private capital would be free to operate in small-scale productive units. Even in the aftermath of political change the market would still be necessary to perform the task of production and distribution.

Two important points have to be made here. First, in political terms, although a form of pluralism has been envisaged, this would not be the same as the *bourgeois* pluralism which operates in the conditions of capitalist hegemony. This democracy of the transitional period would be a pluralism operating in a political system in which exploitative and oppressive classes were no longer dominant and the state apparatus was at their disposal.

In the economic sphere, although we are talking about a mixed economy, it would be a mixed economy unlike that which operates under capitalism. While the latter is based upon private/state ownership plus private and/or individual control from above, under the democracy of the transitional period a mixed economy would be characterized by public/ private ownership and collective control (largely in the public sector) through the strategy of workers' participation.

Thus, I am envisaging a social organization in which the bourgeois class still exists but is subordinated to a revolutionary structure of popular political power; there is private ownership in the means of production but restricted to small-scale operations, and subject to the activities of labour unions; the market does function, but is counter-balanced by the intervention of the state. In short, Iran can no longer afford to be an Indonesia (an authoritarian capitalist state) or another Ethiopia (an authoritarian one-party state) but it can try a Nicaraguan road.[4]

Undoubtedly, the transitional period is characterized by tensions and contradictions. If the new state can maintain its hegemony through its reliance upon an active popular participation; if in political and cultural domains, the state can provide viable alternatives to those of the bourgeoisie; if, in the economic sphere, the labour councils and unions can sustain their momentum, then the transition to a socialist society may be possible. Otherwise, once again, capitalistic values and/or an authoritarian rationale will inevitably be brought to the fore in order to 'save the revolution'.

In this process, the operation of the labour councils in industry, the service sector, state administration, educational establishments and in local neighbourhood councils and among the ethnic minorities would be of immense value. Amongst these, the grass-roots and independent labour councils can play a vital role, for they can contribute to the cause of democracy both directly (as an independent and unified organization of the working people) and indirectly (as democratic institutions in which employees would experiment, practice and learn democracy in a systematic way). Labour councils also would provide an institution of collective control in the public sector.

Through the medium of workers' councils workers would be actively involved in production and administration, and would comprehend the problems involved in the administration of affairs and the possible conflict between their own immediate interests and the interests of society. This involvement and understanding is politically crucial. An authoritarian one-man management, unlike the system of collective control, will rapidly lose the confidence of the workers when it fails, for economic reasons, to respond positively to the demands of the workers. If workers continue to press, the management's response is likely to be use of force.

How to Reproduce Workers' Control

If workers' control is fundamental to the consolidation of political democracy in a transitional society, then the basic question is how to bring it about and maintain it; how to preserve its institutions from degeneration to powerless and merely formal bodies.

The workers' councils in Iran, the *shuras*, failed to reproduce themselves effectively not only because of external pressure (political repression), but also because of their own internal contradictions and the inherited division of labour.

The internal problem was a conflict between the long-term and short-term interests of the councils. For the Iranian workers the *shuras* were the institutional manifestation of their keen desire to determine the process of production and administration. In practice, they demonstrated a real enthusiasm for making decisions and taking part in future planning; they struggled to direct the factory operation. Their efforts, however, brought them into conflict with the traditional capitalist division of labour. The workers who had fought so dramatically against the professional managements, and who had put the latter on trial and dismissed them, later requested the state to send back these professional managers after running the industrial workplaces for months! This contradiction in the workers' behaviour reflected the dual function of management — co-ordination and control. The function of co-ordination is related to the technical co-ordination of affairs, that is, maintaining harmony, avoiding waste and so on. It is required in all complex forms of organization. The function of control, on the other hand, is to preserve the power relations within the production process. This function is specific to authoritarian forms of organization. The two functions can be separated only at the level of abstraction. In reality they reproduce each other.

The workers transformed the existing management system. In so doing, however, they felt that they needed, in the short run, the skills of professional managers, simply in order to maintain production. But the re-instatement of the very same managers meant, in effect, the re-establishment of the same technical and social (or power) relations. So the workers both wanted and at the same time did not want the existing management system. Thus, on the one hand, restructuring or modifying the existing system of the division of labour was essential for the survival of the councils in the long run. The consolidation of the councils, therefore, required new relations and a new system of management. On the other hand, their survival, in the short run, depended on the traditional forms of managerial competence. In short, the councils wanted the same managerial functions without the associated power relations. Obviously this was unrealistic. In the hierarchical structure of management the position of each agent carries a specific degree of power which is exerted objectively.

The fact is that the working class as broadly defined does possess a power of negative control, in the sense that it can *subvert* the control of capital over the enterprise or the whole economy through strikes and sabotage (and over the whole society through revolution). This is indeed a gigantic power. The point, however, is to translate that negative control into a positive control in the sense of a theoretical and practical capacity to produce and reproduce a new order which can provide the conditions for, and be based upon, the exertion of real power (as opposed to formal power) by the working people, that is, to bring about in Bahro's terms a 're-division of labour' (1978).

Marx's conception of the division of labour, according to Rattansi (1982a, 1982b), evolved in three stages. Initially, Marx equated the division of labour with class and exchange. In the second stage, beginning with the *Poverty of Philosophy*, he developed the two concepts of 'social division of labour' and the 'division of labour in manufacturing'. In his later works, notably in *Capital*, he took the sphere of production as his point of departure for an analysis of capitalist economy. Marx then abandoned his earlier ideas on class and the division of labour, attributing a transhistorical and at times natural character to the division of labour — even if classes were dissolved, the complete abolition of the division of labour would not necessarily follow. Yet the crucial question remained: to what extent was it feasible to fight against relations of subordination and to secure the exercise of workers' power without abolishing or restructuring the division of labour?

To transform or modify the existing division of labour is something which is beyond the capacity of theory alone. Practice, experience and learning are vital. Unfortunately the fate of workers' revolutions in contemporary history have been such that we cannot learn much from them. In post-revolutionary Russia, despite a fundamental change in power structure and social relations, forms of the division of labour characteristic of capitalist organization of production remained. East European countries have followed a more or less similar path (Bahro, 1978). Yugoslavia has developed a unique model of self-management in which relatively autonomous and democratic enterprises (local democracy) operate under the conditions of market relations.

In China, the Cultural Revolution, according to Bettelheim, attempted to revolutionize the division of labour within the enterprises through ideological struggle. Bettelheim has suggested that in the transition to socialism it is possible to transform the division of labour by an ideological-political struggle, that is, by rejecting productivism and by putting proletarian politics in command (1974, pp. 74, 102). The question of why workers' participation in Chinese industry did not continue is beyond the scope of this book. Bettelheim attributes that failure to the rise of the right and the strategy of what he terms the 'great leap backward' (Burton and Bettelheim, 1978). In contrast, some writers, including the activists of the present-day Chinese Democracy Movement, have questioned the whole project of the Cultural Revolution itself, describing it as a form of feudal-fascist dictatorship (Chen, Erjin, 1984, pp. 16-17) in the context of which popular participation was no more than 'mass regimentation dosed with terror' (Benton, 1984, p. 65).

It seems that at least two conditions have to be met to facilitate a gradual development of workers' control: a) the direct involvement of the working people in their own affairs, developing a learning experience and, b) the state's strategic support.

a. In industry and service sectors, the councils, by involving the mass of the employees in the process of production and administration, can learn and experience the ways in which the traditional division of labour can be restructured. Once they have removed the political obstacles, the workers may discover an alternative organization of production and develop alternative forms of production and socialist management. All this would mean that the mass of the workers would no longer be the powerless tools and mere appendages of machines and bureaucratic structures, but labourers with manual capacity and intellectual knowledge who would acquire the power of determination not only of an enterprise's affairs, but in the long run, economic planning process. This would mean the gradual conquering of new domains of authority.

This process would involve a long-term strategy of permanent class struggle by introducing a new culture of production as a viable alternative to the dominant hierarchical division of labour. This new culture of production would necessarily be related to the changes in other domains of social life — culture, social and individual values. Here, then, as Bahro (1978) argued, the concept of (economic) growth would have to change from quantitative orientation to qualitative orientation. With the same token, the concept of need, luxury and comfort would also have to change. The question then would be 'to create objective conditions so that everyone *can* prefer to know and to be, instead of to possess' (1978, p. 281)

b. We have already assumed that the future Iranian government, at least at the level of intention, would be democratic. In addition, we discussed the pre-conditions under which such a state form might be sustained, concluding that the extensive empowerment of popular organs (in production units, enterprises, state administration and educational establishments and among ethnic minorities) could guarantee a popular democracy in Iran in future. It follows then that the councils are both the pre-condition and product of the popular struggle. Political pre-conditions for workers' control are that not only would the *shuras* not be destroyed by external pressure, but that the state would provide conditions for their self-development. At the macro-level, the state would have to tailor various dimensions of socio-political and cultural life to the requirements of workers' participation. The education system would have to be transformed to respond to the requirements of this strategy. A constant connection between the educational institutions (schools, colleges, research centres, etc.) and workplaces would be necessary. Within the industrial units there might be organized technical-educational classes on production, management and administration to bridge the gap between the spheres of conception and execution. At the level of social relations, social status based upon the existing hierarchy, and differentiated salaries, would have to be eliminated. The mass of the labourers in industry, state institutions and so on would be encouraged to organize in political, social and cultural groups.

These developments at the workplaces would underline the social role and social acceptability of the working class among the rest of the population. Thus, the changes would not be simply technical, but also provide conditions for ideological changes. Here, my stress is upon the significance of the cultural hegemony of the working class, in the sense of the capacity of this class to offer a viable alternative way of life to be desirable and practised freely by the whole civil society.

Notes

1. For an historical survey on this issue see Therborn (1977).
2. Here we are concerned not with the *emergence* or *establishment* of democracy — democratic constitution or institutions — but rather the *continuation* and *reproduction* of democracy in a given country.
3. See a valuable article by Therborn (1979). Therborn says that 'where it has been strong — in Argentina, Bolivia, Cuba and Chile . . . the working class has been an important democratic force in Latin America' (ibid, p. 85). Bolivia and Turkey exemplify two different and interesting situations in which the combination of the rule of weak capital and prevalence of popular struggle has resulted in successive military coups as well as fragile democracies since the 1950s. For Bolivia, see an excellent study by James Dunkerley (1984), and for the case of Turkey see Keyder (1979) and Taylan (1984). I have discussed the relationship between labour and democracy in post-revolutionary Iran in my 'Labour and Democracy in Post-Revolutionary Iran' in Amirahmadi and Parvin (eds), *Post-Revolutionary Iran*, USA: Westview Press, 1986 (forthcoming).
4. For post-revolutionary Nicaraguan political economy, see Petras (1981, 1984), Nwafar (1984), Weber (1980), Irvin (1983), Black (1983).

Bibliography

Abrahamian, E., (1974) 'Oriental Despotism: The Case of Qajar Iran', *International Journal of Middle Eastern Studies*, vol. 5.

Abrahamian, E., (1981) 'The Strengths and Weaknesses of the Labour Movement in Iran, 1941-1953' in M.E. Bonine and Nikki Keddie (eds), *Continuity and Change in Modern Iran*, New York.

Abrahamian, E., (1982) *Iran Between the Two Revolutions*, Princeton University Press.

Abu-Lughod, J. and Hay, J.R. (eds), (1977) *Third World Urbanization*, Maavoufa Press.

Aglietta, M., (1979) *A Theory of Capitalist Regulations: The US Experience*, London, New Left Books.

Alavi, H. and Shanin, T. (eds), (1982) *Introduction to the Sociology of 'Developing Societies'*, Macmillan, London.

Amsden, A.H., (1980) *The Economics of Women and Work*, Penguin, London.

Anderson, P., (1977) 'The Limits and Possibilities of Trade Union Action' in T. Clark and L. Clements.

Anthony, P.D., (1977) *Ideology of Work*, Tavistock, London.

Aref, A., (1982) 'Kargaran va Kontrol-i-Kargari dar Iran' (Workers and Workers' Control in Iran), *Dawlat va Enghelab*, no. 1, London (in Farsi).

Aref, A., (1983) 'Daramid-i bar Mabahes-i Jonbesh-e Kargari-e Iran' (An Introduction to Debates on the Iranian Labour Movement), *Dawlat va Enghelab*, no. 6, London (in Farsi).

Arrighi, E. and Saul, J.S., (1968) 'Socialism and Economic Development in Tropical Africa', *Journal of Modern African Studies*, vol. 6, no. 2.

Avrich, P., (1963a) 'The Russian Factory Committees in 1917, *Jahrbucher fur Geschischte Osteurpas*, no. 11.

Avrich, P., (1963b) 'The Bolsheviks and Workers' Control', *Slavic Review*, vol. 22, no. 1.

Azad, S., (1980) 'Workers' and Peasants' Councils in Iran', *Monthly Review*, October.

Bahro, R., (1978) *Alternative for Eastern Europe*, Verso Press, London.

Baldwin, G., (1967) *Planning and Development in Iran*, Baltimore.

Banaji, J. and Subramanian, A., (1980) 'A New Strategy for Indian Unions', *Newsletter of the International Labour Studies*, no. 8.

Banisadre, Abolhasan, (1980) *Kar va Kargar dar Islam* (Work and Workers in Islam), Teheran, Payame Azadi (in Farsi).

Bank Markazi Iran, (1978-81) *Annual Reports*, Teheran.

Barrett, B. *et al*, (1975) *Industrial Relations and the Wider Society*, Collier

Macmillan, London.

Barret, M. *et al*, (1975) 'Workers' Control Versus "Revolutionary" Theory', *Socialist Register*, vol. 1975.

Bartsch, W., (1968-70) *Labour Supply and Employment Creation in the Urban Areas of Iran, 1956-1966*, unpublished PhD thesis, University of London.

Bartsch, W., (1971a) 'Unemployment in Less Developed Countries: A Case Study of Poor Districts of Teheran', *International Development Review*, vol. 3, no. 1.

Bartsch, W., (1971b) 'Industrial Labour Force of Iran: Problems of Recruitment, Training and Productivity', *Middle East Journal*, Winter.

Baumgartner *et al*, (1979) 'Self-Management, Market and Political Institutions in Conflict: Yugoslav Development Patterns and Dialectics', in T.R. Burns *et al* (eds).

Bayat, Assef, (1984) *Workers and Workers' Control in the Iranian Revolution, 1979-1982: Implications for the Third World*, PhD thesis, University of Kent, UK.

Bayat, Assef, (1983) 'Iran: Workers' Control After the Revolution', *MERIP Reports*, no. 113.

Bayat, Assef, (1983-4), 'Proletarianization and Culture: The Case of Factory Workers of Teheran', *ALEPHBA*, no. 4, Winter, Paris (in Farsi).

Bayat, Assef, (1986a) 'Labour and Democracy in Post-Revolutionary Iran', in M. Parvin and H. Amirahmadi (eds), *Post-Revolutionary Iran*, Westview Press, Boulder.

Bayat, Assef, (1986b) 'The Politics of Economic Disorder in Post-Revolutionary Iran'. Paper presented at the 4th Annual Conference of the Center for Iranian Research and Analysis (CIRA), Washington DC, 5-6 April 1986.

Beiler, Andre, (1983) 'Work and Religion: A Protestant Outlook', *Labour and Society*, vol. 3, no. 19.

Benton, G., (1984) 'Chinese Communism and Democracy', *New Left Review*, no. 148.

Bernstein, H. (ed.), (1976) *Underdevelopment and Development*, Penguin, London.

Bernstein, H., (1982) 'Industrialization, Development and Dependence' in H. Alavi and T. Shanin.

Bettleheim, C., (1974) *Cultural Revolution and Industrial Organization: Changes in the Management and the Division of Labour*, Monthly Review Press, New York.

Bettleheim, C., (1978) *Class Struggle in the USSR, 1917-1923*, Harvester, London.

Bettleheim, C., (1979) *Economic Calculation and Forms of Property*, Routledge and Kegan Paul, London.

Beynon, H., (1973) *Working for Ford*, Penguin, London.

Bharier, Julian, (1971) *Economic Development in Iran, 1900-1972*, Oxford University Press, London.

Bharier, Julian, (1972) 'The Growth of Towns and Villages in Iran, 1900-1966', *Middle East Studies*, vol. 8, no. 1.

Black, G., (1982) *Triumph of the People*, Zed Press, London.

Blackburn, R.M. and Mann, M., (1979) *The Working Class in the Labour Market*, Macmillan, London.

Blumberg, P., (1973) *Industrial Democracy: The Sociology of Participation*, Schocken Books, New York.

Bologna, S., (1976) 'Class Composition and the Theory of Party at the Origin of the Workers' Control Movement', *The Labour Process and Class Strategies*, CSE, London.

Braverman, H., (1974) *Labour and Monopoly Capital*, Monthly Review Press, New York.

Breman, J., (1976) 'A Dualistic Labour System? A Critique of the "Informal Sector" Concept, *Economic and Political Weekly*, 4 December.

Brinton, M., (1970) *The Bolsheviks and Workers' Control, 1917 to 1921: The State and Counter-Revolution*, Solidarity, London.

Bricianer, S., (1978) *Pannekoek and Workers' Councils*, Telos, USA.

Burawoy, Michael, (1978) 'Toward a Marxist Theory of the Labour Process: Braverman and Beyond', *Politics and Society*, vol. 8, nos. 3 & 4.

Burawoy, Michael, (1980) 'The Politics of Production and the Production of Politics: A Comparative Analysis of Piece Work Machine Shops in the USA and Hungary', *Political Power and Social Theory*, vol. 1.

Burawoy, Michael, (1982) 'The Hidden Abode of Underdevelopment: Labour Process and the State in Zambia', *Politics and Society*, vol. 11, no. 2.

Bureau for Mobilizing and Developing the Islamic Culture of Workers, (1982) *Rahnamoud-i bar Tashkil-e Anjomanha-ye Islami (A Guideline for Formation of the Islamic Associations)*, Kane-i Kargar (Labour House), Teheran.

Burns, P. and Doyle, M., (1981) *Democracy at Work*, Pan Books, London.

Burns, T.R. *et al* (eds), (1979) *Work and Power: The Liberation of Work and the Control of Political Power*, SAGE, London.

Burton and Bettelheim, C., (1978) *China Since Mao*, Monthly Review Press, New York.

Calvert, P., (1982) *The Concept of Class*, Hutchinson, London.

Carchedi, G., (1975a) 'The Economic Identification of New Middle Class', *Economy and Society*, vol. 3.

Carchedi, G., (1975b) 'Proletarianization of Employees', *Economy and Society*, vol. 3.

Carciofi, R., (1983) 'Cuba in the Seventies', in G. White *et al* (ed.).

Chaqueri, C., (1978) *The Conditions of the Working Class in Iran*, Mazdak, Italy.

Chen, Erjin, (1984) *China: Crossroads Socialism*, Verso Press, London.

Clark, Martin, (1977) *Antonio Gramsci and the Revolution that Failed*, Yale University Press, New Haven and London.

Clark, T. and Clements, L., (1977) *Trade Unions under Capitalism*, Fontana, London.

Clegg, Ian, (1971) *Self-Management in Algeria*, Allen Lane, London.

Coates, Ken (ed.), (1968) *Can the Workers Run Industry?*, Sphere, London.

Coates, Ken, (1975), 'Democracy and Workers' Control', in J. Vanek (ed.).

Coates, Ken and Topham, T., (1968), 'Participation or Control?', in K. Coates (ed.).

Coates, Ken and Topham, T. (eds), (1970), *Workers' Control*, Panther, London.

Coates, Ken and Topham, T., (1972) *The New Unionism: The Case for Workers' Control*, Penguin, London.

Cohen, Robin, (1972) 'Class in Africa: Analytical Problems and Perspectives', *Socialist Register*, vol. 1972.

Cohen, Robin, (1980) 'Hidden Forms of Consciousness Amongst African Workers', *African Review of Political Economy*, no. 18.

Cohen, Robin, (1982) 'Workers in Developing Societies', in H. Alavi and T. Shanin.

Cohen, Robin, Gutkind, P. and Brazier, P. (eds), (1979) *Peasants and Proletarians*, Hutchinson, London.

Cole, D.H., (1975), 'Collectivism, Syndicalism and Guilds', in J. Vanek (ed.).

Comfort, C., (1966) *Revolutionary Hamburg: Labour Politics in the Early Weimar Republic*, Stanford University Press.

Communist Platform, (1978a) 'Working Class History as a Learning Process', *Bulletin of Communist Platform*, no. 2, June-September.

Communist Platform, (1978b) 'Debate on the Nature of Trade Unions', *Bulletin of Communist Platform*, no. 2, June-September.

Communist Platform, (n.d.) 'Workers' Communism Against Doctrinalised Leninism', *Bulletin of Communist Platform*, no. 2, June-September.

Connel, J., (1973) 'Teheran: Urbanization and Development', IDS Discussion Paper, no. 32, Sussex University.

Cooley, Mike, (1981) 'The Taylorization of Intellectual Work', in L. Levidow *et al* (eds).

Cooley, Mike, (n.d.) *Architect or Bee? The Human-Technology Relationship*, Langley Technical Services, Slough, UK.

Corrigan, P., Sayer, D. and Ramsay, H., (1978) *Socialist Construction and Marxist Theory: Bolshevism and its Critique*, Monthly Review Press, New York.

Cressey, P., and MacInnes, J., (1980) 'Voting for Ford: Industrial Democracy and the Control of Labour', *Capital and Class*, no. 11.

Crouch, C., (1983) 'The State, Capital and Liberal Democracy', in D. Held *et al* (eds).

CSE, (1978) *Workers' Inquiry into the Motor Industry*, a pamphlet of the Conference of Socialist Economists.

Daftary, F. and Borghaii, M., (1976) *Multinational Enterprises and Employment in Iran*, ILO Working Paper.

Daftary, F. and Borghaii, M., (1981) *Sherkatha-ye Chand Melliat-i dar Sanaye-i Iran* (Multi-National Enterprises in Iranian Industry) in *Ketab-i Agah*, no. 1, Teheran.

Das, N., (1964) *Experiments in Industrial Democracy*, Asia Publishing House, New York.

Davis, Mike, (1982) 'The Retreat of American Labour', *New Left Review*, no. 136.

De Chungara and Domitila, Barrios, (1978) *Let Me Speak*, Zed Press, London.

de Vroey, Michel, (1980) 'A Marxist View of Ownership and Control', in T. Nichols (ed.), (1980) *Capital and Labour*, Fontana, London.

Dillon, Robert J., (1976) *Carpet Capitalism and Craft Involution in Kirman, Iran: A Study in Economic Anthropology*, unpublished PhD thesis, Columbia University.

Doeringer, P. and Pior, M., (1971) *Internal Labour Market and Manpower Analysis*, D.C. Heath, London.

Draper, Hal, (1978a) *Karl Marx's Theory of Revolution: State and Bureaucracy*, vol. 1, Monthly Review Press, New York.

Draper, Hal, (1978b) *Karl Marx's Theory of Revolution: The Politics of Social Classes*, vol. 2, Monthly Review Press, New York.

Dubetsky, A., (1976) 'Kinship, Primordial Ties, and Factory Organization in Turkey', *International Journal of Middle Eastern Studies*, vol. 7.

Dunkerley, J., (1984) *Rebellion in the Veins: Political Struggle in Bolivia: 1952-1982*, Verso Press, London.

211

Economic Intelligence Unit, (1985) *Quarterly Economic Review: Iran*, London.

Edwards, Richard, (1979) *Contested Terrain: The Transformation of the Workplace in the 20th Century*, Basic Books, New York.

Elbawm, Bernard *et al*, (1979) 'The Labour Process, Market Structure and Marxist Theory', *Cambridge Journal of Economics*, vol. 3.

Elger, Tony, (1979) 'Valorization and "de-skilling": A Critique of Braverman', *Capital and Class*, no. 7.

Elger, Tony, (1982) 'Braverman, Capital Accumulation and De-Skilling', in Stephen Wood (ed.).

Elger, T. and Schwartz, B., (1980) 'Monopoly Capitalism and the Impact of Taylorism: Notes on Lenin, Gramsci and Sohn-Rathel', in T. Nichols (ed.), *Capital and Labour*.

Elkan, Walter, (1977) 'Employment, Education, Training and Skilled Labour in Iran', *Middle Eastern Journal*, vol. 31, no. 2.

Ershad, F., (1978) *Migration and Life Style: Work and Leisure in an Industrialized City (Arak)*, Sociology thesis, Chelsea College, London.

Fanon, Frantz, (1967) *The Wretched of the Earth*, Penguin, London.

Fedaeen (OIPFG), (1978a) *Gozaresht-i az Mobarezat-e Dalirane-ye Mardom-e Kharej az Mahdoudeh* (Reports on the heroic struggles of the shanty-town dwellers) (in Farsi), Teheran.

Fedaeen (OIPFG), (1978b) *Land Reform in Iran and its Direct Effects*, (private publishing), London.

Fedaeen (OIPFG), (1981) *Barrasi va Tahlil-i az Jonbesh-e Kargari dar du Sale-ye Gozashteh* (An analysis of the Workers' Struggle in the last two years) (in Farsi), Teheran.

Ferro, M., (1972) *The Russian Revolution of February 1917*, Routledge and Kegan Paul, London.

Ferro, M., (1980) *October 1917*, Routledge and Kegan Paul, London.

Fine, B. and Harris, L., (1979) *Rereading Capital*, Macmillan, London.

Fisher, W.B. (ed.), (1968) *Cambridge History of Iran*, vol. 1, Cambridge University Press, Cambridge.

Forseback, Lennart, (1980) *Industrial Relations and Employment in Sweden*, The Swedish Institute, Uppsala.

Foster, J., (1974) *Class Struggle and Industrial Revolution*, Weidenfeld & Nicolson, London.

Fox, Alan, (1971) *A Sociology of Work in Industry*, Macmillan, London.

Friedman, M., (1962) *Capitalism and Freedom*, Chicago University Press, Chicago.

Friedman, Andrew, (1977a) 'Direct Control and Responsible Autonomy', *Capital and Class*, no. 1.

Friedman, Andrew, (1977b) *Industry and Labour: Class Struggle at Work and Monopoly Capitalism*, Macmillan, London.

Gardner, W. and Taylor, P., (1975) *Health at Work*, London.

Geary, D., (1976) 'Radicalism and the Worker: Metalworkers and Revolution, 1914-33', in R. Evans (ed.), *Society and Politics in Wilhelmine Germany*, London.

Gallacher, W.M. and Campbell, J.R., (1977), 'Direct Action', in T. Clark and L. Clements (eds), (1977) *Trade Unions Under Capitalism*.

Ghasim, A., (1979) *Shuraha va Democracy-e Mostaghim* (The *Shuras* and Direct Democracy) (in Farsi), Teheran.

Ghotbi, A., (1978) *Iran: Where to Begin?*, Committee for the Restoration of Trades Union Rights in Iran, London.

Ghotbi, A., (1979) *Shuraha dar Iran va Socialim-e Elmi* (The *Shuras* in Iran and Scientific Socialism) (in Farsi), Teheran.

Ghotbi, A., (1980) *Kargaran-e Kafsh-e Melli: Agar Iran Hamintour Bemanad, Soghout Mikonad* (The Workers of Melli Shoe Plant: If Iran Remains Like This, It Will Collapse) (in Farsi), Teheran.

Gilbert, A., (1981) *Marx's Politics; Communists and Citizens*, Martin Robertson, Oxford.

Godelier, Maurice, (1980) 'Work and its Representations: A Research Proposal', *History Workshop Journal*, no. 10.

Goodey, C., (1974) 'Factory Committees and the Dictatorship of the Proletariat', *Critique*, no. 3.

Goodey, C. *et al*, (1975) 'Workers' Control in the Portuguese Factories', a pamphlet of Institute for Workers' Control, Nottingham.

Goodey, C., (1980) 'Workers' Councils in the Iranian Factories', *MERIP Reports*, June.

Goodrich, C., (1975) *The Frontier of Control: A Study in British Workshop Politics*, Pluto Press, London.

Gorz, Andre, (1973) 'Workers' Control is More than Just That', in G. Hunnius *et al* (eds).

Gorz, Andre (ed.), (1978a) *The Division of Labour: The Labour Process and Class Struggle in Modern Capitalism*, Harvester, London.

Gorz, Andre, (1978b) 'Technology, Technicians and Class Struggle', in A. Gorz (ed.), *The Division of Labour*.

Gorz, Andre, (1982) *Farewell to the Working Class*, Pluto Press, London.

Graham, R., (1979) *Iran: The Illusion of Power*, Croom Helm, London.

Gramsci, A., (1977) *Political Writings 1910-1920*, Lawrence & Wishart, London.

Grayesh-e Socialisti (Socialist Tendency), (n.d.) *Taraz nameh va Cheshm Andax* (The Balance Sheet and the Prospect), published by a political group split from the Fedaeen (in Farsi).

Halim, Fatimah, (1983) 'Workers' Resistance and Management Control: A Comparative Case Study of Male and Female Workers in West Malaysia', *Journal of Contemporary Asia*, vol. 13, no. 2.

Hall, Stewart, (1981) 'Notes on Deconstructing the "Popular" ', in R. Samuel (ed.), *People's History and Socialist Theory*, Routledge and Kegan Paul, London.

Halliday, F., (1977) 'Labour Migration and the Formation of the Working Class in the Oil Producing States of the Middle East', *MERIP Reports*, no. 59.

Halliday, F., (1978a) *Iran: Dictatorship and Development*, Penguin, London.

Halliday, F., (1978b) 'Iran: Trade Unions and the Working Class Opposition', *MERIP Reports*, no. 71.

Halliday, F., (1983) *The Making of the Second Cold War*, Verso Press, London.

Haraszti, M., (1977) *A Worker in a Workers' State*, Penguin, London.

Hartman, H., (1975) 'Co-Determination Today and Tomorrow', *British Journal of Industrial Relations*, vol. 1975.

Hatef, A., (1982a) 'Teory-e Dawlat dar Radde-e Economism: Teory-e Bonapartiti-e Dawlat' (A Theory of State in Refutation of Economism: The Bonapartist Theory of the State), *Dawlat va Enghelab*, nos 1 and 2 (in Farsi).

Hatef, A., (1982b), 'Naghdi bar Jam, handi-e Yeksale-ye Moghavemat-e

Mosallehaneh', *Dawlat va Enghelab*, no. 2, London.

Haydary, G., (1951) 'The Agrarian Reform Problem in Iran', *Middle Eastern Journal*, vol. 5.

Held, D. *et al* (eds), (1983) *States and Societies*, Open University Press, Milton Keynes.

Henson, D., (1978) 'Trade Unionism and the Struggle for Liberation in South Africa', *Capital and Class*, no. 6.

Hill, Stephen, (1981) *Competition and Control at Work*, Heinemann, London.

Hinton, James, (1973) *The First Shop-Steward Movement*, Allen Lane, London.

Hobsbawm, Eric, (1979) *Labouring Men: Studies in the History of Labour*, Weidenfeld & Nicolson, London.

Holubenko, (1975) 'The Soviet Working Class Opposition', *Critique*, no. 4.

Hooglund, Eric, (1973) 'The Kuhshnashin Population in Iran', *Iranian Studies*, vol. VI, no. 4.

Hooglund, Mary, (1982) 'Religious Ritual and Political Struggle in an Iranian Village', *MERIP Reports*, no. 102.

Hosseini Kazerouni, M.R. and Ghaleh Golabi, H., (1980) 'Barrasi-e Amari-e Sharayet-e Hashieh Nashinan' (Statistical Investigation of the Conditions of the Shanty-Town Dwellers), *Kitab-i Jomeh*, no. 12 (in Farsi), Teheran.

Hoyles, A., (1969) 'The Occupation of Factories in France: May 1968', in K. Coates *et al* (eds), *Trade Union Register*, Merlin Press, London.

Humphry, John, (1980) 'Labour Use and Labour Control in the Brazilian Automobile Industry', *Capital and Class*, no. 12.

Hunnius, G., Garson, G.D. and Case, J. (eds), (1973) *Workers' Control*, Random House, New York.

Hyman, Richard, (1974a) 'Workers' Control and Revolutionary Theory', *Socialist Register*.

Hyman, Richard, (1974b) *Marxism and the Sociology of Trade Unionism*, Pluto Press, London.

Hyman, Richard, (1975a) *Industrial Relations: A Marxist Introduction*, Macmillan, London.

Hyman, Richard, (1975b) Foreword to the 1975 Edition of C. Goodrich, *Frontier of Control*.

Hyman, Richard, (1979) 'The Politics of Workplace Trade Unionism: Recent Tendencies and some Problems for Theory', *Capital and Class*, no. 8.

Hyman, Richard, (1983) 'Andre Gorz and his Disappearing Proletariat', *Socialist Register*.

Irvin, G.W., (1983) 'Nicaragua: A Note on the Political Economy of Transition', Institute of Social Studies, The Hague.

Islamic Society of the Employees of Insurance Organizations, (1981) *Shuraha-ye Islami (Islamic Shuras)*, Teheran.

Issawai, C., (1971) *The Economic History of Iran, 1800-1914*, Chicago University Press, Chicago.

Ja-far, M. and Tabari, A., (1981) 'Iran: Islam and the Struggle for Socialism', *Khamsin*, no. 8.

Jalil, T., (1977) *Workers Say No to the Shah: Labour Law and Strikes in Iran*, London.

Javadi Najjar, Z., (1974) *Barrasi-e Nahve-ye Gozaran-e Awghat-e Faraghat-e Kargaran-e Karkhanejat-e Gharb-e Teheran* (A Survey on the Leisure Time of the Factory Workers of Eastern Teheran), BA Dissertation in Sociology,

Teheran University.

Jenkins, D., (1973) *Job Power: Blue and White Collar Democracy*, Gordon Fity, New York.

Jessop, B., (1984) 'Capitalism and Democracy: The Best Possible Political Shell?', in D. Held *et al* (eds).

Johnson, C., (1980) 'The Problem of Reformism and Marxist Theory of Fetishism', *New Left Review*, no. 119.

Jones, C. and Novak, T., (1980) 'The State and Social Policy', in Corrigan, P. (ed.), (1980) *Capitalism, State Formation and Marxist Theory*, Quartet Books, London.

Kaplan, F.L., (1969) *The Bolshevik Ideology: The Ethics of Soviet Labour, 1917-1920: The Formative Years*, Peter Owen, London.

Karpat, K., (1979) *Gecekondu*, Cambridge University Press, Cambridge.

Katouzian, H., (1981) *The Political Economy of Modern Iran, 1926-79*, Macmillan, London.

Kavousi, Freydoun, (1976) *Kargaran dar Iran-e Emrouz* (Workers in Present Iran) (in Farsi), Teheran.

Kay, G., (1975) *Development and Underdevelopment*, Macmillan, London.

Kazemi, F., (1980) *Poverty and Revolution in Iran*, New York University Press, New York.

Kazemi, F. and Abrahamian, E., (1978) 'The Non-Revolutionary Peasantry of Modern Iran', *Iranian Studies*, no. 11.

Keddie, N., (1972) 'Stratification, Social Control and Capitalism in Iranian Villages: Before and After the Revolution', in R. Antoun and I. Harik (eds), *Rural Politics and Social Change in the Middle East*, Indiana University Press.

Keyder, C., (1979) 'The Political Economy of Turkish Democracy', *New Left Review*, no. 115.

Khomeini, R., (1980) *Valayat-e Faghih* (The Rule of the Theologician) (in Farsi), Teheran.

Kidner, Richard, (1980) *Law at Work: Trade Unions*, Sweet and Maxwell, London.

Kinnersley, Patrick, (1979) *The Hazards of Work: How to Fight Them*, Pluto Press, London.

Lambton, Ann, (1953) *Peasant and Landlord in Persia*, Oxford University Press, London.

Lajevardi, H., (1985) *Labour Unions and Autocracy in Iran*, Syracuse University Press, New York.

Larijani, H., (1974) *The Effects of Middle Managers on the Safety of Workers in the Manufacturing Industry in Iran*, unpublished PhD thesis, University of Missouri, Columbia.

Lee, Everett, (1966) 'A Theory of Migration', *Demography*, vol. 3.

Lenin, V.I., (1960a) *Collected Works*, vol. 4, Moscow.

Lenin, V.I., (1960b) *The Development of Capitalism in Russia*, Moscow.

Lenin, V.I., (1961) *Collected Works*, vol. 6, Moscow.

Lenin, V.I., (1964) *The State and Revolution, Collected Works*, vol. 25, 1964.

Lenin, V.I., (1965) *Collected Works*, vol. 10, Moscow.

Lenin, V.I., (1966) *Imperialism the Highest Stage of Capitalism*, Moscow.

Lenin, V.I., (1973a) *What is to be Done?*, Peking.

Lenin, V.I., (1973b) *Collected Works*, vol. 33, Moscow.

Lenin, V.I., (1974a) *Collected Works*, vol. 30, Moscow.

Lenin, V.I., (1974b) 'A Great Beginning', in *Collected Works, vol. 29, Moscow*.

Lenin, V.I., (1978) *On Trade Unions*, Moscow.

Levenson, D., (1977) 'Workers' Movement in Chile 1970-1973', unpublished MA thesis, University of Massachusetts.

Levidow, L. *et al* (eds), (1981) *Science, Technology and the Labour Process*, CSE, London.

Liebman, M., (1975) *Leninism Under Lenin*, Merlin Press, London.

Lipietz, Alain, (1982) 'Towards a Global Fordism?', *New Left Review*, no. 135.

Littler, C.R., (1982a) *The Development of the Labour Process in Capitalist Societies*, Heinemann, London.

Littler, C.R., (1982b) 'Deskilling and Changing Structures of Control', in S. Wood (ed.), *Degradation of Work?*

Lloyd, Peter, (1979) *Slums of Hopes? Shanty Towns of the Third World*, Penguin, London.

Lloyd, Peter, (1982) *The Third World Proletariat?*, Allen and Unwin, London.

Lomax, Bill, (1976) *Hungary 1956*, Allison and Busby, London.

Looney, R.E., (1973) *The Economic Development of Iran: A Recent Survey with Projection to 1981*, Praeger, New York.

Lubeck, Paul, (1975) 'Unions, Workers and Consciousness in Kano, Nigeria: A View from Below', in R.O. Sandbrook and R. Cohen (eds).

Lusinde, J., (1979) 'Workers' Participation in Industrial Management in Tanzania', in H. Mapolu (ed.) (1976).

Luxemburg, Rosa, (1971) *Trade Union Struggle and Mass Strike*, Merlin Press, London.

Mallet, S., (1975) *The New Working Class*, Spokesman Books, London.

Mandel, Ernest, (1973) 'The Debate on Workers' Control', in G. Hunnius *et al* (eds).

Mapolu, H., (1976) 'The Organization and Participation of Workers in Tanzania', in Mapolu, H. (ed.).

Mapolu, H. (ed.), (1976) *Workers and Management*, Tanzanian Publishing House, Dar es Salaam.

Marchetti, P., (1982) 'Church and Revolution: An Interview with Peter Marchetti', *Monthly Review*, vol. 34, no. 3.

Marglin, S.A., (1978) 'What Do the Bossed Do?', in A. Gorz (ed.), *The Division of Labour*.

Marx, K., (1962a) *Class Struggle in France, 1848-1850*, in Marx and Engels, *Selected Works*, vol. 1, Progress Publishers, Moscow.

Marx, K., (1962b) *The Eighteenth Brumaire of Louis Bonaparte*, in *Selected Works*, vol. 1, Progress Publishers, Moscow.

Marx, K., (1963) *Theories of Surplus Value*, vol. 1, Progress Publishers, Moscow.

Marx, K., (1964a) *Economic and Philosophical Manuscripts*, Internal Publishers, New York.

Marx, K., (1964b) *Anarchism and Anarcho-Syndicalism*, Progress Publishers, Moscow.

Marx, K., (1976) *Poverty of Philosophy*, in Marx and Engels, *Collected Works*, vol. 6, Lawrence and Wishart, London.

Marx, K., (1977) *Capital*, vol. 3, Progress Publishers, Moscow.

Marx, K., (1979) *Capital*, vol. 1, Penguin, London.

Mason, Tim, (1981) 'Workers Opposition in Nazi Germany', *History Workshop Journal*, no. 11, Spring.

Mattick, P., (1979) 'Workers' Control', in P. Mattick, *Anti-Bolshevik Communism*, Merlin Press, London.

Mihyo, Paschal, (1975) 'The Struggle for Workers' Control in Tanzania', *Review of African Political Economy*, no. 4.

Miller, R.F., (1978) 'Workers' Self-Management in Yugoslavia: The Current State of Play', *Journal of Industrial Relations*, September.

Ministry of Economy, (1966) *Industrial Statistics*, Teheran.

Ministry of Industry and Mining, (1977) *The Statistics of the Large-Scale Industries in Iran*, 2533 (1974/75), Teheran.

Ministry of Industry and Mining, (1980-81) *Karkhanejat-e Jadid va Tawse-eh Yafteh, 1358* (Modern and Developed Plants, 1980), Teheran.

Ministry of Industry and Mining, (1980) *Sanaye-i Khodrow Sazi-e Iran* (Car Industry in Iran), Teheran.

Ministry of Labour, (1964-65) *Majoue-ye Barrasiha-ye Masael-e Nirou-ye Ensani* (A Collection of Surveys on Manpower Problems), 3 vols (in Farsi), Teheran.

Ministry of Planning and Budget, (1982) *Productive Resources and Industrial Employment* (in Farsi), Teheran.

Mitchell, A., (1965) *Revolution in Bavaria, 1918-1919: The Eiser Regime and the Soviet Republic*, Princeton, New Jersey.

Molyneux, J., (1978) *Marxism and the Party*, Pluto Press, London.

Monds, J., (1976) 'Workers' Control and the Historians: A New Economism', *New Left Review*, no. 97.

Montgomery, D., (1979) *Workers' Control in America*, Cambridge University Press.

Moore, B., (1969) *Social Origins of Dictatorship and Democracy*, Penguin, London.

Moorehouse, B., (1978) 'The Marxist Theory of Labour Aristocracy', *Social History*, vol. 3, no. 1.

Mudjahedin (OPMI), (1979) *Rahnemoud-i baray-e Tashkil-e Shuraye Vagheii dar Karkhanejat va Moassesat* (A Guideline for the Formation of Genuine *Shuras* in the Factories and the Offices), Teheran.

Murray, Robin, (n.d.) 'Imperialism and the Labour Process', discussion paper.

Neal, R.S., (1983) *History and Class*, Basil Blackwell, Oxford.

Neumann, Franz, (1969) *Behemoth, the Structure and Practice of National Socialism, 1933-44*, London.

Nichols, T. and Beynon, H., (1977) *Living with Capitalism: Class Relations and the Modern Factory*, Routledge and Kegan Paul, London.

Nichols, Theo (ed.), (1980 *Capital and Labour: Studies in the Capitalist Labour Process*, Fontana, London.

Nima, R., (1983) *The Wrath of Allah*, Pluto Press, London.

Nore, P. and Turner, T. (eds), (1980) *Oil and Class Struggle*, Zed Press, London.

Nowshirvani, V. and Bilder, R., (1973) 'Direct Foreign Investment in the Non-Oil Sectors of the Iranian Economy', *Iranian Studies*, vol. vi.

Nwafor, A., (1984) 'The Nicaraguan Revolution' (Review Essay), *Third World Book Review*, vol. 1, no. 2.

Nyerere, J.K., (1976) 'The Establishment of Workers' Councils, Executive Boards and Boards of Directors', in H. Mapolu (ed.).

Pakdaman, N., (1980) 'Ettehadieha-ye Kargari: Sazmandehi-h Tajrobeh-e Bozorg-e Enghelab-e Iran' (The Trade Unions: Organization of the Great Experience of the Iranian Revolution), *Kitab-i Jom'eh*, no. 33 (in Farsi), Teheran.

Palloix, C., (1976) 'The Labour Process: From Fordism to Neo-Fordism', in *Labour Process and Class Strategies*, CSE pamphlet no. 1, London.

Pannekoek, A., (1959) *The Way to Workers' Control*, London.

Passerini, Lussia, (1970) 'Work Ideology Under Italian Fascism', *History Workshop Journal*, no. 8, Autumn.

Pelikan, J., (1973) 'Workers' Councils in Czechoslovakia', *Critique*, no. 1, Spring.

Pelling, H., (1983) *A History of British Trade Unionism*, Penguin, London.

Peoples Fedaean Guerrillas of Iran, (n.d.) 'A Report on Yamaha and Peugeot Motor Cycle Plants', appendix *Khabar nameh*, no. 29 (in Farsi).

Pesaran, H., (1981) 'The System of Dependent Capitalism in Pre- and Post-Revolutionary Iran', working paper, Trinity College, University of Cambridge, August.

Pesaran, H., (1982) *Income Distribution in Iran*, Cambridge University Press, Cambridge.

Petras, J., (1981) 'Nicaragua: The Transition to a New Society', *Latin American Perspective*, no. 29.

Petras, J., (1983) 'Workers' Democracy: The Key to Defending the Revolution and Developing the Productive Forces', *Latin American Perspectives*, no. 36.

Plan Organization, (1973-74) *The Results of Manpower Census in 1351 (1972-3)*, Teheran.

Plan Organization, (1977) *The Statistics of the Large-Scale Industries 1356*, Teheran.

Plan Organization, (1978) *A Survey of Population Growth in Iran: Final Report 1973-76*, Teheran.

Plan Organization, (1980-81a) *Narasaiiha va Vabastegihay-e Kargahhay-e Bozorg-i Keshvar dar Sal-i 1358* (A Survey on Shortcomings and Dependency of the Large Industries in 1979-80), Teheran.

Plan Organization, (1980-81b) *Statistical Year Book*, Teheran.

Plan Organization, (1981-82a) *Annual Economic Report*, Teheran.

Plan Organization, (1981-82b) *Teheran Census (1980-81)*, Teheran.

Poulantzas, N., (1975) *Classes in Contemporary Capitalist Societies*, New Left Books, London.

Poulantzas, N., (1979) *Fascism and Dictatorship*, Verso Press, London.

Pouyan, A.P., (1975) *On the Necessity of Armed Struggle and Refutation of the Theory of 'Survival'*, New York.

Rah-e Kargar Organization, (1980-81) *Shuraha va Mavaze-i Ma* (The *Shuras* and our Stand), Teheran.

Rajavi, Kazem, (1980) 'Naghsh-e Amrica dar Enghelab-i Safid-i Iran' (The Role of the USA in the Iranian White Revolution), *Ayandegan*, 25 & 26/3/1359.

Rakovsky, C., (1980) *Selected Writings*, Allison & Busby, London.

Ramondt, J., (1979) 'Workers' Self-Management and its Constraints: The Yugoslav Experience', *British Journal of Industrial Relations*, vol. 17.

Ramsay, H., (1980) 'Participation: The Pattern and its Significance', in Nichols (ed.), *Capital and Labour*.

Raptis, M., (1973) *Revolution and Counter-Revolution in Chile*, Allison & Busby, London.

Raptis, M., (1980) *Socialism, Democracy and Self-Management*, Allison & Busby, London.

Rattansi, Ali, (1982a) *Marx and the Division of Labour*, Macmillan, London.

Rattansi, Ali, (1982b) 'Marx and the Abolition of the Division of Labour', in A. Giddens and G. Mackenzie (eds), *Social Class and the Division of Labour*,

Cambridge University Press.

Reich, M., Gordon, D.M. and Edwards, R., (1980) 'A Theory of Labour Market Segmentation', in A.H. Amsden (ed.).

Rene, K., (1978) 'Democracy and Council System', in T. Bottomore and P. Goode (eds), *Austro-Marxism*, Oxford.

Richards, Frank, (1979) 'Revisionism, imperialism and the state: A Critique of the Revisionist Dogma of State Monopoly Capitalism', *Revolutionary Communist Papers*, no. 4, February.

Roberts, B., (1979) *Cities of Peasants*, Edward Arnold, London.

Rose, M., (1975) *Industrial Behaviour*, Penguin, London.

Rosenburg, W., (1978) 'Workers and Workers' Control in the Russian Revolution', *History Workshop Journal*, no. 5, Spring.

Rostami, T. and Alvandi, M., (1980) 'Mohajerat-i Fasli-e Roustaiian va Ta'sir-e an dar Toulid-e Keshavarzi dar Dasht-i Esfehan' (The Migration of Peasants and its Impact on the Agricultural Production in Dasht-i Esfehan), Ministry of Agriculture, Centre of Rural Research, Teheran.

Rubery, J., (1980) 'Structured Labour Market, Worker Opposition and Low Pay', in A.H. Amsden (ed.).

Samuel, Rafael, (1980) 'British Marxist Historians, 1880-1980', *New Left Review*, no. 120.

Sanavandi, S., (1974) *Sharayet-i Eghtesadi va Ejtemaii Zanan-e Kargar dar Iran* (The Socio-Economic Conditions of Women Workers in Iran), BA dissertation, (in Farsi), University of Teheran.

Sandbrook, R., (1981) 'Workers' Consciousness and Populist Protest in Tropical Africa', in R.L. Simpson *et al* (eds), *Research in the Sociology of Work*, A Research Annual, no. 1.

Sandbrook, R. and Cohen, R. (eds), (1975) *The Development of an African Working Class*, Longmans, London.

Santamaria, V. and Manville, A., (1976) 'Lenin and the Problem of Transition', *Telos*, no. 27, Spring.

Schafar, W., (1982) 'Collective Thinking from Below: Early Working Class Thought Reconsidered', *Dialectical Anthropology*, vol. 6, no. 3.

Schaur, Helmet, (1973) 'Critique of Co-Determination' in G. Hunnius *et al* (eds).

Seabrook, J., (1978) *What Went Wrong: Working People and the Ideals of the Labour Movement*, London.

Seidman, M., (1982) 'Work and Revolution: Workers' Control in Barcelona in the Spanish Civil War, 1936-38', *Journal of Contemporary History*, vol. 17.

Shoar, Ja'far, (1981) *Sanadha-ye Shura dar Quran* (The Quranic Documents on *Shuras*) (in Farsi), Teheran.

Simpson, R. and Simpson, I.H. (eds), (1981) *Research in the Sociology of Work*, A Research Annual, no. 1.

Singer, Daniel, (1981) *The Road to Gdansk*, Monthly Review Press, New York.

Siriani, C., (1982) *Workers' Control and Socialist Democracy: The Soviet Experience*, Verso Press, London.

Smirinow, Gabriel, (1979) *The Revolution Disarmed: Chile 1970-73*, Monthly Review Press, New York.

Smith, S.A., (1980) *Russian Revolution and the Factories of Petrograd 1917-1918*, PhD thesis, University of Birmingham. This has been published under the title *Red Petrograd*, Cambridge University Press, 1983.

Smith, S.A., (1980) 'Craft Consciousness, Class Consciousness: Petrograd 1917',

History Workshop Journal, no. 11.

Smith, S.A., (1983) 'Taylorism Rules OK? Bolshevism, Taylorism and the Technical Intelligentsia in the Soviet Union, 1917-1941', *Radical Science Journal*, no. 13.

Sodagar, M.R., (1979) *Roshd-i Sarmayehdari dar Iran: Doure-ye Enteghali: 1322-42* (The Development of Capitalism in Iran: The Transitional Period 1943-1963) (in Farsi), Teheran.

SOGAT, (1982) *General Rules 1982*, SOGAT, London.

Spiriano, Paolo, (1975), *The Occupation of Factories*, Pluto Press, London.

Standing, Guy, (1981) 'Migration and Modes of Exploitation: Social Origins of Immobility and Mobility', *The Journal of Peasant Studies*, vol. 8, no. 2.

Stein, Margaret B., (1978) 'The Meaning of Skill: The Case of French Engine Drivers, 1837-1917', *Politics and Society*, vol. 8.

Stephen, H., (1981) *Competition and Control at Work*, Heinemann, London.

Stewart, Frances, (1977) *Technology and Underdevelopment*, Macmillan, London.

Sticher, S., (1976-77) 'Imperialism and the Rise of a "Labour Aristocracy" in Kenya, 1948-1970', *Berkeley Journal of Sociology*, vol. xxi.

Storey, J., (1983) *Managerial Prerogative and the Question of Control*, Routledge and Kegan Paul, London.

Sutton, L.P.E., (1950) *Labour Conditions in the Oil Industry in Iran*, ILO, Geneva.

Sweezy, P. and Magdoff, H., (1979) 'Iran: The New Crisis of American Hegemony', *Monthly Review*, vol. 30, no. 9.

Tabari, A., (1981) 'The Role of the Shi'i Clergy in Modern Iranian Politics', *Khamsin*, no. 9.

Tabrizi, Ali, (1982) 'Teheran: Dou Yad'dasht Darbare-ye Tahavvol-e Jammiat va Taharrok-e Ejtemaii' (Teheran: Two Notes on Population Growth and Social Mobility), *Ketab-i Aghah*, no. 1 (in Farsi), Teheran.

Tampke, Furgen, (1979) *Ruhr and Revolution: The Revolutionary Movement in the Rhenish-Westphalian Industrial Region, 1912-1919*, Croom Helm, London.

Taylan, T., (1984) 'Capital and the State in Contemporary Turkey', *Khamsin*, no. 11.

Therborn, G., (1975) 'The Working Class and the Birth of Marxism', *New Left Review*, no. 79.

Therborn, G., (1977) 'The Rule of Capital and the Rise of Democracy', *New Left Review*, no. 103; and in D. Held *et al* (eds) (1983).

Therborn, G., (1979) 'The Travail of Latin American Democracy', *New Left Review*, nos. 113-114.

Therborn, G., (1983) 'Why Some Classes are More Successful than Others', *New Left Review*, no. 138.

Thompson, E.P., (1978a) *Poverty of Theory*, Merlin Press, London.

Thompson, E.P., (1978b) 'Eighteenth-Century English Society: Class Struggle without Class?', *Social History*, vol. 3, no. 2.

Thompson, E.P., (1979) *The Making of the English Working Class*, Penguin, London.

Tiktin, H., (1973) 'Towards a Political Economy of the USSR', *Critique*, no. 1.

Tiktin, H., (1974) 'Socialism, the Market and the State', *Critique*, no. 3.

Todaro, M., (1969) 'A Model of Labour Migration and Urban Unemployment in Less Developed Countries', *American Economic Review*, no. 59, March.

Todaro, M., (n.d.) 'Income Expectations, Rural Migration and Employment in Africa', *International Labour Review*, no. 104, vol. 5.

Topham, Tony, (1964) 'Shop Stewards and Workers' Control', *New Left Review*, no. 25.

Topham, Tony, (1975) 'Democracy and Workers' Control', in J. Vanek (ed.), *Self-Management*.

Trotsky, Leon, (1973) *1905*, Penguin, London.

Turner, T., (1980) 'Iranian Oil Workers in the 1978-79 Revolution', in P. Nore and T. Turner (eds), *Oil and Class Struggle*.

US Department of Labor, (1964) *Labor Law and Practice in Iran*, BLS Report, no. 276.

Van der Molen, G., (1979) 'Economic Impacts of Education and Personnel Management: Case Studies from the Industrial Sector in Iran and Surinam', *Development and Change*, vol. 7, no. 1.

Vanek, J. (ed.), (1975) *Self-Management: Economic Liberation of Man*, Penguin, London.

Van Onselen, C., (1976) *Chibaro: African Mine Labour in Southern Rhodesia, 1900-1933*, Pluto Press, London.

Vieille, Paul, (1980) *Paygah-i Kargaran-e Teheran* (The Position of Teheran Workers) (in Farsi), University of Teheran.

Walker, J., (1981) 'Markets, Industrial Process and Class Struggle: The Evolution of the Labour Process in the UK Engineering Industry', *The Review of Radical Political Economy*, vol. 12, no. 4.

Walton, T., (Pesaran, H.), (1980) 'Economic Development and Revolutionary Upheavals in Iran', *Cambridge Journal of Economics*, September.

Warren, B., (1980) *Imperialism, the Pioneer of Capitalism*, Verso Press, London.

Waterman, P., (1977) 'Workers in the Third World', *Monthly Review*, September.

Waterman, P. (ed.), (1979) 'Strikes in the Third World', a collection of essays in *Development and Change*, vol. 10, no. 2.

Waterman, P., (1983) *Aristocrats and Plebians in African Unions*, Institute of Social Studies, The Hague.

Weber, H., (1981) *Nicaragua, the Sandanist Revolution*, Verso Press, London.

White, G. *et al* (eds), (1983) *Revolutionary Socialist Development in the Third World*, Wheatsheaf Books, UK.

William, Gwyn A., (1979) *Proletarian Order*, Pluto Press, London.

Wise, A., (1975) *Eye Witness in Revolutionary Portugal*, Spokesman Books, London.

Wood, Stephen, (1982) *Degradation of Work? Skill, De-skilling and the Labour Process*, Hutchinson, London.

Wright, Eric O., (1976) 'Class Boundaries in Advanced Capitalist Societies', *New Left Review*, no. 98.

Wright, Eric O., (1979) *Class Structure and Income Determination*, Academic Press, London.

Zabih, S., (1982) *Iran Since the Revolution*, Croom Helm, London.

Zelinsky, W., (1971) 'The Hypothesis of the Mobility Transition', *The Geographical Review*, no. lxi.

Zeitlin, A., (1980) 'The Emergence of Shop-Steward Organization and Job Control in the British Car Industry: A Review Essay', *History Workshop Journal*, no. 10.

Zimbalist, A. and Petras, J., (1977) 'Workers' Control in Chile', pamphlet of the Institute for Workers' Control, Nottingham, UK.

Documents, Journals and Newspapers in Farsi

Ayandegan	Daily morning paper (now banned and stopped).
Enghelab-i Eslami	Daily evening paper (now banned and stopped).
Ettelaat	Daily evening paper (legal).
Jomhouri-e Eslami	Daily morning paper (the organ of the ruling IRP).
Kayhan	Daily evening paper (legal).
Dawlat va Enghelab	Independent Marxist journal (London).
Farhang-i Nuvin	Monthly radical journal (now banned and stopped).
Kar	Organ of the Fedaian (both 'Minority' and 'Majority') (banned, but published).
Kargaran	Leftist workers' journal (now banned and stopped).
Khabar-i Kargar	*Ad hoc* labour report during the Revolution.
Khabar-nameh	Occasional newsletter of the Fedaian in 1979.
Paykar	Organ of the leftist Paykar organization (banned).
Rahaee	Organ of the Communist Unity (banned, occasionally published).
Rah-i Kargar	Organ of the Organization of Revolutionary Workers (banned, but published in exile).

Annual Reports, Bank Markazi Iran, Central Bank of Iran.
Internal Bulletin, Organization of Industrial Development and Reconstruction.
Kar, Jelve-ye Hagh Taala, Monthly labour report of the ruling party (IRP).
Economic Reports, Plan Organization.
Salehan-i Sazandeh, Weekly labour report of the ruling party (IRP).

Index